Strategic Negotiation

For Felix and René

Strategic Negotiation

GAVIN KENNEDY

GOWER

Published by
Gower Publishing Limited
Gower House
Croft Road
Aldershot
Hampshire GU11 3HR
England

Ashgate Publishing Company
Suite 420
101 Cherry Street
Burlington, VT 05401-4405
USA

Gavin Kennedy has asserted his moral right under the Copyright, Designs and Patents Act, 1988, to be identified as the author of this work.

British Library Cataloguing in Publication Data
Kennedy, Gavin
    Strategic negotiation : an opportunity for change
    1. Negotiation in business
    I. Title
    658.4'052

    ISBN-13: 9780566087974

Library of Congress Cataloging-in-Publication Data
Kennedy, Gavin.
    Strategic negotiation : an opportunity for change / by Gavin Kennedy.
      p. cm.
    Includes index.
    ISBN 978-0-566-08797-4
    1. Negotiation in business. I. Title.
    HD58.6.K48 2007
    658.4'052--dc22
                                     2007002015

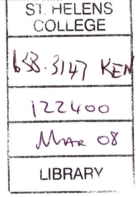
Printed and bound in Great Britain by TJ International Ltd, Padstow, Cornwall.

Contents

List of Figures

List of Tables

Preface

No matter how skilled at negotiation you might become, if you are pursuing inappropriate strategies, your negotiation skills won't pull rabbits out of a hat (like magicians who amaze children); conversely if you have brilliant and appropriate strategies, but do not have the requisite negotiation skills to implement them, you will not succeed unless you have the good luck to choose negotiating partners with even fewer skills than your own. Relying on luck is the antithesis of strategy; if you have poor strategies and poor negotiating skills, you will reap what you sow.

Interest in negotiation strategy follows naturally from interest in the process of negotiation. Teaching negotiation skills to managers soon raises questions about how and why they are pursuing this or that objective for which they wish to deploy their improved negotiation skills. If not clearly separated, arguments about appropriate skills easily become confused with implicit differences in strategic objectives.

Strategic Negotiation is different from my other books on negotiation (such as *Kennedy on Negotiation*, Gower, 1998 and (with Florence Kennedy) *Kennedys' Simulations for Negotiation Trainers*, 3rd Edition, Gower, 2007); it is a step up from introducing negotiators to negotiating skills to introducing them to the different task of preparing them to apply their skills to serve their strategic purposes.

Strategic Negotiation is for practitioners and is based on an elective written for postgraduate MSc management courses at Edinburgh Business School (Strategic Negotiation, EBS, 2005). Its focus is on the generation and implementation of negotiation strategy in business and public organizations and is based on many years of practical experience.

Teaching strategic planning effectively is extremely difficult. Strategy is not a series of axioms to be rote learned; it is about the application of thoughtful analysis to real world problems, with the added complication that there is vast room for error both in the selection of the tools of analysis and in the identification of the real world problem. *Strategic Negotiation* offers advice in the implementation phase of strategy. It is organized around case examples that demonstrate the application of its Process Model to the real world. The cases are drawn largely from my consultancy work in various industries and business situations, without any pretence to comprehensive coverage; and I also draw upon the work of colleagues who have demonstrated competence in this field. To cover all, or even most, potential applications of negotiation strategy would produce a multi-volume text, which is neither appropriate nor necessary for most purposes. The cases illustrate the application of the core concepts and provide a framework for understanding how the strategic negotiation process can be applied to general situations.

It is important in *Strategic Negotiation* to remember that you are approaching fairly generic business situations from the functional point of view of a negotiator and not that of other professions such as a lawyer, accountant, finance specialist, marketeer, production engineer, human resource management specialist, or any other of the many functions with which you may be concerned in your organization. It is true that you will touch on many of these functions in this book but you will not, so to speak, be touched by any one of them alone. The negotiation strategist approaches business problems from a different angle to those working exclusively in other functions. It is often a question of 'Which of my objectives are possible in this situation and how will they be achieved?'

As Chester Karrass puts it, though for a somewhat different purpose: 'You get what you negotiate, not what you deserve', or, as I heard a hard-boiled streetwise person, experienced in the ways of the world, put it: 'Sometimes you get what you want, sometimes you get what you need, and other times you get what you get.' Negotiation is about trying to do better than just getting what you get. Negotiation strategy is about creating the conditions that enable you to get (closer) to what you want. Anybody who tells you that negotiation is easy is obviously the kind of person who makes do with what can be got, which is not quite the same.

You should enjoy reading *Strategic Negotiation*. As a leading salesperson once put it: 'Successful selling is the best way to have fun with your clothes on.' I believe negotiation strategy and process runs successful selling a very close second.

Acknowledgements

My late business partner and friend John Benson was for many years a major influence on me in negotiation strategy and he contributed immensely to our work on strategic negotiation consultancy projects. He was Chairman of Negotiate Ltd (founded in 1986; www.negotiate.co.uk), our consultancy, and we worked together over a decade earlier to devise and deliver one of the early UK negotiation skills courses ('Workshop Bargaining') for the Management Programme at Brunel University, and later at Scottish & Newcastle Brewery from 1974–80. From these, John and I delivered consultancy and training courses in many companies in the UK, the rest of Europe and in Australia, and trained many others to do so too.

John's distinguished career took him to the main boards of three major PLCs: Scottish & Newcastle, Nabisco and Reed Packaging. In 1980, we co-authored *Managing Negotiations*, published by Business Books (now Random House), which went through four editions and placed our Eight Steps/Four Phases model of the negotiation process into the public domain (reinforced when the Rank Organization made a highly successful training video from it, *The Art of Negotiation*).

Our last co-authored book was *Local Pay Bargaining* (J. Benson, L. Helme and G. Kennedy), published by the Management Development Group in Scotland, in 1994, which I draw on in Chapters 4 and 11 for examples of the Strategic Negotiation Agenda model applied to a set of negotiation problems in publicly-funded hospitals (and elsewhere since, in the public and private sectors). It is illustrative, also, of the high professional standards of competence John brought to his negotiations. John died suddenly in February 2000.

Friendly advice from Louise Hart, at the time a group projects manager at Railtrack UK, now returned to her home country, Australia, prompted me to follow up her suggestions when she noted that my negotiation course at Edinburgh Business School was limited to basic skills and to fairly non-complex negotiations, and she asked why 'the course had nothing to say about the particular problems posed by very large and complex transactions, which are becoming increasingly commonplace'. I was aware vaguely of this need from repeated runs of our strategic negotiation consultancy work and I am grateful to Louise Hart for her timely suggestions that prompted me to commence writing.

Professor Lumsden, Director of EBS, gave me space to work on the book between negotiating assignments for EBS prior to my retirement, and my family were as accommodating as ever when my writing intruded into their notions of the appropriate work-life balance. The early removal of my howlers by Charles Ritchie, the editor, is responsible for any literary merits found in the text, but all remaining howlers that have slipped back in remain solely my own work.

Professor Alex Scott, ever interested in anything strategic, also cast his professional eye over my approach, applying his notorious fastidious taste for rigour and clarity, always with good humour, qualities for which he is tolerably well known. What you are about to read was re-arranged into a more coherent order following his advice.

As ever, I am grateful to Jonathan Norman of Gower Publishing for encouraging me to adapt *Strategic Negotiation* from a distance-learning text into a book suitable for the discriminating readers of Gower Books. It joins my two other Gower books on negotiation, plus our training CD/video, 'Do We Have a Deal?' As with negotiation, long-term business relationships are always more rewarding for both parties.

Similarly, long-term relationships are also rewarding in a different sense for families. As always, my family have long supported in myriad ways my consultancy and training assignments, which occasioned many long absences, and my writing occasioned many absences too, while I was in the same house with everybody. With my daughter Florence now in charge of Negotiate, what goes round comes round, so to speak, and the next generation has taken over. We celebrated Negotiate's 20th birthday in October 2006, and we hope that the next twenty-year anniversary in 2026 will produce as much fun, excitement and satisfaction for our colleagues and clients as we have generated during our first twenty years.

Gavin Kennedy
www.negotiate.co.uk

Introduction

Strategic Negotiation is about the middle- to long-term strategic context in which the tactical skill sets of negotiation are applied. Strategy is about what you want to happen; tactics are about making it happen. Hence, there are few overlaps between this book and the typical book on negotiation skills. Competence in negotiation is properly a complement to competence in strategy, but they do not substitute for each other.

Strategic Negotiation corresponds to Figure 1.1 in Chapter 1, which provides an overview of the Strategic Negotiation Process Model. The foundations of the Process Model rely on knowledge-based information and primarily they cover the kinds of content with which every strategic negotiator has to be familiar. A set of tools is introduced that are used in strategic negotiation processes, particularly in the analysis and diagnosis of the negotiation problem in its strategic context. The strategic process is essentially a practical exercise that applies the strategic process model to business problems, mainly through the implementation of the steps necessary for the achievement of the organization's business plan, identified, analysed and negotiated using the Negotiation Agenda method.

For each chapter there is a set of concepts, chosen for their relevance to the strategic context, and these are applied to cases drawn from a range of business activities to illustrate the strategic approach. *Strategic Negotiation* assumes familiarity with business practice at a level expected in mature people experienced in business and organizations. Most of you will already have worked on business problems of sufficient complexity to be able to bring your experience to bear on the types of problems I address.

This is a practical and applied, not a theoretical, book. It is for practising managers operating, or wishing to operate, at a senior level where negotiations by their nature are high value, complex, multi-level and often multi-party. Obviously, it would be unrealistic to be encyclopaedic and cover every possible circumstance where the methods associated with strategic negotiation would be useful, so I have included enough elements of a generic model, plus an assumption of your experience, to make it adaptable to the circumstances likely to be of particular interest to you.

Strategic Negotiation is about learning from mistakes without having to make them first. The method grew out of my negotiation consultancy for businesses and public sector organizations. Many managers contributed to the concepts in the book and many individuals and teams of negotiators have applied its elements in their business practice. When the learning curve is steep and the issues are of great importance, it is sometimes necessary to rapidly adapt to changing circumstances. From these experiences the robustness of the Process Model has been confirmed where it matters, in the world of real organizations run by real people.

The book moves on from purely tactical concerns of negotiation to the strategic contexts, where optimum, even excellent, bargaining skills are insufficient to secure success. The scale and context of complex negotiations require strategic awareness because the interests of the parties are more complex, the options more numerous and the outcomes more critical than at the tactical level. Strategic interests drive proposals and bargains and, beyond a low level of complexity, there are many more significant off-table events, which require coordination with the events happening across the table, than in simple two-person bargaining.

Strategic Negotiation is about higher-level judgement and discusses the interests, issues and positions, and the attendant options, as if we were in the same room. Necessarily, I will interpolate what I think you would ask if we were in live contact. My style is informal, primarily to avoid accusations of pedantry, but also to entertain as well as instruct. The book succeeds to the extent that it creates useful learning opportunities and assists you to achieve fitness in the subject.

Throughout you will find items labelled 'Activities' prompting you to evaluate from your own experiences. You may explore different lines of approach, using the suggestions as to how you might tackle the Activities, which constitute excellent practice in preparing for your live strategic negotiations, and you should attempt these to any degree with which you are comfortable.

That you may disagree with my selections and comments is a perfectly valid behaviour. Strategic negotiation is not an exact science like physics or mathematics. Remember, learning is about your learning and we learn best by correcting our mistakes and clarifying our confusions. That is how we learned to walk, talk and play games (what a bore it would be if every time you played golf you went round getting 18 holes-in-one – though some of my golfing friends may not agree!).

Of course, some mistakes could be fatal – you crash the plane in a flying lesson – but learning from a book is a safe environment, where mistakes are acceptable and where nothing fatal happens to you or anybody else due to your slip-ups and confusion. The real difficulty comes if you keep making the same mistakes dealing with the same problem! A US client firm I spent time at had a poster on a wall stating: 'Stupidity is when you keep doing the same thing and expect a different result!'

My task, as author, is to help you learn from your (and my) mistakes and to show you how to correct them before you make serious mistakes in the real world.

PART I

Foundations

Strategic Negotiation Process Model

Introduction

The Strategic Negotiation Process Model (the 'Process Model') in Figure 1.1 maps the stages of activity.

The Process Model is primarily concerned with the internal affairs of the organization and is expandable to include external affairs of the organization for the obvious reason that a large part of an organization's Negotiation Agenda consists of contracts negotiated with various external parties, for example suppliers, customers, government agencies and regulators, licensees and licensors, alliance partners, joint venture partners and parties involved in mergers and acquisitions. These are entered as items in the preparation phase or on the Negotiation Agenda as appropriate.

I shall discuss each entry in Figure 1.1 because it provides a model within which the concepts and ideas of negotiation strategy are understood. Once you work through the Process Model, you should find it fairly straightforward to apply it to almost any strategic negotiation task, either as a project leader and initiator, or as a negotiator/implementer of the Negotiation Agenda.

Foundations of the business plan

The subjects covered in the framework are the foundation upon which much of the strategic negotiation process rests. Without some basic knowledge of these subjects, not necessarily to the competence level found among professionals who advise senior management (lawyers, accountants, financial analysts and HR personnel), you would be severely handicapped and unable on many occasions to evaluate the advice you receive.

The alternative – hand everything over to the professionals – is not always wise because while authority can be delegated, responsibility for what happens

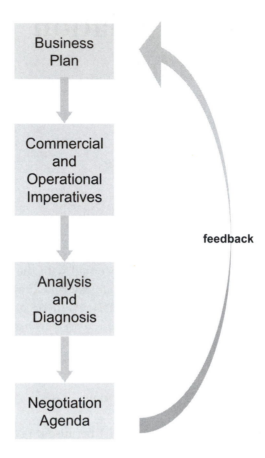

Figure 1.1   Strategic Negotiation Process Model

afterwards cannot. Therefore, it is better to retain close involvement in your operational responsibilities.

Among the framework foundations, you should have a degree of familiarity with the elements of contract law. The legal details vary for different jurisdictions but the fundamental elements are more or less the same: written contracts summarize the basic distrust each party has of the other. No contract at all (a handshake only) means higher vulnerability if the relationship breaks down; highly complex contracts signal high degrees of distrust that cover many contingencies. Prolonged precautionary contingency planning may cause resentment and damage the relationship before it starts.

Two important influences on the organization's people (pay and benefits; multi-parties) are inputs into *business plans*. Organizations consist of people who do the organizing and who determine the organization's pay and benefits regime. They also experience the people-management problems of prolonged multi-party meetings that put together the business plan and negotiate its implementation within the planning horizon.

Though this presentation is heavily focused on the pay and benefits regimes of North American and UK organizations, the framework has enough generic features to be translatable into the remuneration regimes of countries elsewhere.

The main instruments for business growth are licensing, joint ventures (JVs), mergers and acquisitions (M & As), bid management (tendering) and due diligence. The simple tools of bid and tender management are the most common methods for selecting suppliers for all levels of purchases.

Analysis and diagnosis

The tools of *analysis and diagnosis* supply substance to strategizing. The force field using the simplest of tools (or doodles) maps the various parties or personnel (the 'players') engaged for and against a proposition, the arguments used by the players in their attempts to influence the outcomes and the special role played by 'events' (exogenous shocks) that may tip the balance for or against either side.

The force field diagram, originated in Kurt Lewin's *Field Theory in Social Science* (1951), went through many developments and adaptations over the years. Originally it was an organizational change model. The force field diagram rests on the simple idea that at any one moment there are 'forces' operating on a situation, some of which *drive* for positive changes in the status quo and some of which *restrain* the driving forces to maintain the status quo. To the extent that these forces cancel each other, the status quo prevails.

Those who wish to change a situation work to strengthen the forces for the change (drivers) and weaken the forces against the change (restrainers); those who do not wish to change the situation will work to achieve the reverse (weaken the forces for change and strengthen the forces against change). Figure 1.2 shows a generic force field diagram.

Those forces that are highly important will attract the most attention (assuming they can be strengthened or weakened), although a typical error is to attend mainly to those forces than can be easily influenced, irrespective of

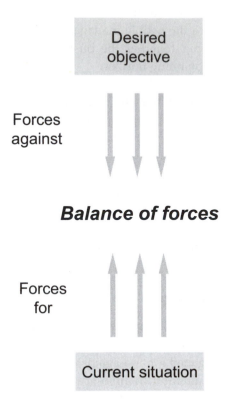

Figure 1.2   Force field diagram

the significance of their impact on the balance of forces. For example, we tend to spend more time influencing people who are already on our side – preaching to the converted – than we do on the more difficult targets entrenched against us.

The expanded force field develops this relatively simple notion for complex cases found in multi-party, multi-level and multi-issue negotiations, and also introduces people, issues and events occurring in the outside world where these can influence the negotiated outcomes.

The power element discusses the illusive question of how power might influence a negotiation using a 'power balance' tool.

The last element provides a tool for handling complex multi-party negotiations where other powerful influences and alliances are present. Long regarded as almost unmanageable in negotiation, McKinsey consultants developed graphical tools to bring into view a manageable instrument with great promise in this field.

Overview of seamless strategies

Problems in advising on strategy begin when the players adopt what is essentially an inappropriate strategic perspective – the strategy they propose is at variance with the goals it is supposed to tackle. This links to the material covered in the business plan.

I favour deriving the important *commercial imperatives* from the business plan because they are pivotal to achieving it. From the commercial imperatives we derive the *operational imperatives* in the three most prominent resources of the organization – finance, people and technologies – for achieving the commercial imperatives.

The operational imperative of human resources provides the detailed example in Chapter 8 of the generic method to determine the data for, and the content of, the Negotiation Agenda.

Also, there is a brief examination of the many complex problems that arise from the management of complex negotiations over long durations, involving multi-parties and interests, subject to great, and not always overt, political pressure, in an environment heavy with legal and regulatory interference.

What follows is a brief summary of elements of the seamless process from the organization's business plan to its implementation. It covers:

- the Business Plan
- Commercial and Operational Imperatives
- Analysis and Diagnosis
- the Negotiation Agenda.

BUSINESS PLAN

The organization's business plan concerns where the organization intends to be over the next 3 to 5 years. It can be a relatively long or short formal written statement, updated regularly, or an informal statement of a decision; even in a generic sense, it is not something conforming to a standard format (I have seen many variations of formats for business plans in organizations). We also consider 'interests and objectives' because an organization's interests are important for negotiation.

Interests are about our motivations for our preferences among various possible outcomes. They summarize our fears, hopes and concerns; they are *why* we negotiate for our objectives. Recalling our interests, stepping back on occasion to reconsider our interests – and theirs – and searching for alternative ways in which our interests can be delivered from among the issues, is or could be a powerful antidote to positional posturing by taking stances and refusing to move, or trying to convince the other party – and ourselves perhaps – that we will not move.

In carrying out the business plan you address your interests. If you don't then it is the wrong business plan. So while you may not have made a contribution to the writing of the organization's business plan, you should still be aware how its objectives reveal the organization's interests – assuming that they do; if they do not, make further enquiries! Hence, the need for regular reviews, using the resultant findings as data. In short, you should read and understand the business plan. As feedback is generated it also invites you to review the business plan (the vertical line to the right-hand side of Figure 1.1).

A general premise of the Process Model is that the organization's business plan is normally a given for those charged with implementing it. Usually, however, business plans are subject to review following feedback on operational performance, or because circumstances have changed within the organization's capabilities, or have changed outside it (competitively, technologically or environmentally).

How strategic objectives might be determined is not discussed here. We can note, however, that overly precise numbers are not congenial in negotiating situations – both sides of negotiators have a veto on the outcome, if only by exercising their right not to agree, and negotiators should always think in terms of ranges rather than single positions.

Individual managers in most organizations, taking as given that the CEO's or the board's business plan corresponds to the reality of everyday experience, accept, without assessing its validity, that the contents of the business plan are the parameters within which they must work. There can be major errors in the derivation of policies supposedly designed to implement business strategy and negotiators should be aware of their need to review proposed policies where they suspect dissonance between the strategic objectives and the policies proposed to achieve them. How they handle evident discrepancies comes under the file marked 'career decisions'!

CASE STUDY

Misleading Precise Instructions

Many years ago, John Benson and I attended a board meeting of a large family-owned shoe manufacturing business. It was our first consultancy assignment. The meeting was interrupted by news that one of the shoe plants was about to go on strike. In this company's 150-year history it had never experienced a strike and, therefore, the managing director (the last of the family members at the top of the company) was perplexed that matters had gone so far that a strike had been called. He asked the personnel director who was present for an explanation.

The gist of his explanation was that he had been instructed by the board to implement the company's voluntary redundancy scheme in the plant and was given the precise number required to take voluntary severance (ten per cent or 115 employees). In the event, only 97 volunteered, so he announced compulsory redundancies for the remaining 18 employees. It was the announcement of the compulsory 18 redundancies that had provoked threats of a strike.

Clearly angry, the managing director commented that the 97 volunteers were sufficient and they should have been processed immediately; also he should have been informed of the small shortfall before any public mention was made of compulsory redundancies.

Our view was that the board, when it set a target of employees to be invited to volunteer for severance, should have made clear that it had in mind a range of possible redundancies (95 to 115 jobs, say) and not a specific number as precise as 115, because a precise number is seldom realized in these situations and, anyway, is too precise – if exactly 95 jobs were to go, the situation was likely to be much worse than the precision suggests.

Also, if a review step had been introduced before action was taken in the event of not reaching a number in the range it would have assisted policy implementation. Ranges and review steps should be the norm, not the exception, in a company's planning process. The managing director's chastisement was itself an acknowledgement in favour of ranges not precision.

In practice, business plans should be subjected to regular adjustments, because time confirms, or otherwise, whether earlier plans continue to be applicable. For example, the dotcom boom-to-bust happened within a 3-year period in the mid 90s, dramatically illustrating the need for sober reassessment of plans once feedback makes it evident that events have changed the original imperatives driving the business.

In this respect, the objectives in the business plan – where the senior managers want their organization to be in a five-year horizon – are not the same as the fashion (indeed, it was once a passion) for mission statements, especially of the motherhood-and–apple-pie variety, that is, full of platitudes so obvious that no one disagrees with them or understands stating a need for them. This is not to say that deriving a mission statement is always unproductive. The Process

Model refers to operational business plans; those that have clearly defined or definable objectives, measured or measurable within the time horizon specified for their achievement, however they are recorded.

A 3- to 5-year planning range is sufficient for most purposes of negotiation planning and implementation. However, many contracts last much longer than five years, and during their operation over ten or twenty years ahead organizations experience many changing influences and circumstances; therefore, plans are best treated as flexible data.

Contracts still operating in years 6 to 20+ (for example, leases of property, patents and copyrights, terms and conditions of business, long-term supply and sales contracts, and, in several countries, public-private partnerships) may be treated for all intents and purposes as requiring new negotiations when operating conditions change, rather than being treated as items from an old Negotiation Agenda which were assembled in different circumstances 10 to 20 years previously.

Fighting old battles makes it all too easy to lose focus and difficult to regain it, partly as a result of poor preparation and partly because we are drawn into debating prominent symbols of our past disagreements. Either party could introduce a prominent number or boundary early into the discussions: 'one penny a quire'; 'draw a line in the sand'; 'indigenous labour only'; 'international wage rates to apply'; 'no re-exports'; 'payment in local currency'; '30 per cent withholding tax'; and such like. What is prominent attracts attention and subjects that attract attention become the foci. Positions for and against old foci are articulated, defended and fortified. Strategic focus is lost in exchanges of rhetoric.

The usual result is for the negotiation to become a single-issue haggle around yes-no stand-offs, with creeping zero-sum feelings about the outcome, if there is one, or a deadlock. Studying strategic negotiation helps to avoid these sub-optimal outcomes by reminding us all of why we are negotiating.

COMMERCIAL IMPERATIVES

You derive your commercial imperatives from the business plan (what you must do if you are to achieve it) and you derive your operational imperatives from the commercial imperatives, subjecting both sets of imperatives to analysis and diagnosis.

It is from your diagnosis of your operational imperatives that you determine what your organization must do to achieve the commercial imperatives that achieve the business plan. From these imperatives you compile your Negotiation Agenda, which facilitates senior management's endorsement of your negotiation objectives because you can demonstrate their credible and seamless link to their business plans.

To prepare for analysis and diagnosis, it is necessary first to derive the imperatives. Typical commercial imperatives might be:

- reduce bad debt provisions;

- reduce the labour cost base;

- extend distribution nationally/internationally;

- improve profitability to cover debt interest;

- reduce dependency on foreign agencies.

A rule of thumb, when presented with what appears to be a large number of possible commercial imperatives, is to prioritize those that have the most impact in achieving the objectives of the business plan.

For example, it may be that a commercial imperative of lowering the labour costs in a business where they account for 80 per cent of total costs (such as in a people-intensive hospital or education service) may be considered of higher priority than where they are only 8 per cent of total costs (such as in an oil refinery). In the latter case, priorities may be directed at capital costs and consumables used as throughputs in the refining of oil. The relationship between factor costs and their importance is not always proportionate, by the way, particularly where substitution between factors is possible (new technology or new ways of organizing labour) and where the next phase of the business plan aims to take advantage of such developments.

There are circumstances where labour costs in an oil refinery would be the priority commercial imperative, such as when data from other comparable refineries show that your operation has significantly higher labour costs than in refineries producing the same or greater output. A few years ago, British oil companies assisting the new Kazakhstan Oil Ministry noted that refineries there employed up to 15 000 people compared to similar (as measured by output, but definitely not in the technology used) refineries in Western Europe employing 1500 people.

Maybe a chosen commercial imperative, such as an increase in the proportion of patients admitted for day surgery and a reduction in multi-day in-patient care, should be considered of higher priority than lowering the labour cost base in surgery, because the employee resource implications of switching to a higher proportion of day surgery admissions are calculated to be significantly more important than its labour cost implications, given the impact of the change on other non-surgery costs, including labour pre- and post-treatment procedures.

Knowledge of an organization's commercial imperatives is usually widespread among experienced employees once they are asked to identify them. In most cases that I have worked upon, I found it takes less than a half-day session for employees to derive a long list of commercial imperatives for their organizations, even when working with fairly junior staff. Of course, arriving at a list does not prioritize the items appropriately, but it does show that there are untapped reservoirs of knowledge in organizations, even where it is not usual for them to be asked to use such knowledge for these purposes.

OPERATIONAL IMPERATIVES

Which resources will deliver your commercial imperatives? The Process Model concentrates on three functional imperatives of an organization:

- *people* – those who do the work and receive remuneration;

- *finance* – how and on what terms it is resourced;

- *technology* – what it does for the organization and what it costs (including how resources are organized and managed).

The resources at the disposal of an organization consist of three main types:

- Organizations work through people and can hardly function without at least one person in them, and despite companies having the separate legal status of being a 'legal person' in their own right, some real person's name must appear on the legal paperwork that ultimately defines the beneficial owner(s).

- Organizations do not function for long in a market without access to and use of some minimum level of finance, even if run by unpaid volunteers.

- Organizations use some kind of technique, embodied in technology protected by or using somebody's intellectual property rights or know-how from the public domain.

The basic operational resource questions for strategic negotiation are:

- People: What people mix must we assemble and retain?

- Finance: What capital mix should we assemble and pay for?

- Technology: What technology mix should we use and is it affordable?

The same person, or same small group, in small organizations (the most common organizational form of market capitalism) negotiates for its resources. In larger organizations different specialized functional managers negotiate for each resource heading. Essentially, whether a single individual or a specialized functionary, they have answered and continue to answer these questions in their managerial roles. The existing organization is the summation of the answers made to these questions in the past.

Typical people imperatives include:

- lowering the labour cost base

- 'decruitment'

- recruitment

- training

- remuneration packages

- outsource operations.

For finance imperatives you might choose from:

- in-house sources including from revenue or asset disposals

- initial public offering (IPO)

- new share issue

- joint ventures (JV), including outsourcing

- merger or acquisition (M&A)

- licensing

- franchising

- borrowing.

For technology imperatives you have many choices because under technology all manner of material and non-material inputs and organizational forms deliver commercial outputs.

CASE STUDY

Informed And Focussed

In negotiation it is easy for the wood to obscure the trees. For example, during an intense and expensive skill-enhancement programme for diagnostic engineers, it was noted that as their comparative pay rates fell behind other firms this hampered their retention, which in turn slowed the transition to the rescheduling of work processes and the introduction of new plant. The personnel director decided to address the pay issue by raising pay rates for those employees who had completed enhanced diagnostic skills training.

Oblivious of its strategic purpose, local (junior) personnel negotiators treated the exercise as a typical zero-sum pay bargain and succeeded by their normal standards by holding the increases of pay to about half the level needed to bring them into line with comparable rates in the district. With the disincentive to remain employed by the company that had trained them still in place, retention continued to be a problem, and it required swift remedial (and more expensive) action to correct.

The withholding of the strategic requirement (raise the remuneration of diagnostic engineers to enhance retention) could have been avoided if the personnel director had shared her knowledge of the business plan's intentions with the negotiators.

Technology can cover sophisticated IT through to hand axes, and basic teamwork and organization through to high-level managerial performance of large enterprises. Taking the broader idea of 'technology' we can generate considerable imperatives from which headings for the negotiation agenda are derived. Among these we have:

- intellectual property rights (IPR)

- R & D

- licenses and royalties

- JVs and M & As to gain access to needed technologies

- all aspects of people management and organizational change

- know-how

- innovation

- organizational forms.

To change the technological processes of the organization, you are not negotiating for change in the use of inanimate material objects and systems: you negotiate with people to adapt to changes in the way they work and cooperate, as well as with people in other organizations who supply the inputs of people and materials embedded in the technologies required for the resource mix.

The involvement of a wider range of personnel in the development of the organization's Negotiation Agenda (using the strategic negotiation approach) than is normal in traditional forms of preparation for major negotiations has the significant effect of improving the implementation phase of whatever is agreed. By enabling managers to see how their roles and the changes within them contribute to the success of the organization as the business plan unfolds, they see how a wider than normal spectrum of strategic thinking comes to be appreciated throughout the organization.

ANALYSIS AND DIAGNOSIS

What about non-commercial organizations in the public or non-profit-oriented sector? Can we identify meaningful commercial imperatives for them? At first sight it might not seem appropriate to label something as a commercial imperative in a non-commercial organization. But if you think about so-called non-commercial organizations, speaking about their commercial imperatives is entirely appropriate.

No publicly funded non-commercial organizations are immune to the iron law of the scarcity of resources. Governments, though perceived as such, are not bottomless pits for unlimited finance for the purposes of any organization, public or private. They are constrained by budgets, levels of politically acceptable taxation, and the competing demands of other organizations, many of which feel just as passionate about their aims and objectives and all of which articulate their demands through political rather than market forces.

This means that the commercial model of scarce resources competing for alternative uses is relevant. Of course, in some cases this is sensitive to the language of people managing publicly-funded organizations, though having conducted strategic negotiation concepts for charities and public sector organizations I have found little hostility towards the commercial language because they understood it was about enhancing their viability to undertake the social tasks they had set for themselves.

For example, when commercial language was introduced to the managers and their sponsors in a large public hospital, they expressed discomfort over the use of the terms 'business plan' and 'commercial imperatives' in a discussion of priorities in the funding of medical procedures ('money should never come into the treatment of illness'). For a while, 'business plans' became 'budget plans' and 'commercial imperatives' became 'targets'. In a short time, however, when the benefits of strategic negotiation preparation became apparent, these objections were first muted and then completely absent in their planning meetings.

In commercial organizations the imperatives relate to the matching of expenditures to what the markets will (eventually) pay for; in non-commercial organizations the imperatives relate to the matching of expenditures to what the budget holders (donors and the government) might renew in future budgets. Failures to perform in both types of organizations are punished by either markets or budget holders withholding resources. The imperatives to perform according to the business plan/budget plan have the same impact on any organization. Essentially, what you call them is less important than that you recognize them as 'imperatives'.

The analysis and diagnosis of the necessary operational imperatives that must be assembled to allow the commercial imperatives to deliver the business plan may be undertaken by business planners or delegated to staff and functional line managers. There are advantages in delegating the detailed staff work downwards to senior management and their staff. The greater the number of people who contribute to planning the implementation of the business plan, the more they are likely to align their activities afterwards to secure its successful outcome within the scheduled planning period. The fewer people – and the more senior – who are privy to the business plan, the more its realization is vulnerable to the distractions of daily management and the slower the necessary imperatives are mobilized to achieve the plan's objectives.

NEGOTIATION AGENDA

Management should take regular surveys of the future of the enterprise. Important as wage costs are, they are not always decisive, because other costs, including the level of productivity, may be as important. A failure to tackle a need to restructure the composition of a business, should it be necessary because of the changing markets, changing technologies or changing sources of finance, could have a devastating effect.

The Negotiation Agenda is a well-thought-out proactive strategy for conducting relationships with employees, suppliers and customers. It always contains a longer list of potential issues than the number raised for a specific negotiation. Should it be necessary or helpful, unused items from the Negotiation Agenda may be entered into current negotiations in pursuit of an agreement. No management should be stuck for ideas about what they can put forward should opportunities or difficult circumstances arise in which they do not know how to put a price on the other party's demands.

It is an assertion of the strategic negotiation approach that the derivation of the Negotiation Agenda adds greatly to the smoother implementation of the necessary changes and to the flexibility with which adjustments can be made should events show them to be necessary.

Policy choices made in the pre-negotiation phase are costed carefully and integrated into the Negotiation Agenda. Should the agenda items be agreed, allowing for adjustments that may be necessary in the light of negotiated changes in the original proposals, their implementation should follow the plan discussed during preparation for the negotiations.

Negotiation of changes in working practices is bedevilled by poor preparation by those making proposals for changes. If the details prove overwhelming, timelines slip and the exceptions so corrupt the proposed changes that people lose interest in continuing with the meetings and the changes never materialize.

One of the many benefits to management of having a Negotiation Agenda is that its derivation requires consideration of the organization's objectives as specified in the business plan and of the identification of imperatives of performance. This moves negotiation from being a routine chore (something that interrupts the proper work of management) to itself delivering the organization's objectives.

The Negotiation Agenda imposes its own discipline on the time allocated to preparation and the tasks associated with it. The old routine of waiting to respond to a wish list of demands from employees' representatives, or to demands and loaded suggestions from business partners, or simply relying on the lazy habits of preparing by waiting to hear what they have to say and grabbing an unopened file of recent correspondence, handing the initiative to the other party, is just not good enough. Everybody knows this, but few avoid such bad habits on some and sadly more than some occasions. Negotiators instead, who always take the time to gain command of the details, to cost the various options and uncover potentially useful variations in what they may want to achieve, consistently do better than those who don't.

Moreover, because the Process Model requires current negotiation objectives to be linked seamlessly to the organization's business plan, it facilitates gaining the approval of higher management for the objectives of the Negotiation Agenda. Post-negotiation feedback and review is also enhanced and future negotiation performances are thereby improved.

IMPLEMENTATION

Changes in an organization's policies may be prompted by:

- changing environments in which the organization operates (examples: market competition, government regulations, taxation policies, trade regimes, exchange rates, labour and other laws, job security);

- changes in an organization's strategic focus (examples: national or international markets, diversification, consolidation, vertical or horizontal integration or disintegration, growth through mergers or acquisition, profitability through spin out and disposals, cost cutting and retrenchment);

- changes in the organization's technology (examples: IT, online publishing, online banking, online sourcing, insurance, borrowing, screening, profiling; bar coding, POS; JIT, TQM, wireless connectivity, satellite, cable, digital entertainment; mobile phones, video, text messaging, Internet, synthetic materials, prescription drugs, R&D, organizational change, and so on).

These changes (too many to enumerate) place constant pressure on the organization and the way it functions. Some of the changes may have distinct competitive advantages, which could affect the future of the enterprise. If, for whatever reason, you do not implement the necessary changes and one of your competitors does, then any competitive advantage you have over your rival could be eroded. To complicate your decision making, not all changes that promise competitive advantage fulfil their promises – an anticipated first-mover advantage could become first-mover folly.

The changing policies agreed with those affected by them are assessed by how they affect the mix of people, finance and technology that constitute what the business is about, how it operates, its success or otherwise and the contribution each makes to the organization's varied purposes.

In any negotiation, not all proposed changes are agreed in their original form. Proposals have to survive the scrutiny of others. Some bring their experience to bear in the form of advice; for others, their interests lead them to propose amendments or, indeed, to signify outright rejection of what is suggested. And this is not the case only where trade unions exist to protect, as they see it, their members' interests, including at the expense of other employees. There may be explicit negotiations and implicit influence games underway among any group of employees. All kinds of people, besides militant trade unionists, can offer awkward opposition to whatever you propose.

Finding reasons to say no to change in any organization is among the easiest of reactions to all proposals to change anything, trivial or serious. The management of change is still under-researched. One thing we do know for certain is that in any change programme, as in the management of existing and well-established programmes, there are distinct roles for negotiation and influence techniques in implementing the changes.

REVIEW AND FEEDBACK

Securing board-level approval (and commitment) for the Negotiation Agenda is facilitated by its demonstrated seamless connection to the organization's business plan. This is an important benefit of undertaking the preparatory work to procure the Negotiation Agenda. Managing change to assemble the appropriate resource mix has cost implications, which normally are under the discretion of the organization's board or devolved to senior management functions. Fully-costed options from the Negotiation Agenda have a greater chance of securing higher-level approvals where they directly support or deliver the objectives of the higher-level's specified objectives.

Feedback is part of the implementation phase and it is an important and integral part of the Process Model. If there are discrepancies in any of the negotiable issues beyond those planned by the negotiation team, an explanation should be offered (it should certainly be required by higher-level management), with details of the likely consequences for the realization of the business plan and what suggestions the negotiation team has to recover, rectify or remedy each discrepancy, and over what time period.

Some of the items in the feedback report will have obvious quantitative discrepancies compared to the original negotiation plan submitted to the board or CEO for sign-off prior to the negotiations. These will be clearer from negotiations on finance than on human resources or technology. How far the tolerance of the top-tier managers extends for bottom-of-the-range achievements on quantitative finance issues, allegedly compensated by softer, less-tangible gains in terms of future relationships, goodwill and cooperation, is an open question, much dependent on the general environment in which the organization finds itself. This goes back to the manner in which the Negotiation Agenda is drawn up and the attention it pays to these softer achievements.

Feedback is directed at all those involved in the strategic negotiation process, as well as being an input into the review process. Experience suggests that it is better to be able to show positive improvements, no matter how small or intangible, across all targets, than a mixed set of major improvements in some dimensions mixed with significant negatives in others, particularly if the former are confined exclusively to the softer targets and the latter exclusively to the harder numbers.

Post-negotiation reviews should also provide feedback on the negotiation process as a whole, what worked well, what not so well, and what lessons may be learned for future negotiations of the Negotiation Agenda.

CASE STUDY

Ripe For Change

The case illustrates the need to prepare properly in complex negotiations. It also illustrates the consequences of treating a large cost element in an organization's activities as a residual.

A large organization involved in providing higher education services for many years approached the annual pay negotiations by the residual budget method – labour costs were treated as an aggregate expenditure, to which a range was added to cover likely increases in pay for the coming year and this was the extent of the preparation for the annual round of wage negotiations! The organization's remuneration strategy was based on the arithmetic of a percentage increase in labour costs unrelated to the business needs of the organization (including the suitability of the current employment structure for identified future developments within the organization). It was woefully inadequate.

A similar treatment was given to other budget headings, such as capital, buildings, maintenance and repairs, and marketing.

What was left over after each item was allocated its increase – the residual – was squeezed to fit the remaining headings. Because labour negotiations tend to continue past the start of the budget year, it was common for the budget for pay increases to be derived from a residual amount after every other heading had been determined.

The main weakness of such a process was obvious. With two thousand employees, labour costs were a high proportion of total costs. Because blanket percentages were usually applied covering most, if not all, of the functional groups and grades, these percentages tended to be small for everybody, irrespective of the changing needs for labour.

While small increases in pay are not wrong in themselves, they do not allow for differentiation among employee groups or sub-groups, and this inhibits using pay as an instrument to adjust the size or the rewards of those groups that contribute to the growth of and changes within the organization, and those which add only to costs and contribute little to the future of the organization. Also, in periods of budgetary restraint – a not uncommon feature of publicly funded organizations – low and unchanging pay levels contribute to loss of morale and inhibit employees exercising their initiative, either to seek and participate in retraining or to seek employment elsewhere. Good employees tend to leave for better-paid jobs elsewhere, and poorer employees tend not to move because their options are limited. Thus, the average quality of employees, with exceptions of course, declines without new-blood infusions.

In addition to the budgetary-driven pay policy, the organization practised an annual automatic increment policy – most people were placed within narrow pay bands or grades and received annual increments in pay, independent of negotiated annual increases within the pay ranges of the grades and independent of individual or group performance, but wholly dependent on length of service. Combining the two policies of negotiated increases in pay and automatic annual increments merely for being employed, the organization had a poor pay system because it made employment and its rewards independent of personal effort, initiative and contribution to the changing future of the organization.

The organization decided it needed a pay strategy related more closely to its organizational objectives. The major obstacles to change included the inflexibility of employees across all grades. Many employees had reached the top of their pay grade and were thus ineligible for automatic annual increments. For them, annual negotiated increases were important because they were the only routes to higher pay. As the negotiated increases were relatively small, they were dissatisfied and unwilling to cooperate in necessary change programmes the organization needed to implement, if it was to justify its budgets to achieve its agreed objectives.

For those employees benefiting from annual increments as they passed through the pay grade, their pressure for higher annual increases was modified, but their pressure to prevent changes was enhanced (until they reached the ceiling for their grade). Changes meant redesignating their employees' functional grades, which could end their upward movement through the grade. The result was general inflexibility in the employee grades. The situation was ripe for the application of the Strategic Negotiation Process Model to its remuneration and reward policies.

The Model starts from the organization's business plan – what it intended to achieve within a five-year horizon. In education, such a plan could include a target of transforming its catering programmes into wider hospitality management programmes (which is much more than a mere change of name) and changing its secretarial, mainly typing, programmes into IT literacy programmes for modern office computer networks, and so on. Immediately, in human resources terms, the Strategic Negotiation Process Model identified a need to retrain and replace traditional cookery and typing teaching resources with the requisite skills for teaching hospitality management and IT. This led to thinking about how these types of transformations of resources (there were many more than only the two of them identified here) could be managed and over what time period, in part by using the pay and reward negotiations to support the changes.

What began as a simple pay and reward strategy, soon involved management in a total review of all aspects of the educational institution, and from the mass of data collected it became a useful educational exercise for the institution's employees at all levels. It certainly motivated senior management in the immense tasks facing the organization if it was to adapt to a changing educational environment hitherto ignored in previous isolated pay negotiations.

Instead of more of the same, which manifested itself in too cosy an acceptance of the decline of the relevance of the institution to the changing educational needs of the community in its current configuration (which it could only serve poorly, thus opening a future threat, evident from a SWOT – strengths, weaknesses, opportunities and threats – analysis), the institution acquired an insightful vision of what it should be doing with which employee mix. Some were retained and retrained, and others phased out with natural wastage, retirements and transfers, to meet the imminent and future challenges. Changing a situation over time is usually more productive and less costly than changing one relatively suddenly amidst a crisis.

Crucially, it also acquired the determination to undertake the change programme to rejuvenate the institution's relevance to the local community, based on a realistic and manageable strategy. Comparing the change programme's effects on the institution with similar unchanged institutions in the country, the differences were almost all positive. Of the negatives, these were not fundamental and were manageable because they were not left unattended and allowed to fester.

Activities
for Chapter 1

Activity 1.1

Make a list of the items about which you or your organization negotiates with both internal and external parties.

COMMENTS ON THIS ACTIVITY

You may list any formal negotiations (remuneration and staff conditions, budgets, project management schedules, contracts, licences, service level agreements, property purchases and disposals, and so on) as well as the informal negotiations you undertake from time to time, such as between departmental responsibilities, staff-related issues, inter-departmental relations, coordination meetings and reviews, rearrangements of location, activity and appraisal reviews, and so on.

A fairly common conclusion is the surprising extent to which most managers are engaged in negotiation in their work roles.

Activity 1.2

Think of a current discussion about a problem in your work role where there are competing solutions. To what extent can you identify the people who are in favour of and those who are against the competing solutions to the problem under discussion?

COMMENTS ON THIS ACTIVITY

If there is disagreement over a solution it should be a fairly simple task to divide those for and against the proposed solution into two groups. Think of the people who oppose the change in the status quo as being resisters to those favouring the change. There are also people driving for the change.

To change a situation, drivers must overcome restrainers. In principle, you could visualize the two groups (restrainers and drivers) as counterpoised to each other in a diagram, much like two teams of competing sports personnel drawn on a diagram representing their locations on the field of play.

Activity 1.3

What contribution did you make to your organization's business plan?

Have you had access to it (normally these documents, which vary in design and content, are treated as 'commercial in confidence')?

Have any of its contents percolated down to your pay grade?

If you were involved in compiling your organization's business plan, what arrangements were made to involve the staff in understanding their roles in achieving the plan's objectives?

COMMENTS ON THIS ACTIVITY

Working at the strategic level in an organization requires that you are guided in some way by the organization's business plan, or its equivalent, even if it is only a statement about where the organization's leadership wish the organization to be within the next five years. If you were involved in contributing to the business plan then you should be well placed to make a practical contribution to the implementation of the strategy, using some of the techniques and tools of Strategic Negotiation.

Activity 1.4

In the organization that employs you, how would you distinguish its fundamentals from other organizations (labour–capital balance; business-to-business or business-to-customer; active in the primary, heavy/light industry, service, government agency or voluntary sector)?

From these fundamentals, what might constitute necessary imperatives to improve the survivability of your organization?

In what order would you prioritize the various fundamentals associated with your organization?

COMMENTS ON THIS ACTIVITY

If your organization is in the voluntary sector and you rely on part-time unpaid volunteers to carry out its functions, with a small core of paid employees, you may have a different requirement in terms of training and discipline than if you employ all staff on a full-time paid basis, working under the direction of a volunteer policy-making charity.

Government organizations are part of the country's public services and subject to political management (keeping the politicians at bay and the public on board could be the priority, and the reverse, of course).

Activity 1.5

Survey your organization and consider if there is anything you would like to change as a manager for the benefit of the organization but, because you anticipate resistance from individuals, the departments affected or for some other reason, you feel helpless to try.

COMMENTS ON THIS ACTIVITY

Management seldom has unilateral discretion to change current working arrangements without at least consultation with the managers and employees affected and, where the changes are fundamental, without some version of a negotiation of what is intended (that is, the consent of the majority of those affected by the changes). In unionized environments, negotiation is mandatory, but it is not uncommon for managements to feel discouraged from attempting to open negotiations on certain issues because the anticipated resistance could be more trouble than they believe the outcome is worth.

You have been asked, in effect, to identify any such changes that you believe would improve operational efficiency. Do not select changes by first assessing your chances of obtaining them. Of course there are issues of resistance, but until you have compiled the Negotiation Agenda it is not possible to judge what you will trade for cooperation.

Basics of Contracts

CHAPTER

2

Introduction

This chapter covers the basics of written contracts. In my experience, knowledge of the basics is not widespread amongst negotiators, who usually leave all contractual matters to professional lawyers. While it is always advisable to involve lawyers early and at every subsequent stage in a major negotiation, it is also an essential part of the strategic negotiator's toolkit to have a working knowledge of what is involved in a written contract, just as a basic knowledge of human resources management, accountancy and finance, marketing and economics is deemed useful to manage at most middle and senior levels. Contracts summarize the distrust of each party of the other.

I shall provide a *negotiator's* (not a lawyer's) perspective on some main contractual clauses and their importance. It won't get you through any law exams, but it will give you some idea of what your lawyer is talking about when they have a word with you during a break in the negotiations, and indeed when they whisper advice during a session. It might be useful too when you have to assess and respond to a proposition that has legal implications for your deal.

Promises, promises

Promises are the lifeblood of relationships. Friedrich Nietzsche, the philosopher, claimed that humans were the first animals to learn to keep their promises; he added, more for dramatic shock than literal accuracy, that the earth was drenched red with the blood of those that failed to keep theirs.

Times change. Nowadays, written contracts summarize the residual distrust each party feels about the other's promises. Contracts are enforceable in law. And they are negotiable; hence, as a business negotiator you will not negotiate for long before you come across a written contract.

CASE STUDY

Incentivizing Honesty

An elderly Arab trader I met in Kuwait in the late 90s described to me how his great-grandfather had left his grandfather, then only 12, with an Emir's family as surety that he would return from a trading voyage for the Emir to East Africa. His gesture of drawing his fingers across his throat made brutally clear the fate of his grandfather, should his great-grandfather have failed to return for any reason.

For many reasons, you ought not to leave contractual matters entirely to your lawyers; nor do you need specialized legal training to contribute to or judge the merits of a contract's contents. There is much to be said for negotiators becoming familiar with the elements of contract law – not to replace your lawyers (perish the thought!) but because lawyers must interpret your intentions; the more clearly these are expressed, the more likely it is that the papers you sign will accurately represent your promises and protect your intentions.

Anatomy of contracts

I start with a brief run through the basic principles of contracts because contractual promises (obligations) underpin almost all business transactions. This is true of relations between independent parties (two separate organizations) and between people and departments within the same organization. A promise to perform (and to pay for performance) is an obligation which the enforceable contract summarizes and records. There are penalties for failing to perform as promised: in legal contracts these are specified in the contract or in general law; in informal contracts or understandings the penalties suffered may be political in terms of your career prospects.

The ten main elements of a contract are:

- the identities and addresses of the parties;

- statements of their expertise and their explicit wish to contract;

- definitions and meanings of words used throughout the contract;

- promised obligations and warranties, and indemnities for not keeping them;

- rewards for performance;

- penalties for non-performance;

- duration and termination of the contract;

- 'boiler plate' clauses (for example, governing jurisdiction);

- schedules supporting the contract;

- signatures of the parties and witnesses.

No matter who drafts a contract you should read every clause carefully for understanding, and you should cross-check every reference made to other clauses (when you first come across them). This might mean occasional awkward page turning, but the advantages of checking the connections together when first mentioned outweighs relying on reading the clauses in sequence and memorizing earlier references where the significance of related clauses may be missed.

What is standard, even innocuous, to a lawyer may have unexpected consequences for you (due to your misunderstanding) when you operate the contractual terms over the duration of the contract. The basic rule for all negotiators is: what you include you live with; what you do not include, you live without.

Taking each element in turn, you should soon appreciate its relevance to your negotiations. Remember, however, that I provide a negotiator's generic perspective on the ten elements of contracting and not a set of robust legal interpretations for all jurisdictions and circumstances.

NB: *Qualified lawyers experienced in the jurisdiction of your business should always be consulted for authoritative guidance and advice.*

After many years experience of training lawyers in negotiation, I found that lawyers and (non-legally minded) negotiators think differently when considering a negotiable legal point. The lawyer places the negotiable point in the context of the law on the legal point; the negotiator places the legal point in the context of its contribution to a negotiated solution.

For example, in discussing with managers the choice between 'stalling in the payment of an invoice containing a disputed item' and 'paying the invoice minus the disputed item', the usual view of lawyers is that because the law (in the UK) requires the latter course of action only and not the former, therefore that is what you should (must!) do.

To contemplate stalling on the whole amount of the invoice would be wrong in law; therefore, negotiators are advised by lawyers to avoid the stalling option. The perspective of a negotiator could be different.

To stall is not necessarily to refuse payment explicitly (that would be illegal) but stalling is of vague meaning and duration. Delaying payment on the whole invoice for any plausible reason ('our accounting system does not allow part payment of an invoice once it is presented and as our policy is not to pay for disputed items, we can only expedite matters if you re-issue separate invoices or issue a credit note for the disputed items') may put pressure on your supplier to come to a settlement sooner rather than later. In other words, the negotiator seeks actions that maximise leverage on them to come to a satisfactory settlement, without provoking legal retribution.

THE PARTIES

Contracts are between parties (of which there may be two or more). The names and addresses are identified at the head of a contract. Where it is a standard licence for, say, a software package, the licensor is identified by name. The licensee may only be identified as the 'licensee' and not by name because thousands buy and use the product and printing out licences for thousands of different people would be cumbersome administratively.

You should check carefully the names and addresses of the parties as a matter of routine. Banks do. If companies with famous names are subsidiaries of the main company with the same name, the holding company may not accept recourse by creditors to recover contractual debts incurred by its subsidiary. This might be important if there were a need to seek recourse for non-performance or breach of a bank covenant (such as a requirement to maintain a profit level that covers a multiple of bank interest on its loans). Linking in the title and address of a subsidiary to its head office or holding company, especially if in another country or legal jurisdiction, may have useful consequences if a dispute arises over recourse. What is included in this clause – as in other clauses – is in principle negotiable.

STATEMENTS AND EXPLICIT WISHES

The recitals usually begin with 'Whereas' as in:

> *Whereas Acme Investments Limited specializes in raising and investing venture capital and wishes to invest in Omega Electronics Pty., Limited, and Omega Electronics Pty. Limited, a long established innovator and installer of security devices for protecting commercial property, wishes*

CASE STUDY

No Recourse

For many years a consortium of large independent brewers, which also owned thousands of branded retail outlets across the country, jointly owned a soft drinks company trading under the brand name Britvic, which manufactured and supplied its products to all the retail outlets of the otherwise competing members of the consortium. But Britvic creditors did not have legal recourse to its ultimate owners or their assets. The owners of the consortium specifically excluded liability for Britvic's debts in their terms of business. While Britvic was highly profitable and covered its debts comfortably, there was unlikely to be a problem with this arrangement.

Nevertheless, many of the banks involved in financing Britvic's multiple manufacturing plants and distribution fleets were keen to persuade the various owners to allow them legal recourse, which the owners as earnestly (and politely) refused to contemplate. The debt figure totalled many tens of millions of pounds and was based solely on the security of the cash flow from multi-million sales of Britvic's products.

So check your rights of recourse in your contracts – the large brand name with which you draw comfort in your dealings with a similar sounding name may not be guaranteeing your deal to the extent that you imagine. Note that banks lend to small limited liability businesses, but usually only on the security of their owners' homes.

---

to commission Acme Investments Limited to raise funds for the Chimp Drive, a patented product.'

This clause has a clear enough purpose. It states that Acme contracts wishes to raise investment funds and place them with Omega, and Omega contracts wishes to use the funds for the Chimp Drive. The precise wording of 'Whereas' clauses is negotiable.

The rest of the contract states the terms under which both parties promise to carry out their intentions and what happens if they do, or fail to do, what they promised.

DEFINITIONS AND MEANINGS

Often skimped by the careless. Yet the definitions and explicit meanings of the words used in a contract could have serious consequences. They are usually listed in alphabetical order but they can also follow an order related to their first appearance in the text of the contract.

Definitions, you should remember, are negotiable. You can change the wording, or add limitations to clarify their meaning and the scope of their applicability.

CASE STUDY

Check Their Definitions

A Publisher asked an Author to amend his book contract to allow it to produce and sell a PDF version on a CD. The Author had reserved his book's electronic rights with a view to selling them separately if a market for e-books materialised. Providing the Publisher's rights to a CD version were restricted, and did not include electronic rights over the Internet, the Author was agreeable to an amendment (note the conditional proposition).

Close examination of the Publisher's definitions showed an attempted sleight of hand, or at the very least carelessly drafted definitions! The definition of a 'CD' (compact disk) referred to 'electronic formats'. Innocuous enough, except that among the other definitions, 'electronic formats' were also defined to include 'electronic rights in the World Wide Web'.

The Author struck the subsequent definition of 'electronic formats' and required that the CD definition dropped its reference to 'electronic formats'. If he had failed to read the definitions carefully he would have inadvertently signed away the electronic rights.

OBLIGATIONS, WARRANTIES AND INDEMNITIES

These clauses are usually presented as 'Obligations of Party A' (the first party mentioned in the list of the parties) followed by 'Obligations of Party B'. Together these state the parties' promises within the terms of the contract. Often, phrases like 'use best endeavours' (even 'reasonable endeavours') are sprinkled about and you should consider the degree to which these loosen or tighten your obligations. Relying on obligations wrapped in terminology like 'use reasonable endeavours' may not be wise; offering obligations qualified by 'best endeavours' may not be prudent. Of course, an obligation not qualified with 'best' or 'reasonable', however tightly or loosely these are interpreted, becomes mandatory in effect – a commitment like 'will deliver' is unqualified (except by a *force majeure* clause).

Warranties and indemnities go together. They can be and are often meant to be extensive and draconian. They are also negotiable up to a point, depending on how vulnerable you feel about diluting the meaning of a warranty or an indemnity.

You may not know how much reliability to place on another party's statements and, where the risk of default is high it is prudent to discourage false and misleading affirmations of performance. Requiring warranties and indemnities discourages tendencies for parties to be economical with the truth.

CASE STUDY

Show Me The Contract!

In 1994, a large multi-hundred-million-dollar hidden black hole in the audited accounts of the International Signal and Control Company (ISCC), Lancaster, Pennsylvania, forced Ferranti, a leading UK defence technology firm, into liquidation after it concluded a merger deal in 1987. Investigators found that ISCC had knowingly overstated forecasted business volumes and profits, thus raising the acquisition price of its shares.

Alleged multi-million-dollar firm orders for defence products by the Pakistan government turned out to be verbal, non-binding understandings, between ISCC executives and certain members of the military government. The death of President Zia of Pakistan in 1988 in a ('suspicious') air crash revealed the fantasy nature of these sales in the ISCC accounts, not assuaged by fraudulent denials by the military officers who negotiated the fantasy deals. The warranties and indemnities given by the ISCC executives did not save Ferranti because ISCC went bankrupt (though several ICCS executives were convicted of defrauding Ferranti of US$1.1 billion and were jailed by US Courts).

Due diligence procedures have limitations, especially when conducted under severe time pressure (sellers do not always give bidders enough time) and there is little protection when there is deliberate and fraudulent intent on the part of the sellers. Ferranti sought damages from the accountancy firms and the lawyers who conducted the due diligence, because they were not diligent enough.

Detecting fraud on the ISCC scale requires the most scrupulous and time consuming of due diligence investigations ('show me the contracts!'). Warranties do not deter fraudsters who believe they can grab the money and hide. Indemnities are worthless if they cannot be collected. ISCC is a rare example of breach of faith on a grand scale!

For example, a seller of a business is required to warrant that their disclosure of sales, profits, costs, cash in hand, creditors and pending litigation are truthful and fully stated. Because of your rigorous 'due diligence' searching of the seller's accounts, titles to property and lists of creditors, assuming there is sufficient time, you may decide to purchase their business on the basis of their statements. Black holes hidden from you in the accounts have a habit of causing unpleasant surprises. Adding warranties and indemnities to protect you from the consequences of making assumptions on what they say and what you have not found out may well be prudent.

REWARDS

Commercial contracts seek commercial gains for the parties. Sellers seek commercial gain from selling products, services or tangible properties for more than they cost to acquire; buyers seek commercial gain from using or exploiting what they buy to create in due course sellable outputs (products,

CASE STUDY

Perils Of Plagiarism

New authors are shocked sometimes (assuming they read their contracts) by the severity of the warranties and indemnities (no resort to 'best' or 'reasonable endeavours' here!) that they are required to give when asserting that their work is original and belongs entirely to them, except for written permissions from third party copyright owners (other authors' work quoted or included in their text). From the publishers' perspective, warranties and indemnities need to be unduly severe to deter plagiarism.

If the author's work turns out to be somebody else's, in whole or in part (plagiarism), it could cost the publisher dear. Apart from the monetary costs in damages to the original author, legal fees, costs of pulping the offending copies, and reprinting a clean edition, there is the damage to the publisher's good name and reputation. Hence, should authors breach their warranties; publishers can enforce tight indemnities from them to cover their costs.

When authors realize the severity and blanket coverage of their warranties and indemnities in standard authors' contracts, they have the obvious choice of not plagiarising the works of other authors (though some new authors naively try to negotiate to weaken the severities of these clauses). If they ignore their vulnerability, should they be exposed as plagiarists, they bring upon themselves the avoidable pain occasioned by their wilful negligence of the property rights of others.

services or tangible properties) realized from adding value to the purchased inputs.

The benefits could include: the seller constructs a tunnel which the buyer uses to enable trains to take fare-paying passengers to their destinations. The seller gains the construction cost of the tunnel, plus a profit; the buyer uses the facility of the tunnel to collect revenue, plus a profit, from its users.

PENALTIES

Penalties can be monetary or terminal (or both). They are also negotiable. The first kind features in oil and gas contracts and is quite draconian, though equitable.

Excluding limited *force majeure*, 'send-or-pay' is the supplier's penalty for non-delivery of oil or gas to, say, a power station customer. Send-or-pay compensates customers for having to purchase supplies from elsewhere, which allows power stations to avoid breaching their contracts for delivering fuel to their customers.

'Take-or-pay' is the customer's penalty for non-acceptance of oil or gas delivered by a supplier. Take-or-pay compensates oil and gas suppliers that have to reschedule delivery of their output to other customers, or to storage, with consequential additional costs. Both parties to these contracts expect to maintain their outloooked incomes over a production period. The alternative would be endless disputes between suppliers and customers over who owed what to whom.

In construction, penalties include 'liquidated damages' clauses specifying a maximum amount that may be charged for non-performance, often capped at a percentage of the contract value, payment of which liquidates further penalties (it not being in the normal interests of a client to bankrupt a contractor in the midst of a project by imposing large compensation claims).

The most draconian penalty would be to impose claims for 'consequential loss', that is sufficient to cover all the losses attributed, and attributable, to a failure of a contractor to perform. Where these are unlimited, the viability of a firm is at risk and often becomes the focus of intense negotiation whenever consequential loss clauses are proposed. You do not have to agree to a consequential loss clause, or any clause, and to agree to one suggests a lack of understanding on your part of what 'consequential loss' means, or perhaps your utter desperation to win business. The existence of consequential loss clauses in your contracts should be reportable to a buyer under prudent due diligence procedures, supported by your warranties that you are fully disclosing all known risks to the viability of the business, enforceable by tight indemnities in case you forget, or make incomplete disclosures, about them.

Other financial penalties include various forms of 'performance bonds'. These include the sum of money you must deposit with the buyer's bank, which amount may be drawn upon by the buyer should there be a failure to perform. In recent years, performance bonds have acquired an association with corruption on the part of government ministers and officials in some countries. Corrupt governments demand performance bonds allowing the customer department to order the release of the bonds to the minister or senior official. Such bonds are collusive invitations to theft. Sometimes the supplier connives at the corruption; other times the officials mislead suppliers into believing their bonds are safe. Again, don't whine over what you shouldn't sign.

The original intention of performance bonds was to ensure satisfactory performance by government suppliers, predicated upon an honest government, the highest probity of the officials and the independent rule of law. Properly performing contractors received their bonds back in full; those that allegedly did not perform were assured of legal due process through independent courts before any sums were released from their bonds to the clients. Where these conditions do not apply, do your business elsewhere.

A milder version of a performance bond is a 'retention money' clause in building and construction contracts. This allows the client to hold back about five per cent of the contract value until some specified time after completion of the work. The idea is that to receive final payment of the total agreed amount, the contractor has to attend to all snags (unfinished items of work listed by the client's architect, and inspected and agreed with the contractor), including cleaning up and making good the usual messy detritus of a building site.

Amounts of retention money and conditions for their release to the contractor are negotiable, as is the definition of material non-performance during a contractor's schedule of work.

DURATION AND TERMINATION

Non-performance of a material contractual obligation, if not remedied, could result in termination of the contract should the offended party push for it. Every contract should contain this provision (if it does not, it should not be signed – though remember, don't just complain about its absence, propose an amendment). Occasionally, the drafters of contracts include a termination provision for themselves by a one-way provision in their favour only. As always, propose an amendment to make the termination clause two way, not just one way.

Other standard termination causes include when:

- a party goes into administration, bankruptcy, or liquidation;
- there is a takeover by new beneficial owners or competitors;
- there is a breach of 'fiduciary duty';
- a party is brought into disrepute by the other party;
- there are 'material breaches' of the contract's provisions.

Some termination clauses in contracts (for example, employees' and directors' service contracts) distinguish between:

- 'termination for cause';
- 'termination without cause'.

CASE STUDY

Expensive Error

An HR department agreed to a bonus deal for drivers related to the value of their deliveries of its products to customers, but it did not mention the duration in its agreement. As time went by, the formula to calculate the amount of the bonus escalated the amount to be paid, boosted by price inflation, which distorted the company's intended remuneration policies. The union refused to renegotiate the bonus formula. The employer eventually had to buy out the bonus at considerable expense.

CASE STUDY

'In Perpetuity' Is Not Forever

A US lawyer's firm signed a deal 'in perpetuity' for the use of a European firm's intellectual property rights, which a US firm wished to repurpose for Asian markets, while it developed it own versions of the product. The US firm paid $3 million as royalties in advance for the rights to repurpose. In year 3 of the in perpetuity deal, the US firm initiated a series of claims for breach of contract and threatened to sue for the return of its annual licence fees. The European firm challenged the unanticipated claims and the threat to sue for the return of paid IPR fees. Deadlock ensued.

Before going to trial, both sides revised their expectations of success, and its costs, and negotiated a settlement. The in perpetuity deal was terminated, leaving each party with the status quo: the US firm was not liable for further annual royalty payments; the European firm kept the earlier royalty payments, and the US firm relinquished its rights to repurpose the European's IPR. In retrospect, the European negotiators concluded that this was the outcome the US lawyers intended from the start.

The former follows any of the events that cause standard termination. Termination without cause permits a party to terminate a contract – even one nominally in perpetuity – merely by giving notice of an intention to do so (negating the validity of the in perpetuity provision). If the contract includes this provision, no cause need be given, and the circumstances it covers may be reasonable or unreasonable. Contracts including a termination without cause provision usually specify the associated compensation provisions, unlike termination for cause clauses.

In employment or service contracts, one party may come to believe that it isn't working out – you are not getting along with them, or you are not on message regarding their business. Perhaps you have revealed some personal idiosyncrasies, hidden in the recruitment process, felt to be too inconvenient to handle or socially embarrassing to colleagues and customers (lack of cleanliness, picking your nose, spitting, piggish eating habits, unusual allergies, foul language, alcohol or drug abuse, human rights violations, untidy or inappropriate dress, you spout ideas that are considered to be socially or morally repugnant, and so on). Employment legislation, which varies from jurisdiction to jurisdiction, adds complications here and leads to a tightening of recruitment procedures, an unwillingness to take risks with marginal candidates and higher compensation levels for loss of office.

Reasons for dismissal under termination without cause provisions could cover subjective in-the-eye-of-the-beholder performance characteristics such as not being a team player or vague allegations that nobody likes you. Because the employer terminates without cause none of these reasons need be given publicly, though whether they have a legal case for a termination under human rights legislation is another matter. Perhaps someone terminated quietly for these reasons prefers not to have them aired in court and takes the offered package in compensation. Termination of a service contract without cause could be worth at least its unexpired value and might be worth negotiating.

One other termination provision should be mentioned:

•   'cross default' clauses.

These apply when, between two parties, there is more than one contract for related or unrelated services. Each contract should have a termination clause as discussed. In addition it is sometimes proposed to insert a cross-default clause in each of its contracts. This allows a termination of all of its contracts in the event that one of them is terminated for cause.

If the cross-default applies to termination without cause, this amounts to a right to terminate any and all contracts between the parties without cause, raising an issue about the value of the duration provisions in all its contracts. Unilateral rights to terminate without cause undermine the meaning (and worth) of a contractual obligation. On the other hand a cross-default provision may be useful as a protection when several contracts are interlinked and a termination for cause is recommended (for example, financial turmoil and uncertainty in the other party's business makes dependence on it to perform the other contracts too risky).

In a case where a party finds that a contract with a supplier is too generous or its obligations under it are too onerous, it might try to make other contracts with the supplier subject to a cross-default provision, which puts the original contract in jeopardy of a staged termination of subsequent contracts and an enforced termination of all contracts under the cross-default provisions. As always, the best strategy is to seek legal advice on these matters.

BOILER PLATES

These clauses cover a multitude of boring issues that have a habit of biting the unwary. The most obvious is which jurisdiction governs the contract if it goes to law. This is worth negotiating.

Where the legal system is independent of the executive or powerful local interests, it may not matter in legal principle where jurisdiction is located. But the law is not always or necessarily a matter of legal principle – contract law in the USA, Britain and elsewhere is compatible loosely and litigants may rely on the legal probity of judges. In some other parts of the world, legal systems may not be independent of the government or powerful private interests, and the impartiality of its judges may be suspect. Should a serious dispute arise, a foreigner may be advised to cut and run because investments there are vulnerable to legalized theft and there is little point in throwing good money after bad.

Jurisdictions create other problems. Location may be important, not the least for the inconvenience and expense of travelling, and of staying away from your business for long periods and neglecting your business while the case winds it way through a distant foreign judicial process. Complex cases require considerable and, therefore, time-consuming legal argument. Adversarial legal systems (of the Anglo-American variety) allow the drawing out of a court case to wear down the other side in costs and time. This is true within a single jurisdiction, such as the UK, and more so in a large country like the USA. Foreigners litigating in the USA should be aware that each party, win or lose, bears its own costs, unlike in the UK, where the winner may be awarded legal costs from the loser.

Besides jurisdiction, boilerplate clauses apply to innocuous issues such as the headings of a clause not being part of the agreement; the singular including the plural; inclusive references to 'the male' or 'the female'; and that a failure of a single clause to be upheld in a court does not invalidate the entire contract.

An important boilerplate clause states that the agreement covers all the terms agreed by the parties and that no reliance should be placed on any prior statements, offers, understandings or promises made before the agreement was signed and which are not contained within it. This exclusion clause could become troublesome if the negotiations leading to the agreement induced a party to sign under false impressions that the clarifications and explanations offered during the negotiations, though not explicitly stated, were part of the agreement. More than a few cases get into the legal process disputing this clause after it is realized just how misleading were the (alleged) earlier representations of the other party.

Treat such clauses of excluding what the contract does not include as a warning to take care, not to be careless. Your lawyers will not be surprised to see this clause (if they are, they are the wrong lawyers!) but they may not draw your attention to its implications (they may not have been present during the negotiations). Always remember:

> *If you've got it in writing, you have a prayer;*
> *If it ain't in writing, you've got thin air. (Anon.)*

Consider what changes in the agreement by the 'mutual consent' of the parties means or implies. Read negatively, it asserts that 'no change to the terms of this agreement may be made unless mutually agreed in writing by the parties'. By recasting it positively, it also implies that 'changes to the terms of this agreement may be made when mutually agreed in writing by the parties'. Now that is good news, because it states that the agreement is not written in stone: it can be changed by mutual consent and gaining mutual consent should be treated like any other challenge to negotiation – prepare tradables to trade for consent.

It is your responsibility to review the negotiation exchanges carefully and to check that all material interim offerings and clarifications are included in what you are about to sign. Hence, if the agreement is already signed, or you are about to sign it, draft a letter containing any omitted clarifications, undertakings and understandings, state that they are addendums and/or amendments to the agreement, and present it for signature at the signing ceremony or by an exchange of signed letters. Tactically, the earlier you raise items missing from the contract, the more likely mutual consent is achieved; consent is less likely when trying to change an agreement after the missing topics become an issue between the parties.

You can also negotiate 'side letters' to amplify an arrangement you do not wish to make public within the main contract. Confidential side letters outline 'private arrangements' agreed by the parties – these could include a side payment to a party for facilitating a deal, or an agreement to pay one of the parties for 'services rendered'. I have seen a side letter from a chairman, linking an unrelated major private transaction to the successful conclusion of a public deal, which side letter was not reported in detail to the seller's main board, though the main transaction was reported to it when it went through some months later.

SCHEDULES

Schedules are part of the contract. They detail lists of items (for example, trademarks, logos and IPR, properties, agencies and products) too long to place within the clauses of the main agreement and difficult to change without disturbing the pagination of the original agreement should the need arise.

It is neater to change by mutual consent a numbered schedule if the contents, such as a product listing, change, leaving the original pagination intact. A schedule of overseas agents and distributors may change several times throughout the duration of an agreement, as might the numbering and designations of different editions or marques of products.

SIGNATURES

Contracts are 'executed' by the witnessed signatures of the parties. Each party is entitled to possess an original, signed copy of the agreement, from which they may take multiple copies for reference (some agreements have strict confidentiality clauses that severely restrict their circulation).

Contracts may also be copied onto a secure database for ease of reference, including the scanned signatures. All signed letters making changes to any clause, including the schedules, should be kept with the original contract's file. When corresponding about the agreement, reference should be made to all of the dated and signed letters adding to or changing any items in the agreement; this keeps them current and operable.

The signatories should be officers of the organization designated or entitled to sign official documents. This sometimes becomes an issue in legal disputes. Witnesses may be any persons asked to witness a signature; they do not need to be aware of the contents of an agreement because they are only witnessing that a named person signed an agreement on a stated date.

Conclusions

At the strategic negotiation level you deal with contractual obligations of a serious nature and, while access to professional advice from lawyers is always advisable and necessary, you ought to familiarize yourself with how contracts are constructed, in much the same manner as you should be familiar with accountancy conventions. This brief introduction to the main elements of a contract covers the minimum with which you should be familiar and is a foundation for further study from your future experience of contract negotiation.

Activities
for Chapter 2

Activity 2.1

Look over a contract from your line of work, such as:

- your contract of employment;
- one of your purchasing contracts as issued to your suppliers;
- a supplier's sales contract or one used by your sales force for your customers;
- a contract for a corporate loan from your organization's bankers;
- a contract for the hire of your photocopier;
- a lease for property;
- a licence from the owner of intellectual property you use;
- any similar such contracts to be found in most organizations.

Identify and compare the ten elements with their equivalents in your selected contract.

Activity 2.2

Who are the parties in the contracts you selected from your organization? Try a Web search on the identity of the other parties. Try to find out more, using subscriber databases, such as DataStream, *Financial Times*, *The Economist*, Google and so on, about the other parties, especially about who owns which party and who is ultimately responsible for the conduct of each party.

COMMENTS ON THIS ACTIVITY

Sometimes the parties with which you are contractually bound have slightly different names from the organization with which you believe you are transacting. This is because the other party is a subsidiary of another company and the contract is with the holding company. For most purposes this is of little significance, but it could have implications if you need to seek redress for some failing of the other party. This can work both ways: the contract is with the head office organization though the transaction is with a subordinate part of the main organization; or the contract is with a subordinate part of an organization though you think you have been dealing with the main part of the company.

The issue in a dispute could rest on whether you have recourse to the main company and its assets or only to the subsidiary company and its smaller (perhaps, near non-

existent) assets. Also, bear in mind that in some very large construction projects the parent company, with a familiar brand name (The 'Familiar Brand' Company), may have registered a new company for the duration of the contract, also called 'Familiar Brand', but with an added date or location indicating a limited, if any, right of recourse – for example, The Familiar Brand (2009) Company or The Familiar Brand Co., (Lagos).

Activity 2.3

What do you think of the description, probably written in-house in one of your organization's contracts, of your organization's statement of its expertise and its explicit wish to contract?

COMMENTS ON THIS ACTIVITY

These tend to be self-congratulatory or simple bland claims. However, by signing the contract the other party agrees that it recognizes the claimed expertise.

Activity 2.4

Check the definitions and meanings in your contract. If it mentions a meaning that is defined later and it links any two or more definitions, does it expand on the definitions or limit them in some way?

Activity 2.5

How draconian are the warranties and indemnities required in your contracts for both you and the other party? Are they more draconian or less so for you than the other party? (Who wrote the contract?)

Activity 2.6

Compare the rewards received by the parties from the transactions in your organization's contracts. Seller's prices identify the seller's rewards for supplying inputs on time; discounts identify the buyer's rewards for paying on time, online or by regular standing order, and for buying larger volumes. How clear are the reward terms in your contracts?

COMMENTS ON THIS ACTIVITY

The benefits of bargaining include making the parties better off than the status quo before bargaining. The rewards to each party summarize in what manner they may be made better off by implementing the terms of their contracts. It is these benefits, assuming everything happens as intended, that you should become aware of when reading contracts. Sometimes the main contract clauses define the exact terms of the benefits ('the sum of €3.2 million for the property described in the schedule and located at the place marked in red on map 6A'); other times the main contract describes the basis for the rewards (such and such a 'percentage of net revenues') and a schedule shows illustrative figures or the formulae to calculate them.

Much negotiating attention is usually given to the reward clauses. Understanding thoroughly the reward terms in your business transactions is absolutely essential. Sellers tend to sub-divide pricing structures into the smallest identifiable units (that is, the price for one, not for thousands). This has the advantage of encouraging the negotiators to discourse on small numbers that become large numbers when aggregated.

For example, a penny a nail seems more manageable than thousands of dollars per ton, or a year's supply of nails costing $50 000. Likewise, a rental of £20 a square metre seems less burdensome than a £200 000 annual rental for the entire property. Buyers should aggregate small unit prices into normal invoice amounts or annual consumption amounts. The advantage of the aggregate approach is that it makes movement between the parties easier when dealing with large amounts than attempting to trade movement in tiny unit amounts.

A penny a nail moves in halfpennies from half a penny to one-and-a-half pence a nail, producing relatively huge amounts when aggregated (for example, £25 000 or £75 000). Yet, it may be acceptable to negotiate a move from £50 000 a ton to £47 000 or £53 000, or some similar small steps, giving you better savings on negotiated movements.

An international bank, when persuaded to negotiate 'arrangement' and 'non-utilisation' fees in cash terms instead of the traditional quarter-per-cent steps, saw a big improvement in its margins when it switched from changes in percentage rates to small cash steps. Using percentage steps, its average drop in fees per negotiated transaction was worth in cash terms, £10 000; after the change to cash terms, its average concession on fees was less than £2000, with even bigger gains in the high-end loan business.

Activity 2.7

What scope is there in your business negotiations for either disaggregating prices to the lowest unit or aggregating prices to the highest units (total area, not per square metre; annual purchases, not per unit; total pay bill, not per employee per hour; and so on)?

COMMENTS ON THIS ACTIVITY

By convention in the UK, footballer's agents negotiate pay rates for their clients in weekly amounts. Currently, star players receive £50 000 per week or £2.6 million a year, before tax and the agent's commission. Quoting which number, £50 000 a week or £2.6 million a year, has greater shock effect on the owners of the football club?

Activity 2.8

What financial penalties for non-performance are imposable in your organization's contracts?

To what extent are they onerous?

Are they 'one-way streets' (that is, imposable on one party and not on the other)?

Do you know of any requirements for a performance bond? Are they equitable?

COMMENTS ON THIS ACTIVITY

Close attention should always be paid to these clauses even though you do not anticipate their being used (unless recently caught out by cases of their use against you and your client). Euphoria probably dominates the pre-contract mood more than deep suspicion. But the terms of, say, a performance bond in certain countries often leave a lot to be desired where administrative probity is untested. In some cases these clauses are used as conduits for 'irregular' payments'. (Consult your embassy's commercial attaché.)

Activity 2.9

What material non-performance conditions reside in your organization's contracts? Check also the *force majeure* (excusable delay) definitions – are they favourable to one party or are they equitable to both?

COMMENTS ON THIS ACTIVITY

All contracts should specify their duration; otherwise they are 'in perpetuity' by default. It is often safer to have review dates specified, possibly with explicit reference to what is to be reviewed (which aspects of the contract could trigger a termination or non-renewal? – seek legal advice about drafting here). Where it suits the parties, they may be happy to accept the duration as in perpetuity. On the other hand only extreme circumstances may dictate its acceptance. Be aware that acceptance of an in perpetuity clause may be comfortably misleading if the other party intends (or might be tempted) to abscond from their obligations at the first opportunity, once their emergency requirements expire, or your intentions to do so are thwarted because the other party intends to hold you to the deal. (Once again, take legal advice.)

Activity 2.10

What do you think of the termination conditions in your organization's contracts? Are they one-way streets – can they terminate easily but you cannot? Do any allow termination without cause?

COMMENTS ON THIS ACTIVITY

Termination with cause is more secure for the employee up to a point. An employee always has the option to resign without compensation but circumstances change in anyone's life and what seemed to be a dream job can turn out to be a nightmare, or just plain boring and nothing like what was offered. There may be a case for a quiet termination preferred by both parties. If the employer initiates the termination, the maximum compensation cost is known (the salary for the unexpired portion of service); if the employee cooperates in the termination without fuss, there is a case for compensation up to the maximum of the unexpired portion of the contract.

However, if the employee initiates the without cause provision, the case for compensation is less sound unless it coincides with an undeclared wish on the part of the employer for the employee's contract to be terminated with or without cause. For an amicable settlement and mutually convenient termination there is a negotiable price.

Activity 2.11

Do any of your contracts carry mutually agreed addendums, amendments or side letters? Ordinarily they are kept in the same file as the contract, though some sensitive side letters are kept separately without cross-reference to them in any of the paperwork, including minutes of meetings.

Contracting as a
Bargaining Process

Introduction

The drafting of written contracts is a bargaining process in and within which the conditional bargain is conducted.

Contractual bargaining involves:

- offers

- exchanges of promises by amended conditional offers

- acceptance.

Opportunities for negotiation occur at each stage in the contracting process. You may negotiate details of a contractual relationship for some time before you draft a formal written contract, or they may present a draft of a document, or both of you produce rival drafts at the beginning of the negotiation and then negotiate the contents of a composite contract. You should generally prefer a single to two or more, not necessarily compatible, drafts. The first cut at a composite draft should add clauses and sub-clauses from the drafts to the single draft one. Single texts are preferred to multiple texts, which are often a recipe for a muddle.

Negotiations of commercial contracts can become long, drawn-out and complex exchanges, involving a great deal of staff time and perhaps expense associated with activities such as background checks on financial status, proof of title to properties used as security for financial loans or as evidence of a seller's legitimacy, analysis of a company's accounts and budget and market forecasts, and such like (typical of due diligence).

As the expenses of due diligence, or the expenses associated with tendering, mount, parties rely on each other to 'negotiate in good faith', that is, negotiating with a genuine intention of concluding a bargain. Suspicion that a party is not negotiating in good faith, perhaps from gossip or reports in the trade press, or cumulative observation of its behaviour, causes potential partners to withdraw from the process to cut their losses or, if perceived early enough, for them to decline to negotiate or to tender after their first contact.

Memorandum of understanding

In some jurisdictions (for example, parts of the European Union) the lack of good faith bargaining attracts the attention of lawyers, creating a new source of legal fees in pursuit of recompense for 'failures to agree' or deadlock if they can make a case that the other party had little intention of making an agreement or had a hidden agenda.

To obviate the consequences of such practices, you can attempt to handle the problem by means of a memorandum of understanding (MOU). Caution should be exercised in relying on MOUs to protect you and you should be wary if asked to sign one.

In China, and other countries, where the government still dominates the economy and supervises foreign trade contracts, MOUs feature regularly in negotiations. Foreign companies tend to sign MOUs under pressure from their Chinese counterparts.

The argument for signing the MOUs relies on the wish of the negotiators to secure some sign of commitment from the host officials that they support a possible deal 'in principle'. The officials seek MOUs as evidence for their superiors that they conducted the negotiations properly and secured certain useful early commitments on the proposed contract's scope and, where possible, they set down quantitative parameters that effectively bind the foreigners to remain within them in the final contract.

It is best to avoid signing an MOU that includes indicative prices, quantities or delivery dates, and not to accept at face value assurances that the MOU is 'not binding'. These data have the habit of becoming maxima and fixed, to your disadvantage, during later negotiations.

Heads of terms

Frequently presented by negotiators at the start of a negotiation, by default 'heads of terms' acquire a binding status. The very language of heads of terms implies specificity in the headings; and for some negotiators that is exactly their

---

CASE STUDY

MOUs Are Not Contracts

A French aerospace company signed a MOU with a Middle East government to negotiate the sale of a large number of Mirage fighter aircraft. Such was their confidence in the validity of the MOU that the French corporate managers returned home to prepare for the contract negotiations, which, for this kind of order conducted at the highest levels and backed by the French government, involved a huge expense in creating and assembling the documentation. Meanwhile, a British aerospace company, smarting at the apparent loss of the order to its French rivals, kept its sales team in Saudi and attempted to restore its bid into contention.

One part of its strategy was to invite Arab air force pilots to visit Germany where the British fighter jets were in service with the Royal Air Force. The Arab pilots, in small groups, spent three weeks as guests of RAF Germany. The hospitality included their accompanying RAF pilots on missions into the airspace above Germany, close to the then East German borders, which were defended by the aircraft and electronic air defences of the Warsaw Pact countries (primarily the Soviet Union).

The returning Arab pilots lobbied within their defence ministry to downgrade the French MOU. The upshot was that the Arab government signed a purchase contract (not an MOU) with Britain for what became the country's largest ever military export contract.

MOUs are not watertight commitments to conclude a deal; they can be downgraded, and the disappointed party has limited grounds for legal recourse. Besides, future defence orders may be jeopardized if you sue a government for bad faith in downgrading its MOU.

---

purpose. They appear at first to be a list of agenda items ('to be fleshed out later') but the form they are stated in soon sets parameters on aspects of the deal before settling the details of the deal.

Property negotiators use heads of terms to establish a deal's parameters before the real bargaining begins. For example, in a property lease negotiation a short heads of terms could include:

- duration (5 x 5 years);

- upward-only rent reviews;

- rental premium;

- premium for fixtures and fittings;

- acceptability of guarantor of tenant's obligations;

- landlord's legal costs paid by tenant;

- full repair and insurance lease;

- tenant pays own and landlord's costs and state property taxes;

- tenant's compliance with the planning laws and all building regulations.

The acceptability of the implied terms in the list depends on market conditions. In low or falling inflationary cycles upward-only rent reviews should be challenged (the theory of rent reviews implies they could remain the same, and go down as well as up). Agreeing in advance to your paying the landlord's legal costs, in markets flooded by surplus office space, is not advised. The rental premium, paid by the tenant on entry to the property, is negotiable, as are rent holidays to encourage occupation.

Prestigious blue chip retail tenants for a new shopping development can negotiate favourable rental deals *pour encourager les autres*; less prestigious tenants pay the full rental costs, perhaps also a premium, hoping to ride on the coat-tails of the nearby blue chip retailer because it brings many customers into the development.

Heads of agenda

Use of a 'heads of agenda' device could restart stalled negotiations. The differences between the parties could be such that earlier negotiations broke up in acrimony and disorder.

Heads of agenda are popular with diplomats where the parties cannot handle all their differences, or cannot agree in which order their differences should be tackled, or whether certain issues should be tackled at all. Relations may be so poisoned that the parties will not meet in the same room, or if in the same room, the seating may need to be arranged so that neither delegation has to look at the other, as in the V formation, where they look at the chairman, used by the United Nations in the peace talks to conclude the Iraq–Iran war in the 1980s.

The beauty of a heads of agenda approach is that it identifies the agenda topics and does not make any proposals on the substantive differences of the deadlocked parties, nor does it require explanations or the placing of the agenda items in any particular order. They can be placed at points round a drawn circle on sheets of paper with no obvious order, beginning or ending to them.

The idea is to bring the parties to meet without preconditions and to precipitate sufficient momentum to allow negotiations to recommence.

Offers and done deals

The general legal principle is that an unconditional offer unconditionally accepted is a 'done deal' and that its provisions can be enforced.

Lawyers are wary of expressed or implied offers; you should be wary too, and use suitable language developed in practising to dilute the damage caused by your inadvertently making unconditional offers. For example, you should make regular statements when provisionally agreeing to an item in a contract by repeating: 'For the avoidance of doubt, nothing is agreed until everything is agreed.'

Disputes arise as to whether an unconditional offer was made and a legal decision (and legal damages) could turn on evidence of some expression of an intention to enter a contract (a signed MOU for instance, supported by an exchange of letters and e-mails discussing a business arrangement, notes of phone calls and witnessed conversations, minutes of meetings and so on).

Evidence that the terms of a contract had been discussed and negotiated would support a claim that a legal offer had been made. Press reports, media interviews, negotiation papers, e-mails and other correspondence could count as evidence. Visits to sites; requesting access for post-contract suppliers of services, such as architects, interior designers, security, space planners and other specialists, suggest that you were planning for a deal. Correspondence between the offeror and offeree discussing the details of a transfer of ownership after they sign the contract is evidence of purposeful communication between the relevant parties.

To avoid legal controversies on the status of an offer, it is common to find the words 'subject to contract' on every piece of paper (including e-mails) passing between the parties. That way, nothing can be construed as a legal offer and liable to form a contract.

Remember, an unconditional offer unconditionally accepted is a done deal; hence, rapid-talking negotiators should be wary of making offers to buy or sell where they want conditions to be attached but have not yet expressed them. To write (without the usual subject to contract proviso) that you would give them €20 million for their business, risks their accepting before you state your conditions, which, in your mind and intention, were for negotiation.

An offer once made can be withdrawn at any time by the offeror before the offeree accepts it and, if withdrawn before acceptance is made, then no contract exists, even if the offeree subsequently accepts it. It is down to timing. Offers expire if the offer includes a statement that it has to be accepted by a specific

CASE STUDY

A Range Is Not An Offer

I was once asked fairly early in a negotiation exploring my purchase of a small software developer's business: 'How much would you be willing to pay for it, then?' My reply was guarded: 'A sum between £1 and £1 million.'

Evidently, I was too guarded! The seller took umbrage at my insult and shortly afterwards our discussions terminated in acrimony. For some time afterwards, the erstwhile seller told mutual acquaintances of my insulting offer of £1 for his business!

CASE STUDY

Move In, Then Quibble

An experienced senior manager was offered in writing the post of CEO of a prestigious multi-national organization. When he replied with his written acceptance, he included a new condition, not referred to in the offer, which was of moderate importance to him but not necessarily a deal-breaker, suggesting that the organization buy and dispose his current property, as well as fund his relocation expenses to the country where the international corporate headquarters were located. While the organization was willing to fund his relocation expenses, as it was standard practice, it was not inclined to accede to his new condition.

Several members of the board, disillusioned with their choice of new CEO for various reasons, some of them seemingly unsubstantiated rumours about his

working relationships in his current post, others a reaction to what they regarded as his impertinent demands, swung the rest of the board against the new CEO-elect. They revoked the original offer by taking advantage of his new condition for acceptance.

The board wrote to the CEO-elect withdrawing their offer on the grounds that his new conditions constituted non-acceptance of the original terms of their offer.

He should have accepted their offer unconditionally and then, once in post, pursued the novel idea of selling his property to the organization. He may not have achieved his new demands, but he would have kept his job.

time and date and the offeree has not signified acceptance in time and in the appropriate manner, normally stated in the offer or implied by circumstances (an offer to sell a discounted aircraft ticket cannot be valid after the plane has departed). 'First come, first served' is another example of an implied condition – turn up next day and the offer has lapsed because the tickets were sold to people who bought them before you.

What happens if an offer is accepted conditionally? An unconditional acceptance secures the deal, but a conditional acceptance hands the power to revoke the offer back to the offeror.

Exchange of promises

Negotiation usually involves changes to the original terms of an offer, by amending individual terms (raising or lowering prices, for example) or by exchanging conditional propositions that delete or amend linked individual terms. That is what negotiators do across a table.

Lawyers tend to do something quite different. They exchange marked-up drafts of contracts with their proposed amendments to clauses (each using different handwritten colours of ink, or, using their computer programs, different colours of underlining, which leave the crossed out words or lines on the page). Partly, the difference arises from the volume of contract work undertaken by lawyers necessitating them working on several different cases in a business day. Time out for travelling to and from differently located meetings is a rare event. If they do meet to conclude a negotiation it may last all night (there appears to be a universal convention that corporate lawyers conclude complex deals between the hours of 3 am and 6 am!).

The negotiation dance consists of exchanges of 'proposals' (tentative offers) and exchanges of 'bargains' (specific offers). To facilitate movement, negotiators link conditional offers to trade across more than one issue to derive 'package deals', causing negotiation to be described as the 'management of movement'.

Lawyers tend to be wary of anything conditional in an offer and prefer to deal with each issue separately to avoid a sudden withdrawal of commitment to a deal. Their contributions tend to be demand led, rather than exchange led. Now, single-issue bargaining tends to produce zero-sum outcomes (what one lawyer gains the other loses), with a fair degree of failure to agree until time pressure and the impatience of the principals compels both sides to settle. Of course, the notorious penchant of litigators for adversarial (red style) confrontation encourages deadlock, until the brute course of events forces compliance by the 'weaker' party (weaker in law or weaker from circumstance).

Negotiators who, admittedly, may not make tidy deals in law, make progress through exchanging conditional proposals and bargains with greater despatch than lengthy exchanges of correspondence, and usually can accommodate the time needed to conclude a deal, or parts of a deal ('nothing is agreed until everything is agreed'), across a table at single, or continuous, sequential sessions. Amended proposals change the condition or the offer (or both) and provide conduits for the exchange of the negotiators' promises. Lawyers come into their own when they draft what the negotiators agree in language that perfects their intentions.

CASE STUDY

Different Price For Different Package

When conducting a negotiation with a particularly difficult negotiator, I made a conditional proposal, which he rejected out of hand and with much rhetorical vigour. Later, I reformulated my conditional proposal. He observed that my offer was now lower than the earlier one and demanded to know what had happened to the figure of 7 per cent?, snapping that 'We are going backwards.'

I agreed, with mock sadness: 'Yes, I suppose we are. But you rejected my offer of 7 per cent along with my conditions. Hence, my current offer is 3 per cent, with modified conditions. Should, however, you prefer to consider my conditions for 7 per cent, then I would be happy to re-table them.'

What appears to a lawyer to be risky behaviour by a negotiator is in practice safe. Lawyers do not revel in revealing flexibility on an issue; they prefer the other lawyers to move from their positions first (an unfortunate strategy if both parties insist on the mantra 'always move second'!). Negotiators take small risks, protected by their use of conditional propositions, because the condition and the offer are inseparably linked. As the song said: 'You can't have one without the other.' If you want the offer, you must take the condition, or succeed in amending it to the satisfaction of the other negotiator.

It is not, therefore, an ultimatum, because you can always respond with an amended conditional offer, or one that is amended in either the condition or the offer (or both). A futile attempt to ambush me and claim the offer without the linked condition is easily repulsed, because I have not revealed an exploitable flexibility – my movement on an offer is priced in terms of my conditions.

A lawyer, who fears revealing their flexibility on a contractual clause, has good grounds for apprehension. If a litigant's claim for compensation is negotiable downwards, where will it end? Safer to stand pat and await the other lawyer's acceptance of the arguments supported by helpful legal precedents; hence, those prolonged lawyers' arguments over facts, precedents and whether they apply in this case, and their differing estimates of the prospects of success if the case goes to trial.

Linked conditional bargains provide a safe means of indicating flexibility without giving in – every possible offer has a price in terms of their conditions – and negotiators have nothing to fear from revealing their price lists on the basis that a change in the package, changes the price. Linking issues does not jeopardize the integrity of one's promises, nor compromise one's willingness to consider movement.

Acceptance

The end game in negotiation is the making of an agreement. By definition, the close of the bargaining phase ends the negotiation. The outcome is an unconditional agreement because the conditional bargaining has ended. All the terms are agreed and when everything is agreed there is nothing left to negotiate about – for the moment. Other issues may come up during implementation of the agreement and these may be negotiated (or renegotiated).

But for all intents and purposes, the parties who sign the agreement are unconditionally accepting an unconditional offer. The agreement meets the legal definition of a done deal that is legally enforceable in the courts with jurisdiction over it. Negotiators and lawyers eventually arrive at the same destination, having taken, perhaps, different routes to get there and, also perhaps, agreed to different terms on the issues.

Having worked with (and against!) many lawyers during negotiations and in negotiating training sessions, I have noticed differences in how their legal training influences their approach to negotiation. For example, lawyers attend to the legal implications of their offers and proposals because theirs is, necessarily, an adversarial stance. Their basic principle is that an unconditional offer unconditionally accepted is a done deal and, therefore, they do not like putting conditions on their offers or their acceptance, preferring to leave both as they are first presented as demands on behalf of their clients. Anything else, they tend to believe, implies weakness and exposes them to the slippery slope of surrender. This leaves them with narrow options of sticking to their entry positions on issues and waiting for, or forcing, the other party (complicated if it is another lawyer) to move under the pressure of time or events from their current positions.

Lawyers often negotiate by amending single-issue proposals, separated from other issues (note their use of distinguishing colours of ink or underlining draft contracts). This gradually eliminates issues, reducing the residue to difficult issues for both of them. It is a natural zero-sum exchange. It also suits adversarial bargaining; at best it takes time, at worst, it provokes deadlock and they go to trial.

Negotiators, in contrast, make conditional proposals and bargains, linking movement on an issue with movement on a separate but linked issue. They trade things that are of less value to them for things they value more. The conditional proposition links its conditions to its offers. The former is the price of the latter. Revealing a wish to trade does not lead to ambushes by grabbers of the offers who try to discard the conditions. Offers and conditions are inextricably linked and cannot be separated because conditional bargainers are assertive, not compliant (and not naturally adversarial!).

Lawyers avoid conditional offers and revelations of their potential flexibility. Negotiators, on the other hand, base their approach on using their (conditional) offers precisely to reveal their potential for safe and conditional flexibility. Negotiators can reach settlements face to face across a table; lawyers take longer because of their heavy workloads arising from handling simultaneously several cases for different clients, and their ingrained legalistic inhibitions (unless they receive remedial negotiation training!). However, lawyers trained in negotiation make excellent contract negotiators!

Contract negotiation

Contracts, like people, come in all kinds of shapes, sizes and styles. They vary in the degree of negotiable flexibility in them. As do the parties negotiating them. In some cases everything is negotiable, in others nothing is, and in between there are varying degrees of negotiable and non-negotiable terms, plus, as one of Edinburgh's leading investment bankers put it to me, there are those contracts where 'everything is renegotiable'! Because business relationships are expressed in contracts, it is important for you to recognize the types of contracts likely to be presented for your signature.

When strategic negotiation moves from the analysis and diagnosis of a problem or opportunity, to the derivation of policies and their implementation via a Negotiated Agenda, the end product will be a contractual relationship. Negotiators in the Process Model should have a workable knowledge of contracts, their structure, their language and their negotiation (though they should never stray too far from the environs of a lawyer). In this section I review the main considerations in the negotiation of a contract, building on what we have covered so far, and discuss the basic types of contracts.

PRE-PREPARED CONTRACTS

These contracts are pre-prepared for acceptance and signature, though you are advised to read them too. Many organizations use pre-prepared contracts that are closely printed and double columned, implying little or no room for flexibility in their terms of business, such as in car hire, airline tickets, room hire or equipment leases. Some are known to print their terms in faint grey ink on the reverse of their invoices! To access and use computer programs, they make it necessary to indicate acceptance of the supplier's terms before proceeding to open the program, because opening it means you accept their terms.

Where thousands of business transactions are completed per day, the risks to a supplier that ambiguities will emerge by allowing discretion to counter or call-centre staff is too great to be permitted. Hence, pre-printed contracts minimize (but never eliminate) the risks of variations which could create unintended and avoidable legal liabilities arising.

Businesses that pre-print their contracts expect their customers to sign without quibble by accepting the suppliers' predetermined choices. Their contracts express the high-volume nature of their business and they do enough of the same business enough times a day to be reasonably sure that they can impose a virtual take-it-or-leave-it choice, expressed, of course, in the nicest possible way by their usually well-trained highly personable counter staff, to those few customers who baulk at their terms. People in a hurry to hire a car, catch a plane, check into a hotel or use equipment urgently (a common feature of these transactions for most customers) feel the pressure not to debate legal theory – and anyway, counter staff are not given authority to change their company's terms of business.

If you wish to negotiate special deals with any supplier using fixed terms for doing business you have to escalate your point of contact to senior management, from whom almost everything is negotiable. Long-term leases of a fleet of vehicles, multiple aircraft charters, long lets of hotel rooms, significant annual hire of equipment and facilities, and purchases of multiple copies of software are pre-printed from templates with most of the terms negotiable.

PRE-PREPARED TEMPLATES

In this case, the pre-drafted template implies nothing more than that it saves rewriting everything every time it is used, in the reasonable expectation that most of the terms are acceptable for most occasions by most people using their services.

Publishers' contracts are of this type, with room for the negotiation of terms to suit the variables in the book proposition (advance, royalty rates, subsidiary rights, territory, electronic rights, delivery and exclusions). Contracts for screenplays, contributors' releases, hires of facilities, terms for actors, producers and directors' fees, video and repeat fees and rights to screen credits also tend to use pre-prepared templates. However, hot properties and hot stars or hot authors in blockbuster businesses command their own premium rewards and rights, and often write their own contractual terms (or their agent does it for them).

Corporate lawyers store on databases every client's contract they have ever prepared for possible use as pre-prepared templates for any type of contract they might wish to resell to a future client with a similar problem. Such digitised contract libraries store the intellectual capital of legal firms. In the absence of a dedicated contract library, the intellectual capital of the firm remains stored in the heads of its lawyers, which walks out of the building with them when they retire, die in service or switch partnerships.

Some paper-based contract libraries are from the quill-pen age and consist of piles of boxes with the old contracts stacked in random order, and stored in dusty box rooms. Others are modern electronic databases containing digitized and searchable contracts, cross-referenced and recoverable onscreen by the firm's lawyers at their desks or their wireless mobiles. Pre-prepared templates are downloadable (as are the original contracts should they be needed for reference or litigation) and can be used for current clients' purposes. Times and details of who accessed the files on the database are also recorded on a report file for security reasons.

These firms charge clients to see a single template at a time and do not send a selection of possible contracts out because this is equivalent to dispersing the firm's intellectual property, or at best giving it away too cheaply.

SINGLE DRAFT FOR NEGOTIATION

This is the most common type of contract negotiation, usually presented after time spent negotiating the main issues from the parties' prepared agendas and a possible framework for an agreement has emerged or has been identified.

For many negotiations most of the negotiable issues are fairly straightforward and predictable, and while agreement may not yet have been reached, the preliminary meetings suggest that an agreement may be possible if the problem items are settled in further negotiations.

The presentation of an unfinished or incomplete first draft of a possible agreement, reflecting the issues that have been provisionally agreed is an important signal that the parties are moving closer to agreement.

Trying to negotiate the texts of two agreements together leads to confusions and may add to the frustrations of not reaching agreement on individual issues. The clauses of two contracts authored by different persons are unlikely to follow the same order, providing for maximum disorder in cross-referencing between them. You have to decide which of the two texts is the amended version that will constitute the final agreement. In which case, we have a single text authored by one party and amended by agreement, and another text that is used by the other party to propose amendments to the single text.

Experience recommends that a single text be chosen, with parties free to propose amendments to any clauses in it. The source of the amendments, be they from notes, a different draft contract or authored as their need arises in the negotiations, does not cause the confusion of trying to combine multiple contracts.

JOINTLY AUTHORED CONTRACTS

Joint authoring is rarely practical if by 'jointly authored' we mean that the negotiators write the agreed terms line by line and word by word across the table together. For obvious reasons, this would be a slow process even for a single- or limited-issue negotiation; for complex negotiations it would be highly inefficient to maintain two negotiating teams at the table for the long periods necessary to draft and conclude an agreement written in this manner.

The more frequent version of joint authoring, assuming one of the parties has not brought a pre-written template, but has kept side notes on what has been agreed provisionally, is for the parties to adjourn and one of them to draft a single text or to delegate the task to a sub-group of negotiators at which both parties could be represented. If the sub-group, or their lawyers, know what has been discussed, or what is wanted by the parties, they could produce a draft fairly quickly and report on it to a reconvened plenary for further deliberation, amendment and agreement.

In many cases it ought not to be important who drafts the contract provided the draft is carefully scrutinized. Two parties thoroughly acquainted with the idiosyncrasies of a business sector should be familiar with the contents that commercial contracts commonly embody in their sector's agreements. In this case, neither party is likely to be successful in trying to slip anything detrimental past the other. It should not matter therefore whose contract forms the basis of the text to be agreed. Large organizations often insist on the use of their standard contracts that have been 'legalled' by their in-house lawyers, in which they have confidence that they contain no gaps (from their point of view!).

Some organizations like to provide the contract text if they feel it important to be 'the party of the first part', that is, their organization's name appears first, and reflects their claim to be the main party. If you borrow a bank's money, it's their contract; if you hire consultants, it's your contract; if you sell to the government, it's the government's contract ('GCStores 1'); if you sign to play football for Manchester United, it's the 'MU' contract if you are unknown and possibly your contract if you are a world-ranked player, and so on.

In practice, however, none of these factors should be decisive; it is not whose name heads the contract so much as what it contains that matters, and what it contains is down to the attention you pay to what you are signing.

COMPLEX CONTRACTS

The different possibilities for drafting contracts create strategic issues for negotiators. The contracts of the pre-printed type, used for small but numerous transactions like car hire, need not detain us. Pre-drafted contracts and jointly drafted contracts are more likely to be the subject of negotiation for anything complex and some fairly structured contractual processes must be gone through before agreement is reached.

High-value contracts in the construction industry, for example, are subject to formalized government and public agency regulations. The parties acknowledge that these provisions, often minutely detailed, are taken into their contractual relationship and both sides agree to be bound according to their provisions. Many issues are left to the parties to negotiate – the price being an obvious tradable – but others, such as the procedures by which variations in designs ('variation orders') are handled during construction, are also most important. The performance and safety standards of what is constructed by the builders and installers, and paid for by the clients, are laid down precisely by the regulations and monitored in the UK by the Health and Safety Executive (a government agency), and are taken into the main contract.

Because of the nature of construction and the potential damage to people and property if something goes wrong when the building, power station or dam is handed over to the client, a whole host of detailed regulations apply to how the finished structure operates (safety to the user's personnel is one such, its fire safety,

CASE STUDY

Three Is Better Than Two

Publishers dealing with a single, independent author usually present their standard (negotiable) contract for the author's signature. Author's agents normally have their own standard (negotiable) tripartite contract for signature by publishers, authors and themselves.

The agent's contract protects the agent against circumvention by either the publisher dealing direct with the author or the author dealing direct with the publisher, because the agent's contract requires each party to acknowledge and authorize irrevocably that all monies due to the author are paid by the publisher through the agent for the full term of copyright (that is, life of the author plus 70 years) and that the agent must be consulted on any changes made to the contract terms.

anti-pollution integrity and public safety are others) and these form part of the construction contract which binds all those involved (building employers and their employees, the architects, sub-contractors, site visitors and regulatory inspectors).

Major construction contracts consist of at least two sizable documents: the larger covers the technical specifications of the project, and the smaller covers the commercial terms. This applies whether there is a bidding process or not. A group projects manager told me that a major construction contract she was involved in ended up being documented in more than 200 separate agreements filling 22 three-inch ring binders printed on double-sided paper.

Another common problem is that, because of the size and complexity of the negotiations, the composition of the negotiating teams changes, sometimes several times. Because different people bring different experiences and styles to the table in the behaviours they exhibit, it is necessary to be able to adjust to the inevitable changes in personnel. There is also the problem of continuity, or rather its absence, which can cause momentary confusion if you are unsure of what happened or what was agreed or accepted beforehand by others who are no longer at the negotiating table. Misunderstandings may not be examples of bad faith and the act of trying to carry over into subsequent sessions the assumptions and nuances of previous discussions may be well founded, but is always vulnerable to other people not being persuaded that what you say you agreed informally with somebody else has any relevance to them.

Many contracts include a 'whole agreement' clause which specifically attempts to prevent previous representations or arrangements other than stated in the express terms of the agreement from having validity. In short,

CASE STUDY

Beware Of Comfort Zones

A team from a designer and manufacturer of industrial lasers visited Germany to negotiate the sale of six of their automated laser machines to a major car manufacturer. The first week was spent with the technical managers of each side engrossed in the technology of the machines and agreeing the specifications to suit the German production line and their requirements. The teams got on professionally and socially, and a lively camaraderie developed between them. Once their part of the purchase contract was agreed, the German technical managers withdrew after sharing a jolly evening's social at an expensive restaurant.

The British team looked forward to the next day's meeting to complete the commercial terms. From the start of the commercial meeting, however, an entirely different atmosphere prevailed. It was close to being clipped and frosty. The new German team were from the procurement department and clearly knew next to nothing about lasers or how their designs were way ahead of rival products technologically, and they did not appreciate that, with the modifications that had been agreed with the technical managers, the lasers would be practically purpose-built when they were delivered to Germany in three month's time.

The procurement managers pushed the laser company managers on everything. From a certain sale at a good profit, the deal became marginal, largely because the sellers had nothing left to trade. The separation of the technical from the commercial negotiations had been a mistake on the laser manufacturer's part, not easily rectified, as had agreeing to expensive variations in their designs without flagging their provisional agreement as conditional propositions.

One remedy for this problem is to have detailed documentation of all assurances, explanations, representations and such like from previous discussions to hand and entered into the agenda of subsequent meetings, for its status to be recognized by the new players. If they do not agree that the amended proposal is the subject for negotiating its price, then the supplier reverts to the original proposal and offers to negotiate all the changes that the technical people had indicated they wanted.

the agreement as signed is the whole agreement, and anything said by the negotiators not included in the written agreement has no legal standing. Recollect the ditty about 'prayers' and 'thin air'!

The legal technicalities involved in such whole agreement clauses are less important for you (they remain important for the legal advisors) than the fact that you are entitled to seek agreement during the negotiations that all representations are acknowledged in the documentation which goes forward to each subsequent stage of the negotiation. It is the habit of negotiators, feasting on the goodwill generated during the negotiations, not to document such representations that creates the problem of accepting whole agreement clauses too readily.

Activities
for Chapter 3

Activity 3.1

How do you feel when you suspect that a negotiator is not negotiating in good faith? Recall the circumstances from an example and review the factors that led you to your suspicions.

Recall if you have ever acted to instructions to negotiate without an intention to reach an agreement.

Note that recommendations to enforce good faith bargaining, supported by the award of damages, are circulating in Europe and could become law.

Activity 3.2

In what circumstances have you agreed to an MOU? How different from the terms of the final outcome was the MOU?

COMMENTS ON THIS ACTIVITY

In theory, a non-binding MOU provides a degree of comfort, but in certain negotiating situations, and in some jurisdictions, the MOU is regarded and treated by the hosts as a clear mandate for the shape of the ultimate contract. Drafting the MOU requires care, and too casual acceptance of a draft is not advised. The MOU's non-binding status is insufficient protection against an officially presumed mandate.

If you prefer your commitments to be vague, then they must be written in vague language; to constrain your vagueness they will try to lay down indicative numbers as markers. Government officials, adept at manipulating the language of MOUs, constrain or burden future contractual outcomes. They present indicative prices or shares of the revenues as broad indicators but, once your signature supports the MOU, in practice these numbers have limited scope to be changed.

Activity 3.3

What potential use could you make of a heads of terms or heads of agenda in your line of business?

Activity 3.4

How does your organization store its contracts?

Who is in charge of them?

What scope is there for suggesting that they be digitized and stored on a database?

Pay, Benefits and Union Negotiations

CHAPTER 4

Introduction

This chapter is about the human resource environment in which we might apply the Strategic Negotiation Process Model. While heavily influenced by North American and UK labour markets and the formal structures and conventions associated with them, I suggest that elements of a generic approach, from which you may usefully apply selected concepts to the dissimilar structures and conventions applicable to other jurisdictions, are also present.

If you are to negotiate for the objectives in the business plan through the Negotiation Agenda, you should have a basic knowledge of the labour environment in your country and industry, including some understanding of how it has evolved and how it operates in practice, and this chapter provides an illustrative guideline to the minimum knowledge of the employer–employee structures you must attain to accomplish your objectives in the labour market and in labour management.

The main focus is on how the framework of labour negotiations operates in the comparatively freer Anglo-American labour markets with fewer regulations imposed by law (that is, fewer compared to those operating in continental European countries such as Germany, France, Belgium, Netherlands and Italy). The regulatory situation is fluid at present and in the course of the next decade or so, it may change incrementally, but even with foreseeable changes there is a clear demarcation between two models, broadly characterized as Anglo-American ('market capitalism') and continental European ('social capitalism') as measured by differences in their labour market rigidities, unemployment rates, growth rates, interest rates and hours of work.

Those countries in continental Europe with high labour market rigidities, such as the presence of laws severely inhibiting rapid redundancies, which make it more difficult to fire staff with or without cause, and which enforce statutory consultation before management decisions may be implemented, also have higher unemployment rates, lower private investment, higher public spending deficits and shorter legal (though not actual) working hours.

Because all of the countries in the two models are secular democracies, their governments pursue policies supported by electoral majorities and, therefore, it is not a simple matter of examining their data and deciding which model is the best. In any welfare function, the preferences of the electorate must count highly.

National pay bargaining

Many large firms with multiple employment sites operate national pay bargaining arrangements, where remuneration and conditions of employment are set at the national level, usually as part of a general budgeting control process and in some cases through nationally negotiated pay bargaining agreements with trade unions. These nationally determined remuneration agreements apply across all of the organization's local sites. It should be noted that there are fewer instances of management–union negotiations now than twenty years ago, at least in the private sector in the UK and North America, though unions still have a major influence in the rest of Europe, particularly in countries with large public sectors.

A variation of nationally determined pay arrangements includes setting maximum pay guidelines, derived from the organization's national budgets, and communicating these via the human resource director for implementation by local management in the organization's plants. In other cases, local management negotiates with local employee representatives (though not all, or in many cases a majority, of whom are members of trade unions).

Local pay bargaining exists where local organizations and parts of organizations have the freedom to hire and terminate staff, determine how line and human resource managements might better prepare from the strategic perspective to negotiate local pay and conditions with their workforce, including their managers, and, where necessary, negotiate local union recognition and representation agreements.

The laws and practices of trade unionism in individual countries vary – bearing in mind that in the majority of cases in the secular democracies the majority of workforces are non-unionized, but individuals have a legal right to become unionized. In many other countries, national laws heavily circumscribe organizations promoting the interests of labour. It is not feasible to cover comprehensively the impact of all likely variations on the Process Model in a single chapter. The strategic approach, however, is adaptable to deal with many different kinds of environments and, despite myriad variations, much may be gained from treating what follows as illustrative of a generic approach.

HR considerations

Organizations operate in particular market settings and the nature of those settings should be understood if you are to work within them. A company selling tinned soup to repeat customers via large-scale retail outlets operates in a different market setting to a company selling access to cable TV channels direct to households via a sales force. Their sales strategies are different, as are the factors considered to be critical for success, and they require different marketing mixes to achieve that success. Therefore, you should be familiar with your organization's setting.

Some of the considerations for the derivation of HR and reward strategies, albeit at a generic level, highlight the factors you must consider while reviewing past and current strategies. The example I use here is of an organization operating in a unionized or partially unionized environment. While a substantially different analysis would not be required for a non-unionized environment it is certainly the case that unionized environments add complications from their context and circumstances, and that consideration of these complications usefully benchmarks wider applications of the strategic negotiation approach.

In what follows, the aims and objectives of reward systems generally apply to most organizations. Unions, by their presence, impose constraints on management decision making in countries like France, Germany, Italy, Netherlands, Belgium and Spain that is not so evident in more open labour markets in the UK and USA (and many competitor countries). For example, in major social capitalist countries like Germany and The Netherlands, enterprises operate under the direct influence of supervisory boards, supported by associated legislative interventions in the employer-employee relationship which affects the degrees of freedom open to the negotiating parties. I shall discuss briefly different types of pay systems and the design of possible negotiating structures in more open market economies for determining employee pay and rewards.

Objectives of a pay system

Details of the various reward systems that may be applicable are commonly covered in HR management courses and would take us away from strategic negotiation (which is about how to negotiate the implementation of HR and reward policies, and not how to the design them). However, knowledge of the broad aims of pay and reward systems helps to conceptualize the strategies you might want to follow; hence, you require some familiarity with them. Part of this chapter is drawn from *Local Pay Bargaining: an opportunity for change*, by John Benson, Linda Helms, Gavin Kennedy, 1994.

Specifically, pay and reward systems should:

- enable the organization to recruit and retain enough employees of the required standard to carry out its functions;

- reward responsibility and performance;

- create harmonious and productive relationships between the various employees by ensuring that they feel fairly rewarded for their efforts;

- ensure the cost-effective deployment of employees to achieve efficiency in the organization's activities;

- ensure that there is equity in the reward of similar jobs and adequate differentials to reward similar responsibility and the acquisition of skills required to do the job;

- ensure that the organization's overall pay levels are flexible enough to cope with external labour market pressures or organizational change;

- be easily comprehensible and communicable to employees so that links between effort and reward are clearly identified;

- be easily administered, audited and controlled.

Pay structures have different effects on employees and should be designed with these effects in mind. Looking at pay as a package of several measures, rather than as a single line item in a budget, improves the links between pay structure and your sought-for outcomes because each aspect of a pay structure affects aspects of employees' behaviour. Disregarding elements of the package and how they affect the sought-for outcomes may lead to disappointing (and expensive) mistakes. The time taken to think about this possibility could save your organization from avoidable errors. Hence, the need is for you to understand the framework in which such remuneration decisions should be made.

Several factors affect the design of reward systems. Some are shown in Table 4.1:

Table 4.1   Selected factors affecting reward design

Factors	Characteristics
Size of the organization	Large organizations need:
	• formal pay systems
	• to encourage a sense of equity in rewards
	• to provide career progression
	• administrative convenience
Type of business	Farming:
	• agri-business: managers and employees
	• owner managed: itinerant labourers
	Manufacturing:
	• salaried
	• waged
	Service:
	• educated, professional
	• manual, menial
Organizational structure	Employees:
	• highly centralized
	• dispersed
Workforce composition	Employees:
	• large numbers doing the same jobs
	• specialized doing different jobs
Unionized or non-unionized	• unions prefer uniform pay rates;
	• employers prefer pay related to individual performance

Source: Benson, J., Helms, L. and Kennedy, G. (1994), Local Pay Bargaining: an opportunity for change (Edinburgh: NHS), p. 2.2

The three elements of the pay package are:

- those provided to all staff, such as base pay, pensions, holidays and sick pay;

- those provided to certain categories only, such as company cars, performance bonuses, insurances, and share options;

- those provided for some staff categories according to individual need, such as relocation assistance, permanent disability cover, benefits in kind and sabbaticals.

You can expect that items will appear in the negotiations from time to time, some of which will benefit certain staff and others which have little or no effect. How the various elements affect the intended objectives of the management should be considered before responding positively or negatively to proposals for change. The main consideration should be how the proposed elements of the pay package influence the achievement of the management's objectives.

Table 4.2 shows the link between individual items in a pay scheme and their possible outcomes. You may not have sufficient flexibilities in the pay packages for you to negotiate to take advantage of all of these links. During the debate phase of the negotiation, opportunities to explore the actual and potential links with the other side should be taken. Unions tend to focus their demands on what is beneficial to their members without considering the effects on the organization (or on other employees not in their union). You have to take a wider view, which is not the same as using weak arguments to prevent something for which you had not prepared. If you understood the elements of remuneration packages you could prepare properly.

Table 4.2 Correlations between elements and objectives in a pay package

Item	Equity	Competitiveness	Motivation	Retention	Security
Basic pay	H	H	A	A	A
Performance pay	A	A	H	A	L
Deferred remuneration	L	L	A	H	L
Pension plans	A	A	L	H	H
Other benefits	A	H	L	A	H

Key: H = high correlation; A = average correlation and L = low correlation

Source: Benson, Helms and Kennedy (1994), Local Pay Bargaining, Exhibit 2.1

To read Table 4.2, check the row item (pay, pension and so on) against the columns and see how each row item correlates. The data correlates the constituents of remuneration with the qualities of performance they effect; it does not correlate with age, but experienced HR professionals can interpolate the influence of age of a workforce with what is important to that age-group out of those qualities. Younger age groups are interested in basic pay; older with pension plans; younger prefer money now; older are happy to accept deferred elements (for example, end of year bonuses); people hang onto a job if a retained payment is due.

If your negotiation objectives include improving the retention rate because there is an excess of employee turnover, deferred remuneration (such as annual bonuses earned in arrears) has a higher correlation with retention than policies to improve equity (such as narrowing existing differentials). Some share option schemes permit a slower drawdown (the proportion that they qualify for each year) of stock options than others, and employees who have to wait for their bonuses from share options over a number of years are likely to stay longer to collect them.

The organization is assumed to want some mix of the column headings to suit its circumstances and Table 4.2 attempts to show how they may be associated. For instance, individual or group performance pay could be associated with strongly motivating employees to perform but it has weak associations with creating feelings of job security. Compare the role of pension plans, which create the opposite effects.

Union recognition and representation

This section is not about the history, or the deleterious effects, of the need for trade unions. That is a wholly separate subject; your task is to manage the organization to achieve its goals, whatever the existing social, economic or political environment. It is far more important to understand how trade unions function and what effects they have than it is to critique their roles.

Let us begin with recognizing that the highest priority for a trade union is the achievement of recognition and representation rights in an organization in which it recruits. Without recognition rights, unions cannot function; consequently, they would have limited or no value for their members. A few stalwarts may continue to be members of an unrecognized union, but the majority of employees the union wishes to represent will not continue to pay membership subscriptions if the union is not recognized as a bargaining agent by the employer and there appears to be no prospect of it being so.

Where non-recognition is a clash of wills between an obstinate employer and a determined workforce, the resulting dispute over recognition becomes a bitter and destructive struggle. In some prominent cases, these disruptive disputes last for many months – some even last for years. They are extremely costly and take up a large slice of management's time. Most countries avoid damaging recognition disputes with laws stating the conditions under which unions must be recognized as a bargaining agent for those employees who choose to be represented by them.

Unfortunately, mishandling the recognition process passes up a major negotiating opportunity for an employer to establish favourable arrangements for its organization in exchange for according recognition and representation rights to a union. Many union recognition agreements are defective because the management team has not understood just how valuable the recognition agreement is for the union. If you have something that somebody else values highly, then it is a maxim of negotiation practice that you have a greater influence on defining the content of the deal.

It is an all too common feature of human resource practice that this great opportunity is often missed, and the recognition and representation structures, which are introduced at the behest of the trades unions, act to constrain the employer's HR strategies, sometime as far as preventing its business strategies from being realized. The result compromises the business plans of the organization, reduces its competitiveness and makes its survival more difficult if market conditions deteriorate.

In general, the more collective and impersonal the organization's bargaining arrangements, the less performance and individually oriented will be the employees' behaviour and attitudes. As the consequences of this outcome could be serious for the business plan, subsequent realization of the impact of lack of care during the recognition process cannot be changed dramatically in the short run, because negotiated agreements, voluntarily entered into by both parties, are difficult to change, let alone undo, and the organization is stuck with what it agreed, or did not agree when it had the opportunity to trade for more satisfactory agreements.

De-recognition of trade unions, while an option, is fraught with dangers because it strikes at the heart of a trade union's operational existence and it may be resisted fiercely, except in the exceptional circumstances that induce employees voluntarily to forego union membership. The twenty-year-long decline in UK union membership has mostly been by individual attrition, and by new employees not joining a union, rather than from employer driven de-recognition disputes.

Gradations of recognition

There are gradations of recognition. One problem with recognizing unions occurs when employers recognize multiple trade unions in their workplaces without considering or challenging the need for a multiplicity of separate unions. As many as 14 trades unions have been recognized for collective bargaining rights on behalf of various groups of employees, some of whom belong to the same workgroup, such as teachers, nurses, and ancillary workers. The most common examples are mainly in the public sector, or covering various skilled workers in the private sector. Many employers work with multi-union agreements; others have opted for single-union agreements.

Multi-union agreements cause many avoidable disputes and running tensions. HR professionals should understand the problems associated with multi-union agreements at both national and local levels. Multi-union workplaces are associated with:

- recurring arguments over spheres of influence;

- disproportionate numbers of representatives from each separate union;

- disproportionate employer's resources devoted to providing facilities for them to function;

- disproportionate time required by management to attend meetings with them;

- disputes over leap-frogging by rival unions on substantive and trivial issues;

- regular problems associated with inter-union rivalry;

- rashes of competing militancy to recruit from each other's members;

- reduced opportunities for management initiatives on cost controls and new technologies to improve site efficiencies.

These problems, when they occur, are part of the environment in which the management trying to deliver the organization's business plan must operate. Understanding the background to employee resistance to change is an essential component of your basic HR knowledge.

SINGLE UNION

Where a single union is recognized as the sole bargaining agent on behalf of its members, the employer excludes other unions from recognition. The parties to these arrangements avoid the fractious problems associated with multi-union plants. Usually they were able to set up a single-union recognition agreement in the UK primarily because they were new manufacturing plants in greenfield sites. From the trade union side, the proliferation of single-union agreements led to union mergers on a grand scale and has created large single unions in place of the dozens of small unions which were a feature of the UK up to the 1990s.

Adopting a single-union recognition strategy for a new (often foreign) major inward investment (for example, Nissan in Sunderland) is a much easier proposition than ending a multi-union agreement in favour of recognizing a single union in an existing plant. Such a strategy involves de-recognizing all but one of the existing unions in the plant and it could be expensive to buy the consent of those employees in the other unions to leave their current unions and join the single union, or from the associated industrial disruption from strikes and non-cooperation campaigns organized by those unions about to lose their recognition status.

The advantages of single-union recognition for the organization include:

- the efficient use of management resources in dealing with one not twelve unions;

- the absence of inter-union rivalries;

- the likelihood of a single authoritative approach by the union to HR and reward issues;

- the easier introduction of more flexible multi-skilled work practices (because it avoids the loss of jobs from one union to another, always a fractious issue);

- the correction of past inequities in pay and rewards won by separate unions;

- fewer union representatives required to participate in management–union procedures;

- ease of communication.

SINGLE TABLE

Where it is impractical to adopt a single-union strategy, because multi-unions are entrenched (as they are in the UK public sector and in government organizations in France and Italy), the next best solution is to try a 'single-table' approach. In this approach all the recognized unions participate together in collective bargaining with management at the same time – at, in fact, a single table.

The single-table approach is superior, though not as efficient as the recognition of a single union, compared to the multi-union, multi-table approach, with its inbuilt multi-union rivalry and suspicions between white collar and blue collar employees and between craft and semi-skilled workforces (never underestimate the degree of inter-union rivalries on matters which they consider important for their survival as independent unions, or essential to the dignity of their members).

In the debate phases of single-table negotiations there could be occasional semi-humorous banter (a form of friendly teasing scorn), which if carried beyond a level of tolerance can leads to semi-serious flare-ups between representatives of different trades unions, and even to staged walk-outs. You should try to keep out of such incidents.

In exchange for securing a single-union agreement, you should be able to negotiate a comprehensive pay relativity agreement for all employees in the plant, perhaps derived from a simple job evaluation exercise (beware: all overly complex job evaluation schemes are unstable) or from a sensible 'read across' structure. (Some pay scales are vertical; where they overlap they are presented together, so that the top of a grade overlaps with the bottom of another higher grade. This is simpler to read and understand. It is less hierarchical.).

It is also possible to adopt a transitional 'two tiers' approach to single-table bargaining. This combines a single-table approach to all common terms of employment affecting all employees (aimed at harmonizing the terms of employment for example, single staff status, holidays, sick pay, pensions, retirement and discipline) and a second tier composed of sub-groups which have particular interests. Base pay negotiations can be centred at the sub-tier or the main table depending on the circumstances.

It should be your intention to adopt a two-tier approach so that, in due course, the sub-tiers will be absorbed into the single-table negotiations to take advantage of its benefits for the organization. Single-table bargaining:

- is conducive to the efficient use of management resources;

- can facilitate an agreed set of pay relativities (no leap-frogging of small groups over comparable groups of employees);

- provides an authoritative forum for the expression of employee views;

- makes it easier to communicate management views to employee representatives.

Some disadvantages have already been mentioned (latent inter-union rivalry), others include the number of representatives at the single meeting (which is at least an improvement on many meetings on the same issues with different representatives) and the extensive facilities required for several unions to operate (meeting rooms, telephones, copiers, cabinets and such like), plus time off work for official union representatives.

For non-unionized employees the usual representative structure is through a consultative committee, except in small organizations where an individual approach is practicable. Collective consultation is acceptable to management, but can stir up employee dissatisfaction if the consultative process is perceived not to influence managerial decision making to the advantage of employees. To be effective, consultation should take place before a managerial decision is made and not afterwards when it may be unchangeable. Communicating what management has decided already is not the same as consultation before a decision has been made. The former practice and the resultant disappointments may provoke demands for formal collective bargaining rights, with all the attendant disadvantages for the organization.

It may be regarded as better to operate genuine consultation than sham information-only schemes. You should also be ready for the apathetic response from employees who are unwilling to make suggestions. Not every workforce is bursting with enthusiasm to participate in consultation, genuine or otherwise.

In all these existing employee settings the guiding principle is whatever best fosters the delivery of the organization's business plan through its HR and reward strategies.

Formal negotiation procedures

Labour negotiations are normally conducted according to a formal written procedure.

Formal procedures are necessary for the orderly conduct of collective bargaining. Some procedure agreements reserve the negotiation role to professional managers in the personnel or HR function; others make this a responsibility for line managers in the departmental functions, supported by the professionals. The choice comes down to the practicalities of deploying the people with the best skill sets to undertake the preparation and conduct of negotiations for the Negotiation Agenda.

With trade unions the same considerations apply. Full-time union officials conduct negotiations with the employers of their local memberships but this negotiating role can be devolved to local members where the workload would be prohibitive for a few officials covering all the union membership, or when the local employer thinks the presence of outsiders is unnecessary. This last arrangement is usually obtained by including in the recognition agreement the proviso that the presence of full-time union officials at negotiations is preceded by a joint agreement that they attend only at the invitation of both sides. This proviso may be important if the recognized trade union experiences a shift from a professional stewardship of employee negotiations to an overtly political, even extremist approach detrimental to the interests of the organization and the employees in it.

The negotiation procedure agreement should specify how the employee representatives are elected (with provision for the management to approve those elected – a reserve power used, if at all, sparingly), their number and the duration of their appointments, their means of accreditation by the union and a statement of their duties. It should also specify the normal cycle of regular meetings, their purpose (avoiding reference to 'annual increases' – 'review before the expiration of an existing agreement' is preferred), and the choice of ratification process, should one be thought necessary, by the employees, such as group meetings, show of hands (preferred by militants) or by secret ballot (preferred by democrats).

Some formal procedure agreements in the past had escalating tiers of responsibility triggered by a formal 'failure to agree' at the formal meetings of the negotiating body. In practice, failure to agree options followed by escalation to a higher level (senior management with the full-time union officials) encourage routine escalations to seek further opportunities to negotiate further movement (by the management, not by the union). On the other hand, the absence of such escalatory options could lead to an early resort to union sanctions of ballots for strikes or other commercially disruptive activities.

CASE STUDY

Dismiss In Haste, Regret At Leisure

Managers at a car plant (since closed) hit by a number of disruptive strikes led by a union shop steward decided to take speedy action and dismiss the man on a minor technicality. The local union official concurred with the dismissal – he was troublesome inside the union too.

The dismissal led to a strike but a week later the members drifted back to work and the dismissal stood. Two months later, the union had an election for a full-time regional official's post. The dismissed steward and the local official were among the candidates.

The dismissed steward won – the car plant employees making up the largest single branch in the region – and he was able to return to the plant as an official for regular negotiations.

Now that he was no longer an employee, the car plant had no influence on him, and he was even more disruptive than before. Before using heavy sanctions on technicalities and trivial transgressions against troublemakers, the managers should have thought through their interests.

Agreements sometimes specify reference to third-party conciliation, mediation or arbitration:

- Conciliation involves private discussions with a conciliator who explores if there is a basis for a resumption of a deadlocked negotiation and, if there is such a basis, the conciliator informs both parties thus and might agree to chair the meeting, if only to open it.

- Mediation involves an independent third party holding private discussions with the deadlocked parties to review the positions adopted by them and to make non-binding recommendations of possible solutions to the deadlock if the mediator identifies from the private discussions that the negotiating ranges of the parties overlap.

- Arbitration involves independent arbiters (usually three) who make binding decisions on the terms of a resolution of the disagreement, either by compromising between the preferred solutions of the parties (conventional arbitration) or by choosing one of the solutions in total (pendulum arbitration).

As these three examples of third-party interventions are generally written into agreements (though joint consent clauses can also be added to make them options, not binding requirements) there are various considerations in using them.

Any third-party intervention takes decisions away from the parties that are accountable (on the management side to creditors, shareholders, customers, government agencies and to its employees, and on the union side to the union members) for the performance of the organization.

Similar arbitration clauses also appear in commercial contracts, some of which, depending on the wording, have the effect of limiting the rights of a party to have early (or any) recourse to legal redress.

Negotiated agreements are presumed to be superior to third-party arbitration, though difficult to reach on occasion because responsibility for what they have agreed is placed on the parties responsible for their implementation. Accountability gives the agreement greater legitimacy. Unions sometimes also object to binding arbitration clauses that are accompanied by clauses barring sanctions while a dispute is in procedure, which effectively becomes a no-strike agreement.

Communicating for major negotiations

Pay bargaining involves communication between the parties. Direct communication usually is limited to the number of negotiators present. Strategic negotiation requires communication with all those affected by the outcome, prior, during and afterwards. Abandoning communication with the organization's employees to the union or staff side could be a serious error. You do not write the speeches the other side makes to your employees; you do not answer your employees' questions; much better to keep communicating through your own channels.

It is essential always for you to reserve the right to communicate directly to your employees on any subject at any time during their employment, and under no circumstances should you accept that the unions have the sole right to communicate with their members, that is, your organization's employees. When your organization is not normally and regularly communicating with your employees (or only doing so during a tense negotiation incident) such one-sided and dangerous rights of sole communicating can be gained by unions through your default.

Communication beyond the negotiation table is an important part of the Negotiation Agenda and not just for difficult industrial relations situations. It applies to all kinds of negotiations, including commercial, diplomatic and institutional. In pay negotiations (and some price negotiations) it is essential that an attempt is made to structure the expectations of the other side's negotiators because unrealistic expectations, perhaps from exaggerating their party's relative power, or from their excessive ambitions, can lead to deadlock and disruptive sanctions.

When relatively rapid change is under way, those with vested interests in the status quo are minded to reinterpret and reframe the other side's motives and interests, inclusive of circulating outright fictions, untruths and distortions, which have the effect of raising fears, uncertainties and doubts in their constituency. Communicating the main elements of the Negotiation Agenda without ambiguities is an important management task best not left to the unions or to the public media. Negotiations, when they contain insensitive surprises for the other side, are not helpful and they can sour what could be an otherwise positive atmosphere.

It is important to communicate with all levels of management and not just to communicate with those in the negotiation team who prepared the Negotiation Agenda. There is little worse that you can do to demoralize your management colleagues than if, by your neglect, they feel that union members are better informed than they are of what is happening. Where other employees are their source of information, through what is known in the UK as the 'grapevine', the reliability of the information they receive is unlikely to be accurate and their responses to questions may only make matters worse. It is not possible to engage in strategic negotiation without widespread and well-informed support for the Negotiation Agenda by the vast bulk of your management team.

The same is true for employees. You represent the organization, and your behaviours and attitudes influence the outcome of the negotiations. You and your managerial colleagues are in hourly contact with your staff and you can influence many of them with a positive, well-informed attitude to the changes, or, by not being informed yourselves, drive employees to the negative conclusions emanating from the grapevine. Remember, the grapevine is never charitable because everything is always interpreted negatively and it never puts a positive slant on anything it conveys about what management is up to, especially where this involves changes. By responding with factual communication, you can do much to limit the damage of untrue stories and malign interpretations of management motives.

Managerial communication is best conducted regularly and not just when a crisis emerges. Sending letters to employees with dire warnings of the consequences of a current union-inspired event is disingenuous and probably too late. Employees who receive regular communication on major issues affecting them are more likely to react positively, even to bad news, if management has established a reputation for telling the truth and for being honest over the years before something difficult needs to be dealt with. Admitting to a managerial error is appreciated positively and adds to a reputation for honesty and integrity.

In strategic pay bargaining there are three communication phases:

- pre-negotiations
- intra-negotiations
- post-negotiations.

Pre-negotiation communications are an opportunity to spread accurate information (and not a little realism) to the workforce. It is an ideal opportunity to address the 'no surprises' principle properly. Widely representative selections of employees, not necessarily all of them active members of the union (though all union representatives, perhaps officials too, may be invited), should meet for 'away-day' type conferences.

The theme of the conference should be non-adversarial about the situation (positive or negative) facing the organization and all of its employees. A frank exchange of aspirations is its central feature, with presentations from the employees on the improvements they are looking for in their working conditions, including pay rises, and with (equal time) management presentations from the Negotiation Agenda on the key issues as seen by them, such as changes in the way things are done, with emphasis placed on the key principle of affordability in everything that is done or proposed.

The pre-negotiation conference is neither a negotiation nor a substitute for it. Its purpose is to explore perspectives, aspirations and attitudes, and set the scene. There is no need to debate contentious attitudes or to dismiss offhand any employee suggestions. It is nearer to a brainstorming session than to a negotiation debate. By avoiding surprises, accusations of bad faith are prevented and by informing a wider audience than the negotiators accurately about the issues to be negotiated, you should create a more constructive atmosphere for the negotiations.

Pay negotiations typically require more than one meeting and an intra-negotiating communication strategy is required between the meetings. Depending on progress, intra-negotiation conferences can be called by management to inform non-participants about the negotiations. The unions may hold similar meetings with their members.

If serious contention in the negotiations emerges, you may decide to communicate directly with your employees. In this situation, the scripted intra-negotiation briefing used during this period becomes even more important and it should always be seen as reinforcing involvement in the negotiation process and the commitment of both sides to its success. These briefings should not be conducted as a propaganda war, but more as an accurate reminder of what is at stake and where the difficulties reside, always making no mention of your opinions of union behaviours or imputing malign motives to individuals, no matter how well founded you believe your opinions to be. The objective is to influence the influencers with a positive approach to problems and from this to influence the attitudes of employees.

Assuming success in the negotiations – a mutually-agreed negotiated settlement has been achieved - the possibility of a post-negotiation conference should be considered. At this conference, a joint presentation of what has been agreed should be made. It is wise not to gloat over one side's successes or bemoan the other side's obstruction. Agreements are mutually agreed, not selectively, and the agreement becomes the legitimate property of both sides. In all this, the right of management to communicate with its employees is reinforced, subtly.

Organizations have a wide range of instruments for communicating, depending on their size. Starting with the ubiquitous notice boards (which few tend to notice!) it may be useful to audit exactly what communication instruments are available in your organization and decide which are more effective than others. In an age of e-mail it may be that larger numbers can be reached by such means than by other, more traditional means. However, prevent embarrassing errors in your e-mails by proofreading them carefully.

Staff newspapers may not be the most effective of routes to influence and the team-briefing methods of earlier years may have passed their best days. Live conferences may be useful if the presenters are interesting, but video presentations by the CEO may generate cynicism.

Activities
for Chapter 4

Activity 4.1

How would you describe the labour environment in your country?

How regulated is it by law?

Does it lean towards the continental model of social capitalism (for example, Germany, France, Italy, Netherlands and Belgium) or is it more like the Scandinavian variant of 'welfare capitalism')?

Does it lean towards the US-UK model of market capitalism?

Or do you live in a recently-transformed socialist type of economy such as in the former Soviet Union or Eastern Europe?

COMMENTS ON THIS ACTIVITY

There are, of course, other variations on all these models in China, Vietnam, North Korea, Australia, South Africa, other parts of Africa and Central and South America.

Look for instances of market regulation, statutory labour laws governing hiring, firing and redundancies, limitations on working hours and unsocial hours working, and the procedures for the recognition of and negotiation with trade unions.

Do trade unions operate in your organization and have they a legal right to represent employees?

To what extent does the government, through its agencies, intervene in the organization's dealings with trade unions? What legal rights do employees have in your country as a whole?

The purpose of the exercise is not to critique or make a comparison of particular arrangements that exist in your country. It is necessary for you to be aware of the existing arrangements in your country if you are going to mobilize your organization's human resources behind the achievement of your organization's business plan. The choice of a country's labour relations regime is a political decision and not one with which this book is concerned.

Activity 4.2

What arrangements for pay determination across all employee grades operate in your organization?

COMMENTS ON THIS ACTIVITY

This is a more focused activity than Activity 4.1. Begin with your own pay grade and identify how your pay is determined. Is it through a formal system or is it mainly at the discretion of individual managers with individual employees?

Does a systematized performance appraisal procedure operate for your pay grade (that is, one in which you contribute your assessment of your performance against written criteria, perhaps supported by colleagues, managers and employees that you supervise – in a version, say, of a 360° appraisal?

To what extent does a formal system operate for the majority of your organization's pay grades?

Activity 4.3

To what extent do you recognize the objectives in your pay and reward system?

Can you identify any headings under which your pay and reward system acts in a direction counter to any of the objectives? If so, why in your view is that happening?

COMMENTS ON THIS ACTIVITY

Most of the goals in the headings are ideal, much like the standard definition of a perfect procurement regime: to acquire the right goods, at the right time, at the right price and in the right place. Nobody could argue sensibly against any of those applying to the perfect remuneration regime, but the problem with all such goals lies in their achievement, especially simultaneously.

Once we look at existing remuneration regimes, as we will for the Negotiation Agenda, we find some of them do not help the business plan.

If your remuneration regime is in any way a hindrance to your organization's business plan – and you should think carefully about your existing regime in this activity – you should find the Negotiation Agenda approach of great help.

Activity 4.4

If you work in a unionized work environment, ask for a copy of the union recognition agreement. To what extent is managerial discretion inhibited?

Would you consider the agreement to be equitable towards those employees who are members of the union?

What about those employees who are not, or who do not wish to be, members?

Is there a detailed structure for representation, with time off for union duties?

Are union fees deducted from employees' pay and passed to the union, or do employees individually pay the union by their own arrangements?

How broadly are union duties interpreted – within the work place or outside the workplace?

Is there any special protection for union officials who are employees in respect of discipline or grievances?

COMMENTS ON THIS ACTIVITY

Unions seek to be recognized as the sole bargaining agent for the employee grade(s) they wish to represent. It is worthwhile for management to qualify the recognition statement so that the union is recognized as the bargaining agent for its members and not for all the employees in the grade; otherwise the union may be representing numbers of employees when only a few employees in a particular grade are its members.

Unions seek to extend their roles in the workplace by extending the responsibilities of its unpaid officials (shop stewards in the UK) from pay and conditions bargaining into safety, welfare, consultation and business policy. With the amount of time off work for meetings of various committees, internal union member meetings for consultations and external union meetings to discuss union affairs locally and nationally, the unpaid (by the union) workplace officials end up, effectively, as employer-paid union officials whose normal work needs to be done by other employees.

Unions sometimes seek extra protection for their workplace officials by requiring that higher management, in discussion with the paid official of the union, should deal with alleged breaches of workplace discipline, not the immediate line supervision. This protection sometimes results in the union's encouraging disruptive action to reverse a disciplinary decision even in cases where the correctness of the disciplinary decision would not be challenged if it were applied to an ordinary employee. Management may wish to include in the agreement that the organization's disciplinary procedure (lateness, absenteeism, threatening behaviour and so on) applies to all employees, including all union workplace officials.

Remember, because all trade unions value a recognition agreement highly – and some will press for the maximum extension of union powers and facilities – the employer has the opportunity at this time to enforce sensible constraints in exchange for recognition.

Activity 4.5

Which form of collective bargaining structure are you most familiar with in your organization?

COMMENTS ON THIS ACTIVITY

You should familiarize yourself with the existing arrangements; better still become well briefed on its nature, its history and the recent manner in which it has worked. Here you will find the experience of the old hands invaluable, if you can persuade them to take time out to share their experience with you. When it comes to devising strategies for the Negotiation Agenda, a fine sense of what has and has not worked in the past could save time while more informed accounts are addressed.

One good source could be the minutes of the management–union meetings and the correspondence between both sides. Much therein will be meaningless – a measure itself of how short of quality knowledge on the HR environment you are – but persevere.

Activity 4.6

Ask for a copy of your organization's union negotiating procedure agreement(s). How much does it constrain the unions from early disruptive actions by requiring either escalation of the disputed issue to higher levels of management or more senior union officials, or by compulsory arbitration clauses?

Managing Complex Negotiations

CHAPTER

5

Introduction[1]

This chapter covers, briefly, four main topics:

- transaction logistics

- corporate risk management

- public sector transactions

- managing the negotiation team.

It addresses questions such as the following:

- How should the directors of an organization organize the negotiating team, who hold responsible jobs in the organization, to ensure that the organization does not go bankrupt from their neglect of their day jobs?

- How do you ensure that the negotiating team receives enough management attention to ensure that what they commit the organization to deliver is actually deliverable by managers not at the table and unaware of what is being promised in their names?

- How do you get the organization (perhaps acting on behalf of the Government or another organization) to maintain the political will (big or little 'p') for the length of time it takes to do a major transaction (especially when the project is located in another country)?

- How do you deal with third parties engaged in a media war against the project or with a view to influence the outcome of the negotiations?

---

1   I am grateful to Louise Hart for her contribution to the themes of this chapter.

- How do you maintain the focus of the transaction and its momentum in the face of unexpected external events (for example, a multi-fatality from organizational failure elsewhere in its operations)?

- How do you keep track of all the details of a transaction that ends up being documented in more than 200 separate agreements?

These questions will be recognizable by negotiators responsible for complex, multi-stakeholder, high-value deals in which the lives, income and futures of thousands of people, employees, suppliers and customers will be affected one way or another by the outcome.

Transaction logistics

Large complex negotiations will take place over many meetings, certainly for several weeks and perhaps for several months. They may take place in a neutral location, possibly in a different country to the organization's home base. They will involve considerable documentation, which requires to be transported securely to and from the venue. The negotiators will have other resource needs, such as: hotel accommodation; ground transport at the venue; air transport to and from the country; secure meeting places for team review sessions, rest and recuperation facilities, and for communication with corporate headquarters; arrangements for visiting advisers and board members; and arrangements for the inevitable brief absence of key players during sessions.

It greatly facilitates smooth access to such resources if it is recognized that they need managing. The appointment of a 'transaction manager', responsible for all of them, is the best solution. Players under stress do not need the aggravation of inadequate support resources, missing documents, improperly arranged transport and unmet visitors.

The logistics of the whole transaction from preparation through conduct to contract should be seen and run as a major project using the skills and tools of project management. A transactions manager skilled in establishing and maintaining good inter-personal relations with all of the players and the staff who service the facilities they use (a cross between a receptionist, banqueting manager, concierge and travel agent, with the organizational planning skills of an experienced project manager) is ideal – the everyman-for-himself approach is an avoidable disaster.

Transaction management is about the management of the negotiation process and not about the negotiating skills used in the process. Fully-trained soldiers should be proficient in the arts and skills of warfare, but without logistical backup and the management skills to integrate logistics with the battle plans, deployments, and the offensive and defensive stances required by military strategy, it would be a short war, and perhaps a terminal experience for the soldiers, whoever they are protecting, and for the prospects of whatever causes they are putting themselves into harm's way for.

The great land offensives of the First World War, costing tens of thousands of lives, were terminated within days, not for a want of stoic bravery on the part of those unfortunate soldiers conducting them, but from a lack of sustainable supplies of war materials available at the appropriate points at the appropriate times and for durations long enough to achieve the breakthroughs each side desired. As a result, years of static stalemated trench warfare were interrupted by a series of short big-push scenarios until sense prevailed and they agreed an armistice.

A similar problem arises with the management of complex negotiations. When undertaken by poorly-trained negotiators, the results are well below sub-optimal. Lawyers, who prefer to work to precise instructions, are left with imprecise and vague, sometimes contradictory, briefs, and the outcome is no different from what it would be if they were given no instructions at all. The problem is caused by the poor preparation skills of many negotiators. Most negotiators are untrained, except by experience, which is not always an infallible guide to excellence – repeating the same mistakes over and over again could constitute their only experience.

We have to recognize that the transaction itself has to be managed. Negotiations are conducted during negotiation sessions and these sessions take place in real time, spread over many calendar weeks or months, at locations in physical space, perhaps in more than one country. During the spread of sessions there are other events occurring that impinge on the negotiations, the people in them and the arrangements that bring the parties together (or keep them apart).

If the location is the property of one of the parties, the other party has to bring and remove its papers after each session; if it is a neutral venue, this is a burden on all parties, and the burden has to be managed and support staff (supervisors, porters, drivers and filing clerks) assembled and monitored (misplaced or lost files slow down momentum and could compromise security). The degree of security provision needed should be assessed both from a risk assessment of the other parties' arrangements (hopefully, not a serious risk, more of a prudent necessity) and of the various third parties who might intrude on the business of the negotiating teams.

Where the duration of the negotiation is uncertain, calendar events impinging on the sessions, if they drag on, need to be mapped and noted. Certain external dates (board and shareholders' meetings of the parties) and the likely duration of official statutory procedures (regulatory approvals, public enquiries and consultations, licensing courts, parliamentary legislation, court cases and such like) which may intrude at times not always convenient for the negotiators. Festivals, holidays and religious events have to be worked round and it is important to have advance warning of them where they affect transport, access to facilities, service staff and employees. Different days of the week designated as week-end days obviously need to be noted; these could reduce the working week to three days unless sensible compromises are made (a rule of thumb compromise is to abide by whichever two days are the weekend in the country where the negotiation sessions are located, with due allowance for the religious or social imperatives of other parties).

In constitutional democracies, elections may affect the governing party (changes of government may disrupt the negotiations and their outcome) and party conferences may affect the timing of announcements where the negotiation has a high and controversial public profile. Needless to say, military coups, the death of a country's dictator and such like could impinge on the negotiations, as might the attention of demonstrators opposed to the meetings, and incidents of public disorder, kidnappings and terrorism. This raises again the issue of security provision, and professional risk assessment of the threat to the security of the people at the negotiations should be undertaken, especially for known hot spots.

If the negotiations have high-profile implications, the need for a media policy to soften public opinion should be considered. This may already be part of the negotiation planning process where media activity has been judged to be important. It may very well be part of the justification and response process because of the controversial or competitive nature of the subject of the negotiation. Turning public opinion for or against the participants could be something outside the control of the negotiators for ideological, political, religious or ethnic reasons.

Competitors, outside of the negotiations, may still be lobbying to be restored as preferred bidders; ignoring their activities, or activities which would benefit their case but which are not directly sponsored by them, could be careless (for example, the replacement of France's Dassault by the UK's British Aerospace in the Saudi air defence contract). If there is a need for a media team and a media policy closely linked to the negotiation team, then it has to be recruited, assembled, managed and directed from within the negotiation team and not left to its own devices.

The logistics of moving people, documents, files and papers to and from places near or far apart has to be thought through and experienced staff delegated to make the necessary arrangements with travel agents, hotels and facilities managers. There is enough stress generated in prolonged negotiation sessions without adding to it by sloppiness in the arrangements for movement of people and things. Papers missing at the moment they are needed (during a justification exchange, for instance) or people late for a timed intervention cause both stress and embarrassment and undermine the credibility of a party's negotiating stance. A single instance at a crucial moment could be bad enough; constant repetition of such events erodes confidence in a post-negotiation relationship.

All this suggests that a transaction analysis be undertaken and the negotiation treated as a large project that needs to be managed like any other project the party may undertake. Courses in project management cover many of the tools helpful to transaction managers (Gantt charts, critical path analysis, risk management, tree diagrams, PERT and so on). Supporting such technical tools you need common sense and political awareness of the environment outside the negotiation sessions, and how the external environment may change during the course of a long and complex negotiation. The events column in a force field diagram (Chapter 10) should be completed and reviewed regularly.

Corporate risk

Some transactions are so large that getting them wrong could bankrupt the company – a deal too far? In simple deals the tradables are not numerous (in the 10s to 50s) and establishing negotiating ranges from entry to exit points for them is cumbersome but not impossible. What about when there are thousands, even tens of thousands of potential tradables? Should we change the game? Not necessarily. Let's look at the problem from the point of view of the strategy of deriving the Negotiation Agenda from the business plan.

The board's business plan identifies what it regards as the decisive issues important enough for it to consider them a sufficient guide to management charged with achieving them. Boards do not normally go into the fine detail, especially if there are thousands of details associated with the deals it requires to be negotiated. As issues ascend the management hierarchy, they are summarized into key aggregate terms and it is these terms that the board reviews and not the myriad details of which they are comprised. Board reports usually consist of an executive summary on a page of A4, or perhaps in extremis two pages of A4, sometimes backed with many pages of the detailed report; but on most occasions only the executive summary reaches the board for its approval. Fifty-page contracts may only be reported as a line in a manager's report to the board stating that such and such a contract has been signed with the Acme Corporation, and board members who might be interested (rarely) in seeing it can ask for a copy. Few do.

Specifically, the Negotiation Agenda is aligned with the board's business plan. Managers using it do not wander round the business and its markets looking for things to negotiate about: they start with the business plan, identify the commercial imperatives, and derive the Negotiation Agenda to implement the Plan, and then they review the deals they strike and how they deliver the Plan. From the list of items identified in the Negotiation Agenda the negotiation team will derive its Negotiation Plan, which details the fully costed negotiation issues the management will use in the negotiations to secure the Negotiation Agenda's objectives.

Board approvals are obtained because the summary reports seeking them show how the deal implements the Plan's deliberations on the topics for which the negotiation has been conducted. Any gaps between the two are easily exposed; a deal that the board considers does not achieve what the Plan set out to do will not be approved and the management concerned brought to account. Boards should be critical of managerial spin and waffle, and the members of the Board's awkward squad (sceptical non-executives and executives in associated functions) perform a useful service in spotting the gaps and risks in loosely drafted summaries.

Risk management should feature in any competent organization. A note on the risk assumptions in any report on the deals undertaken or concluded should be attached either to the executive report or included in its verbal presentation to the board. That is essential for the larger contracts, where the consequences of risky events occurring are severe, and risks should always be considered for smaller deals where the cumulative consequences of inherent risks could also be serious. This was a feature in the failures of computer leasing companies when, not unexpectedly, lessees took advantage of liberal cancellation clauses in their contracts (drawn up by the leasing companies!) when upgraded systems became available from other companies. This drained cash from the lessors, turning their projected profits into runaway losses.

The negotiation team's report on the outcome of its negotiation plan, drawn from the Negotiation Agenda, lends itself to risk assessment techniques (as illustrated in books on strategic risk management) because the terms of the negotiated contract are seamlessly linked to the board's Plan. Where the prime function responsible for negotiating the agenda overlaps other functions there is a potential for risks to remain assessed inadequately. At a minimum, staff should consult with other functions and receive their advice on the risks, possibly unappreciated by outsiders, inherent in their areas of expertise. If it is accepted that corporate finance and accounts should always cast their eyes over any proposal involving finance, it follows that any function in an organization should do likewise over any proposal involving their services or their knowledge of their part of the business.

Negotiating large deals is expensive. Tendering is expensive. Changes in specifications and design are expensive. Management time away from the day job is expensive. And as the costs pile up, the Concorde fallacy appears in the mind sets of some negotiators: 'We have spent so long on this project that we must conclude it or we have wasted all that money.' They forget the older adage: 'Let's not throw good money after bad' and the economist's dictum: 'Bygones are bygones.' It is not how much has been spent (that is gone now forever) but the marginal cost of completion mediated by the likelihood of the project's profitability.

A possible answer is to establish a separately identified transactionbudget to incorporate all these costs. Left unidentified, and squeezed out of other headings in the negotiator's departmental budget, the momentum for a conclusion to a deal, irrespective of the likely profit, builds up almost irresistibly, and because it is not spoken of as such, it can be presented with glowing reports of future prospects that hide the truth from the board. Once signed, the parties to a contract have to live with what they have signed and without whatever they failed to sign. To remove this temptation for participants to lose their commercial objectivity and get too enthusiastic for the deal's closure for the wrong reasons, a transaction budget acts like a brake as it is drawn down. That very visible reduced budget total alone should promote a risk assessment review, by those not involved closely in the negotiations, of the deal's prospects, within an acceptable period, as a net contributor or otherwise to the fortunes of the company.

CASE STUDY

Expensive Concessions

A well-known case of negotiators committing their company to something they knew little about concerned a negotiation in China by a US computer company. The negotiators were highly competent in computer systems – what they could do and what they cost.

Early in the negotiations, the Chinese oil and gas industry negotiators asked for the operating and maintenance manuals, which were in English, to be translated and printed in Mandarin. The US negotiators agreed, without enquiring of their colleagues in charge of translating manuals into foreign languages the cost of such a free concession.

Eight years later when the negotiations were finally concluded (it took that long in Mao's China) the profitability of the computer deal had been negotiated downwards by the Chinese bureaucrats. The profitability of the deal was made worse by the cost of translation and printing the operating manuals in Chinese by the sum of US$400 000. If they had asked their foreign language colleagues (staff work!) they could have traded this sum against another tradable, but this would have meant also receiving some training in the fundamentals of negotiation.

A feature of the Negotiation Agenda is the inbuilt personal accountability of the negotiation team leader who signs off the board reports, which are countersigned by the CEO or director responsible for the function from which the reports emanate. The need for accountability in negotiated outcomes has two aspects: the negotiation team acts in the board's name in making agreements (promises, warranties and indemnities), and the board may want to know by whom (and why) certain contractual elements were made. Named persons are made accountable for what they do so that praise or penalties fall on the correct persons if events give cause for such reactions. Cynical veterans of the recriminations when things went wrong parody them as a being more like: 'Search for the guilty; punish the innocent!'

Accountability also has a positive role in that it induces those making accountable decisions to constantly check what they are doing against the clear instructions or guidelines laid down by the board. Otherwise, drift sets in between what the board thinks its negotiators are doing and what the negotiators think they should be doing on behalf of the board.

The Negotiation Agenda assists this process of connecting the board's objectives in its business plan (and subsequent elaborations of its instructions) to the planned outcomes for the negotiations. The link is always seamless between the board's Plan and the Negotiating Agenda, through identification of the commercial and other imperatives, the relevant policies and the derived

Negotiation Agenda. To ensure a continuing alignment between them the negotiators constantly check the linkages. The Negotiation Agenda, when compiled by staff work on the relevant data, is signed off by the CEO or the functional director and the leader of the negotiating team. The Agenda consists of objectives, supported by numeric data and the outline of specific proposals, complete with negotiation ranges and costed options.

In this manner there is less chance of the negotiations moving the goal posts such that they end up on a different pitch to that which the board thought they were playing on. The Negotiation Agenda document keeps everybody's eye on the ball.

Public sector negotiations

Two words describe the main problem with negotiating in the public sector: politicians and politics. The main aim of a government is to be re-elected and that of politicians, in democracies and dictatorships, is to remain in or get into power. This makes them unreliable allies in negotiation of large (even little) public contracts and their fickleness pervades all aspects of the negotiation. Because politicians fear (in office) and support (in opposition) the exposure of wrongdoing or carelessness in the handling of public money, they have passed detailed rules for the award of public contracts. The rules have a rationale in past errors of omission or commission by people (contractors, civil servants, ministers) in previous administrations. These rules can create a barrier to a sensible adjustment, or temporary suspension, of a rule when it would be patently in the interest of the government to do so.

Public law rules on contracting (for example, in the UK, GCStores1 and GCWorks1) are difficult to change – they are often taken into the contract intact – but if read carefully they have several invitations to negotiate certain clauses: phrases like 'unless otherwise agreed ... shall apply', lead several of the clauses.

Because public infrastructure projects tend to be large – airport runways, terminals, main roads, bridges, harbours, nuclear power stations – they are subject to various statutory planning regulations for public enquiries and public consultations and these can take years to complete, with the added uncertainty that the Planning Inspectorate could refuse the project or require such expensive alterations to the design as to reduce its profitability, or add to costs if introduced during construction. Organizations hoping to negotiate a contract for such projects may not be able to wait for a go-ahead decision by the

CASE STUDY

Public Probity

A Commonwealth country had a public law against foreign ownership of a commercial entity and required a majority shareholding to be held locally. It also had a public law that large infrastructure contracts were awarded in stages only and not in one contract at the beginning (this prevented poor performance of the contractor being continued into subsequent stages).

The government's negotiators adamantly refused to consider a 51 per cent foreign ownership requirement by the contractor on grounds that this protected its IPRs in an advanced technology, which it was proposing to transfer over the whole contract into the Commonwealth country.

As adamantly, the civil servants refused to consider awarding more than one stage of the contract even though the first stage did not allow enough time for the contractor to cover the set-up capital costs of the first stage. The result – deadlock.

In vain the contractor's negotiators pled with their opposite numbers at least to recommend to the minister they were reporting to for a relaxation of the public laws in these two cases only. They refused to do so.

It took diplomatic pressure from their own government to persuade the Commonwealth member to see the merit in meeting their development interests in preference to their formal rules that inflexibly protected public probity.

public authority, or be willing to take the risk that after great expense in design and tendering, it may be dropped.

Negotiating complex high-value deals with public sector organizations creates special difficulties for other organizations, particularly commercial companies. Negotiators from either side ought to be aware of the operational differences that arise from the different ethos of each organization and the people in them.

Public sector organizations are driven by budgets, which are allocated to them and funded by compulsory taxation and public borrowing. Private sector organizations are driven by budgets too but the difference is that they are funded from net profits and private borrowing, which has to be paid for out of their earnings. If a private sector organization does not spend its net revenue in one year it can spend it in a subsequent year (though it remains under the control of the corporate financial centre); in the public sector an organization or department that does not spend its budget loses it (though limited virement may be allowed) and it is returned to the Treasury or the budget holder and claims on its future use go through the budgetary approvals system as new items.

Awareness of the budget year in the public sector is important because deals that are pending for expenditures in the budget that run over the end of the budget year could be scrapped and the deal fall through. It is not uncommon for public sector bodies to accelerate negotiations near the end of the budget year, and even to ask a regular supplier for invoices for pending deals or to send in invoices before an existing deal has completed its contracted deliveries, so as to use up surpluses in their budget allocation and avoid the penalty of a loss of their allocation.

In the UK, the National Audit Office and the Parliamentary Accounts Committee monitor performance and probity (under the rubric of 'value for money') of the public sector, and public sector organizations take these investigations seriously – apart from departmental pride, personal promotions and public standing could ride on avoiding adverse criticism from either body. Adverse criticism of a private sector supplier – implied in a charge that the public sector purchase did not provide value for money – is best avoided if there is an intention to bid for other contracts in the public sector. Other countries have similar audit systems in place.

In democracies there is always the possibility of a government change and with it the likelihood that policies will change with the departure of the old regime (the same, of course, happens in dictatorships, only less frequently). Where a single party has been in power for many decades (for example, Mexico since the 1920s; Italy from 1945 to the 1990s; India under the Congress Party) the party may stay the same but the persons forming the government are likely to change regularly. Where negotiations are underway for a large-value contract, a change in government or personnel could disrupt the prospect of early celebrations if many matters need to be settled at the time of the change over and the opposition has indicated its intentions to withdraw government support from the project if elected.

Civil or public servants with a degree of sensitivity to these changeovers may speed up the negotiations to conclude them, or back pedal to avoid concluding them, as the date for the change approaches. Bear in mind that public sector bodies are peopled by individuals of diverse views on the interpretation of the 'public good' and the role of your and the minister's project in promoting it, and they have a keen sense of the likely effects on their prospects of promotion (and tenure!) of being closely associated with the policies of the former regime in the eyes of the incoming regime.

If the risk of your negotiations being terminated by an incoming government is high, there may be no point in continuing with them (think of the transaction costs that may be wasted); if you cannot wait the sometimes interminable time that statutory public enquiries and public consultations may take, you should reconsider decisions to bid for publicly funded work or to continue negotiating if negotiations have started.

For some large construction projects there are bound to be many years delay with one or more public enquiries and debates in Parliament, consultations and political haggling among the political parties, local authorities, pressure groups and stakeholders. However, it may still be worthwhile for an organization to keep its name in the sponsor's minds as a potential prime contractor.

Public sector contracts are a special kind in many respects. Defence contracts for large projects come under special requirements on 'transparency' (open books on costs and profits), on bidding for production series of prototypes a firm has built and proved the performance of, and on ever-changing specifications and redesigns of performance criteria. Recent legislation on freedom of information adds a complication in that commercial confidentiality is constrained by the right (not just the need) to know of anything to do with public expenditure and the decisions of public bodies (all adding to costs) on request by the general public. There are also requirements that contractors must meet on a host of subjects on labour policies and employee behaviour.

Politicians often have agendas that the public sector officials have to balance with their professional roles in contests between the politicians' electoral ambitions (they hate losing their seats) and the civil servant's good judgement, with the efficiency of the project in the eyes of the negotiators who bid to build it in the background. When politicians take up a cause against a public project (the building of the Scottish Parliament, for example) both public officials and the contractors are placed under new pressures beyond those that were contained in the negotiations. Contractors who win the public debate earn the eternal enmity of the politicians who lose face, and the public reputation of the contractor is then hostage to the vagaries of future events and the fortunes of the politicians and their access to the media, which are less interested in the facts and more inclined to the unearthing of good stories.

Managing the negotiation team

Negotiation of large contracts must be a team effort, not that of a single individual, but as the team size grows – including its support and resources staff – coordination and communication problems grow. This places a premium on forming a team with the right structure; a written one preferably, which shows each member's responsibilities as discussed and agreed individually, and noted in writing.

Full information on all communication details for everybody on the team (no exceptions) should be produced and circulated, including home numbers (with the necessary permissions from those concerned to conform with recent legislation), mobiles, e-mails and Web sites. Events in long negotiations often intrude at awkward times and it is important to be able to contact team and support members without undue delay (including room and phone numbers in the team's hotel if it is playing away). Film production companies do an impressive professional job on contact numbers, including ex-directory and bolt holes, and negotiating teams for large deals could benefit from copying their normal practices.

If colleagues are nervous about sharing personal data, then the team's transaction manager should act as their contact point and holder of their confidential information. Time away from the negotiations should always be reported and temporary locations noted. The transaction manager is an important member of the team. They should have impressive interpersonal skills and enough assertiveness to ensure people do not easily escape from the manager's reach and discipline. The transaction manager will run the negotiation team's work as a project and will deal with all matters arising in the transaction that require support and resources. The team leader will rely on the transaction manager to keep everything moving smoothly, to sort out snags and to keep them informed about all developments that could affect the negotiation team's performance.

Large-scale negotiations inevitably involve professional advisers – accountants, lawyers, bankers and finance managers, property specialists, valuation assessors, pension managers, insurance brokers, actuaries, surveyors, risk assessors, architects, searchers, due diligence specialists, economists, HRM advisers, translators, and environmental impact assessors – and there are two important things about these people of which your team should be aware:

- Advisers have had professional contacts, often over many years, on various deals, both with and against each other, for other clients. They will probably work with or against each other on future deals. They know each other better than you do and their judgement should be respected, as should their advice on appropriate levels of trust in what you are hearing from the other side, presumably under advisement from their advisers. They are unlikely to want to compromise their professional relationships for your short-term gains (the same applies to the other side's advisers). Bear in mind that when you brief them about your requirements, they will be judging your trustworthiness too.

- The advice you are paying for, especially in due diligence exercises, should be carefully studied and questioned and, where appropriate should be challenged. Make sure that you understand what the data allegedly are telling you about the business and insist on the advisers explaining how they arrived at their conclusions. If you do not bother to do this you give the impression that you do not care whether they bother to do their work properly. Recovering damages for poor quality work is difficult if you only notice errors or dubious conclusions when events have shown them to be erroneous. Questions beforehand might have uncovered the deficiencies.

With many players on both sides of the negotiation and with many advisers on your own side, it is imperative that you select named individual points of contact between your team and your advisers through whom all contacts between you are channelled. Talking to different people adds nuances on interpretation and expression, even worrying contradictions, to what were meant to be definitive instructions because, though several people have been informed of aspects of a decision, not everybody is totally familiar with the final decision. Versions of Chinese whispers (where the message 'send reinforcements I am going to advance' becomes 'send three and four pence I am going to a dance') are replicated when unauthorized people offer opinions on matters upon which they are ill-informed and the message passes through several people, rather than going directly to one.

All members of the team should be kept fully informed of the flows of changing documentation and working papers. A simple, but secure, intranet arrangement would be a great help in keeping the papers in order. A document numbering system should be established and stuck with. Out of date documents waste time and when people are tired, they are easily irritated by such sloppiness. The transaction manager or team secretary can take charge of this function (and tidy up members' folders that need it – you soon identify the tidy ones and those who need help).

When negotiations move from heads of agreement (or heads of terms), it is usual for some team members and advisers to withdraw and be replaced by

CASE STUDY

The Caveat Part Of Caveat Emptor

A financial adviser searched, located and gave the all clear to a firm to negotiate the purchase of a business in Portugal. Some months later the purchaser discovered serious errors in the finances of the business. It had not bothered to check the due diligence reports carefully because a major European accountancy firm, whose prestige induced them to forget about the 'caveat' part of caveat emptor, authored them. Not only did they lose most of their investment, but they received only a small part of their losses in compensation. They would have preferred that the investment had worked for them.

those specializing in negotiation of the detail. The heads of agreement set out in concise form the precise terms of the proposed sale, purchase, contract or agreement and various preliminary matters, or they may be summarized in an exchange of letters. While non-binding legally (save as to confidentiality, exclusivity of the negotiations until a settlement or a withdrawal, and the sharing of costs) they usually carry a heavy moral commitment and a degree of comfort to each side before they embark on costly preparation, including due diligence, and the negotiations proper.

The heads of terms are a useful checklist of the main matters to be decided (the 'subject to contract' part) and the withdrawing team members should thoroughly brief the incoming team members on these matters because not everything discussed or explained during the preliminary negotiations of the heads need appear in the checklist. Yet, some of these discussions may prove to be important and the other side may assume that your side is aware of the importance of some of these matters to them, and therefore to you if they affect the negotiations (say, complications in the approval process for the other side's company, or regulatory inhibitors that affect them). There could be an avoidable negative reaction if they proceed in good faith on the assumption that everybody on your side is thoroughly conversant with such problems and someone from your side proceeds in total ignorance of what they are on about.

Two additional points:

- In big and little deals the same general rules apply: settling smaller issues before big (possibly difficult) ones sounds attractive but experience shows that delaying facing up to the bigger issues is not necessarily good advice. That difficult issues are present should

---

CASE STUDY

On Skipping Legal Advice

A warehouse company sought to acquire a service company, which it considered a good fit with its operations. The service company was a willing seller, its management and owners wishing either to retire or to exit their investments. The owner/manager of the warehouse company was brusque, loud and not given to listening carefully because of his short attention span when listening to legal talk.

As negotiations came towards the end, and a price had been guardedly agreed, the seller's lawyers reminded him that there were complications in the service company's structure in that several of its shareholders had invested under a government tax concession scheme to encourage new ventures in certain regions of the country. Hence, a straight purchase of these shares was not possible; the tax concessions to these shareholders had to be reversed and cleared with the Inland Revenue first, and this could take several months, though the amounts involved appeared to be small compared to the price of the deal.

The warehouse owner reacted predictably, blaming his advisers, accusing the seller of duplicity and castigating the Inland Revenue for interfering in a business decision. The seller and his advisers were not happy with his outbursts, particularly as the nature of the share structure was included in the ten-page written document supplied to the warehouse owner after their first meeting. It was assumed that he would have this complication looked at by his lawyers.

They assumed wrongly. He hadn't taken the matter further and his lawyers had not drawn attention to the tax implications of undoing the concession scheme. To get a quick settlement (in three months instead of six to nine) with the Inland Revenue it cost him £100 000 – his offer document was 'to purchase the entire share capital' of the seller's company, with no reference to the minority shareholders and the tax problem.

---

be acknowledged, at least, early on and probably the earlier the better. Reminding everybody that negotiators are in the solution and not the deadlock business can moderate the impact of your acknowledgement on their deal pessimism. If there is a deal in prospect, it is the negotiators' and their advisers' duty to find it. Build trust in small steps by all means but do not avoid the big issues longer than is necessary. If they are really difficult to solve, spend as much time as it takes understanding why both sides are at an impasse and not as much time as you can avoiding them.

The theory of tackling the easy issues before the difficult ones refers to the goodwill that might develop from agreeing to several issues and which allegedly sets up the players for continuing to be agreeable as they face the issues where disagreement is expected. How realistic this is in practice is not reported – it remains a hope, not an easily recallable experience. There is an analogous assertion, also without researched support, in so-called selling-skills courses where it is alleged that a sequence of questions to which the prospect is bound to give a yes answer can culminate in a yes answer to the 'do you want to buy the product' question.

Contrariwise, in my experience word games are impractical. Professional parties are aware of where the problems lie and while treating preliminary issues in a respectful and cooperative manner is always sensible, expecting goodwill to produce an easier ride on the difficult issues is fanciful manipulation unsupported by evidence.

For a start, in a major negotiation the difficult issues are bound to feature in the discussions on heads of terms (they often are heads of certain terms!). The parties will want to place their markers down on those issues over which they have special requirements or reservations and give notice of where they will want to focus. As everything is (or ought to be) subject to contract there is nothing to be gained by postponing identifying such issues (until when?). Candour is a necessary part of building trust. Statements to the effect that you understand their current difficulties and wish to discuss the identified items as appropriate moves the negotiations towards the detailed discussions, without promoting or risking an early breakdown.

Of course, it would not be sensible to turn anticipated difficulties into a deadlocking insistence on the other side complying with your solution to the difficulties (yours or theirs) as a pre-condition of continuing towards the negotiation of these agenda items. That would be clumsy in the extreme. Outlining certain cardinal principles that are important to your continued participation in an agreement with them may be acceptable provided you understand and make clear you are willing to consider suggestions of how your requirements could be met (we cannot negotiate principles, but we can negotiate how they might best be applied and implemented).

If there are certain showstoppers in the mix, it is no good trying to sweep them under the carpet. A requirement in the request for proposal (RFP) that the computer source code be made available to the buyer would be unlikely to be acceptable to the seller, but when discussed this might be revealed to have a risk management motivation and not a IPR exposure. By discussing alternative ways of handling the issue, the difficulty could be overcome (registered holding of the source code in escrow by an independent third party and provisions for its release in specified negotiable circumstances?) and there would be no need to go to a dominance conflict leading to deadlock in the first session.

- It has become fashionable in international negotiations to work long hours to find a solution to what are or appear to be intractable problems. Committees of the European Commission of the European Union, the United Nations and so on have been known to 'stop the clock' when the statutory time for a decision is approached and to work on non-stop through the night. Major multi-party commercial negotiations last well into the early hours (some wags talk about the '3 am settlement' as being mandatory in deal making) but others bemoan the macho culture of these kinds of deal making. People who have not slept for 24 hours, or longer, are not in the right frame of mind to act responsibly. Best to adjourn, get some sleep and then reconvene. Everybody will feel the better for even a short break and some breakfast.

A final point. In your role as a manager who negotiates you will face many choices before, during and afterwards, and you should realize that whether you choose consciously or otherwise, whatever you do is your choice and will be taken as such by your colleagues on both sides of the table.

This has not been a course on moral issues (though a sense of morality, I hope pervades everything we have covered), but I think it appropriate to state clearly that in my judgement and experience, negotiators who invest in preparation, who identify their interests and search for negotiable solutions that deliver those interests and who behave always on the basis of mutual respect for those with whom they deal, and who seek to establish and prolong trust between the parties in all phases of the negotiation, and afterwards during the implementation of what they have agreed (and always deliver on their promises, even if it becomes inconvenient to do so), are more likely to procure implementable agreements of mutual benefit to those who make them. Attempting red manipulative ploys is a short-term ride to the loss of your reputation, for which no prize you may gain is worth its cost.

As always, my advice is that you guide your negotiating behaviour by strict adherence to: *Ex Bona Fide Negotiari*.

Activity
for Chapter 5

Activity 5.1

What arrangements does your organization make for conducting major contract negotiations both away from your home base and at your home base for the visiting party?

Organic Growth Strategies

CHAPTER

6

Introduction

The concepts and applications in this chapter are necessary background for the commercial and operational imperatives derived from the business plan because you would make little progress in the Strategic Negotiating Process Model without familiarity with them. It is inevitable that the chapter strays over the strict boundaries of what you require to know but this is a useful convenience in the presentation of the large amount of content within the subject headings.

The organization has at least four potential growth strategies:

- organic from within its own resources

- joint ventures and partnerships

- mergers and acquisitions

- licensing, franchises, master franchises and agency distributors.

All of them involve negotiation within and without the organization, including with other organizations and government agencies in the home country and sometimes in foreign countries.

The laws governing a contract may be singular or multi-jurisdictional. The parties can number from two upwards; the negotiations may be simple or complex, and the outcomes may have varying degrees of complexity. Growth can be a normal evolution from a small, local organization progressively towards a global presence in all markets, or a prelude to the organization's demise. The people who start the organization on a growth path may not be with it as it takes off, or for long afterwards; they may drop off as the organization takes a decisive turn to follow a different growth strategy – the organization as predator comes to the attention of another, smarter or bolder predator, better suited to making a success of the strategy than its originators.

Growth strategies can be a fusion of two organizations at the same, or at different stages in their growth cycles – one organisation's distribution negotiation is seen as a prelude to a joint venture and is perceived by the other party as a prelude to an eventual acquisition; and one organisation's merger negotiation is seen by the other organisation as a face-saving step to an outright acquisition; one organization's disposal strategy of non-core businesses is another's integration strategy of compatible businesses; and one organization's negotiated M & A deals for another organization are negotiations about its global growth. From the perspective of those within the organization, the organization grows; to the market, the organization is being absorbed, like the genes of parents dispersing through successive generations. The parents of a global growth strategy may begin their journey in a single department of an organization far from its centre of power, with no vision of what is about to happen to them and the organization. Their vision may be far-reaching; their operational horizons need not.

Alex Scott, an authority on strategic planning explains the dilemma of accounting for rational choice after perhaps a long sequence of unstructured earlier events:

> *The objective of an analysis of choice is to investigate the structures within which choices are made among competing alternatives. Inspection of real-life cases reveals that in many instances no choice was actually made, and that the company was simply carried along by the force of events, perhaps ending up with a dominant market position as a result of good fortune, which it then capitalized on. In other instances choices were made, but on such a non-structured basis that no general lessons can be drawn from the experience. The problem of drawing lessons from the experience of companies is compounded by the fact that different perspectives on the same choice can come to the conclusion either that the outcome was fortuitous or that it was a result of a structured choice approach. This is partly due to the difficulty of determining after the event what actually happened during the choice-making process; managers are as prone as anyone else to justifying their actions. There is a tendency to superimpose a structure on a series of events which, at the time they took place, were unstructured. Probably emergent strategies are the norm, but do not tend to be recognized as such.*

(Scott 2005, Strategic Planning, Edinburgh Business School, p. 7/2)

Strategic negotiation is about the implementation of the strategic choices (usually) already made by the organization, by different people; hence I do not cover the concepts and models, or their evaluation from a strategic planner's perspective. The Process Model takes the business plan's objectives as given and explores and delivers the negotiating imperatives that follow from it. It is an operational activity which implements the necessary decisions that are made as a result of the plans aiming to take it to the organization's planning horizon.

Strategic negotiators, who implement the organization's business plan, in effect, say to the planners: 'OK. If that is what you intend us to achieve then these are the ways we could do it from our negotiations.' In practice, the line between planners and implementers is not always clear-cut and clean. But for our purposes it is better to focus on the merits of the strategically driven negotiating tasks and not on constantly second-guessing the merits of the plan, except where it contains glaring errors or inconsistencies.

A well-known phenomenon associated with 'analysis-paralysis' causes indecision among would-be negotiators preventing them from actually doing anything. As Americans say: 'Are we here to fish or cut bait?' But it is always possible that the items chosen for the Negotiation Agenda cannot help the organization to reach the plan's objectives. It is also likely that any dissonance between method and objectives will be exposed when trying to derive the Negotiation Agenda from the business plan.

For example, the preparatory work, including the due diligence reports, for a negotiation to acquire a business unrelated to the future prospects of the organization – for example, the acquired business is an intercontinental air transport service but the main organization ships its output abroad via container shipping – should highlight for the negotiators that the acquisition is of insufficient positive value to the acquiring organization.

Organic growth

Many organizations do not grow in terms of their sales or net profits; they only age. Their turnover is static. Mom-and-pop stores, small, local wholesale and retail businesses, bars, restaurants, hotels and taxis are among the no- or slow-growth businesses bounded by local market conditions, perhaps seasonal, with little capacity or trading opportunities for growth. Their owners make a living by dint of hard work and long hours; there is an upper limit to the amount of groceries a small corner shop can sell in a district, given all the competing shops accessible to its customers. Reality erodes ambition. Growing from a one-man-and-a-dog business to anything bigger (owning three or four corner

CASE STUDY

Roads To Riches Or Ruin?

On a long taxi journey from Sydney airport to a business meeting in Canberra, Australia (aircraft cabin crews were on strike), I conversed for some hours with the driver as he drove through the night. He told me he had just paid off the loan on his taxi and now owned it, though he still picked up fares for the same taxi company, which had sold him the taxi on their lease-purchase scheme. Not all of their drivers, he told me, were prepared to reduce their net earnings to buy a cab, preferring a higher wage to the responsibilities and burdens of ownership. I was familiar with a similar lease-purchase scheme for wet-cement truck drivers in the UK and we discussed the finances of such schemes.

He was quite clear that he wanted to lease-purchase another, newer, taxi and hire a driver and put him to work. He was looking forward to owning six taxis within two years and then starting his own radio taxi company. He was ambitious, indeed, for his world.

He also intended to negotiate a better lease-purchase deal from the company. We discussed other options for financing a second taxi. He could purchase it in one transaction, paying the finance company off out of the earnings from his two taxis at lower interest rates than the taxi company charged under their scheme.

We discussed why taxi companies (and wet-cement suppliers) encouraged drivers to buy their vehicles. We agreed that because it made them self-employed and no longer employees, it saved the company employee payroll expenses and relieved it from being saddled with social responsibilities, such as expensive contributory pension schemes, holiday pay, plus the infamous Australian scourge of 'sickos' (feigned illness with pay), and, crucially, vehicle insurance for 'smash repairs'. He did not think much of taxi drivers who knew nothing about Sydney's geography, or the behaviours of lazy drivers, his tone suggesting that he did not regard himself as one of them.

Lease-purchase schemes were a reasonably safe growth strategy for the taxi company because it retained a steady pool of good drivers (bad drivers wrecked their cars and went off the road) while they bought their cabs, and meant the taxi company could run more cabs for a self-financing outlay, and more cabs meant higher gross revenues in a shorter time span than otherwise would be financially prudent.

I asked him: would he employ drivers or hire self-employed owners? And how would he motivate them to remain keen, energetic and honest? This meant:

- remuneration negotiations with people who may not share his interests;

- more than two cabs parked outside his suburban house would run up against city zoning or planning regulations and he would need to rent premises and negotiate with landlords and planning officials;

- he would need to negotiate legal, accounting and tax advice to form and run his taxi company;

- he would need to negotiate the purchase/hire of equipment for his radio/telephones;

- he would also need to negotiate paid office help and the purchase/hire of office furniture in his rented office;.

- plus, he would need to negotiate the design of his cab livery, advertising and marketing ('Yellow Pages' adverts?) expenses.

The list of his pending negotiations climbed as fast as he sped his cab and me towards Canberra.

It soon became clear he had some tactical issues to sort out before he did anything else. How was he going to grow from one to six cabs, plus drivers, on the road without his current cab company noticing a potential rival growing up amidst its own operations and privy to its own customer base? They would surely recognize the signs of his growing independence or potential for a breakaway. They might take pre-emptive action to prevent his growing any bigger by his free riding on their customer base. He had to find a market niche to grow from or remain vulnerable to being sacked before he had paid off his debts on his cabs. But what niche could he search for in a highly regulated market like cab services in Sydney?

I began to feel that his chances of success were diminishing as each layer of difficulty was uncovered. Even if everything to be done was confined only to the six negotiation decisions listed above, he would still have problems of coordinating them in such a way that he was not carrying indeterminate costs for long periods without earning compensating revenues, and given that he did not appear to have much capital, it did not look a rosy enough scenario for me to be other than sceptical that he would make it. This left two questions for which I did not have an answer.

- Were his growth plans bankable?

- Would he realize his ambition or realize its impracticality?

The wrecked ambitions of those running small enterprises who test the big challenges of growth deter the risk averse because most fail. A comforting mantra like 'it won't happen to me' is flimsy protection. But for a small minority, success is its own reward. Whether those whose capital the cab driver needed to borrow for his growth plans would share his self-belief in his fate is another (unsentimental) matter.

grocery shops?) is a big challenge, and the big challenges of growth are never easy, no matter how big the business becomes. Truly, growth is risky and can kill a business.

Contract negotiation for non-growth small businesses poses few strategic problems. They tend to be repeat negotiations of standard contracts from suppliers (payment terms, exclusivity, promotion deals, returns policy), including landlords (lease renewal terms, relocation, change of use).

Negotiations for organic growth businesses may have some strategic implications if that growth implies changes of some kind in the product mix or location. A decision to add to the product range requires answers to strategic questions such as, for example, how to extend a common product range or diversify into new products, or how to add enhanced services to existing products, with associated contracts for new employment implications, new leases, and supply and sales.

CASE STUDY

Best Laid Schemes Succumb To Better

Emblem, a leading business hotel chain, chose to diversify by setting up a subsidiary of smaller, 30-bedroom, no-frills budget hotels for business customers. A few pilot schemes located near main roads and large cities proved that the concept worked. Though room rates were a quarter of those in their city hotels, they appealed to budget-conscious businesses, and their room-only, no-restaurant overheads, showed they could achieve almost 98 per cent occupancy rates on weekdays, which was much better than under 55 per cent occupancy rates, plus heavy staffing costs, mainly in the mostly half-empty restaurant and bar facilities, normal for their city locations.

Because the budget business market was likely to be highly competitive, there was going to be a dash to market once word got around about what Emblem was planning. The strategic objective was to acquire suitable locations quickly before rivals appeared. A special 'national site acquisition unit' was set up to begin the programme, located anonymously in a rundown warehouse complex. Later, regional, not national, estate agencies were contracted to locate and acquire sites in their areas to expedite the expansion.

The land negotiators were recruited from experienced property professionals. They sought likely sites, with high volumes of passing traffic (main crossroads and motorway exits) and landowners, usually farmers, who were prepared to sell an acre or two (average value as agricultural land was well under that of a development site), and particularly where local planning authorities were flexible. From the hotel chain's perspective, paying a commercial price per acre, with a small non-returnable deposit for the irrevocable option on the land while planning permission was sought, was sound business. With planning

permission for a budget hotel, a roadside diner and a petrol station, site values could treble. Once built, the complex was a viable and profitable business.

Once Emblem reached over a hundred sites, rivals began to take notice and the race for market dominance began in earnest. Naturally, this raised site-acquisition costs (land agents tend to be savvy about the value of land) making piecemeal growth a slow route to market. Seville, a rival hotel chain, was able to jump into the market quickly by acquiring an existing chain of 350 branded roadside diners (Little Eaters). None of them had hotels near them, but quite a few had petrol stations, and most had spare land attached. Seville expanded most of the several hundred sites it acquired from Little Eaters to produce the proven profitable combination of diner, budget hotel and petrol station. It overtook Emblem, the early mover, within a year to become the largest budget hotel chain in the country

Thus, Emblem, which had at first grown organically, negotiation by negotiation, with small independent farmers an acre at a time, watched Seville, as it scaled up dramatically by negotiating the acquisition of Little Eaters, a large, rather sleepy, but profitable, roadside diner business aimed at motoring families.

Let us explore how the Strategic Negotiation Process Model might have taken Emblem, which initiated the move into budget hotels, straight to the successful growth strategy demonstrated later by Seville, instead of undertaking the stealth-like and ultimately unworkable Emblem strategy.

The decision to develop the budget hotel chain concept arose from an assessment of the competitive downward pressure on room rates at its main chains of hotels from rivals aiming for the same business customers. Discounting was a growing problem on profitability (special offers, weekend 2-for-1 offers, corporate discount rates, lower rates after 11 pm, and so on). The outcome included slowly declining occupancy rates and flattening profitability. Regular sales of marginal hotels reduced some costs, and purchases of small chains improved coverage but none of this altered the obvious fact of a mature business-hotel market in slow decline.

Once the concept of the budget hotel chain, with its stripped down, no-restaurant, no-frills ambience, but comfortable rooms with en suite facilities, pay phones and pay TV was accepted as a winner, the strategic question was surely how fast could they move before the competing hotel chains imitated the concept?

The choice of the organic growth strategy, and its ten or twelve sites a month, built from scratch, may have been necessitated by budgetary restraints and the need to prove the timid strategy before board-level approval for a major change to a bolder strategy. The necessary discussions in the Strategic Negotiation Process Model for the plan would raise the question of the timing of the slower strategy at the start.

The forming of the special acquisition unit to conduct the budget hotel programme and its analysis and diagnosis should have shown that a schedule of targets (10–12 a month) was not going to produce secure, uncontested (and incontestable) first-mover dominance early enough in this market niche because the business plan's horizon of 3 to 5 years allowed imitators to gain a foothold and expand it into a serious challenge.

There was plenty of development expertise available to Emblem for the collective wisdom of this expert group to have noted that once underway, the completion times for each project from greenfield site to a developed operation open for business, depended on the time it took to achieve

planning permission, including the provision of architects' drawings, completing the tendering with builders, time to prepare the site and build on it, recruit staff and to open the sites. This annual total of likely completions for the budget chain opening within the business plan horizon was woefully deficient to deter early and rapid competition from imitators.

Budgeting the necessary finance for the building programme, and for the projections of cash flow of the venture, provides another source that should have warned Emblem of the flaws and the glaring weakness running through the spine of the site-at-a-time strategy. The exposure of major structural weakness should have prompted the senior planners to look for alternatives.

The negotiation load alone would have been formidable, and on the initial site-by-site acquisition approach there was not much scope for scalability. If not anticipated, it must have been apparent in the preparation phases that a slow organic programme would be difficult to keep invisible from potential competitors because recruiting that many developers would soon become news in the trade (people know others and speak about their jobs and who is recruiting).

Public bodies linked to local elected authorities manage planning permission in the UK. The elected authority considering applications for planning permission publishes each application (which any person can read on payment of a small printing fee) and it also writes to those owners with property near a proposed application to notify them of the application and how it might affect them. They have a right to make a written objection to the proposal, which the authority must take into account, though it must accept or reject the objection only on planning grounds. In these conditions, it would not be long before rival hotel chains and land speculators noticed local media reports on current applications. Once they noted applications from multiple sources across the country, and analysed them to derive the details of Emblem's budget chain concept, they would be aware of its strategy.

The Strategic Negotiation Process Model, therefore, would have warned Emblem's senior management that its budget chain programme had little chance of succeeding and this alone should have sparked off the search for an alternative strategy. Given that the rival Seville chain examined the Emblem concept and saw that the best response was not to mimic the 10–12 sites a month programme, but to go instead for a national acquisition for national coverage in one step, suggests that Emblem too would have realized this early in their use of a strategic negotiation approach.

As it was, somebody from Seville on her way to a national strategy meeting stopped by chance at a Little Eater roadside diner, and while eating, contemplated the news of Emblem's budget-hotel chain making loads of cash under its new concept, and picked up a promotional leaflet when she paid her bill. The leaflets showed a map of Britain with the location of every Little Eater diner in the country, marked with a red dot. She noted there were lots of red dots! By the time the Seville manager got to her car, and compared the image of these dots with a map showing the Emblem locations, she was struck by the coverage of Little Eater and Emblem's locations. Bingo! When she attended the meeting on the Emblem initiative, the outline of a daring alternative plan was almost obvious: buy Little Eater's business!

If only – a lament often heard in strategy review discussions – an Emblem strategist had stopped off at a Little Eater (perhaps one of them did – they were very popular) and had read the same leaflet and looked at the red dots on the map, the less costly strategy of growth by acquisition might have been obvious too. Winning strategies are not always the result of high-level intelligence.

Changing scale changes perspectives, complicated by timing. Rapid expansion of sites in retailing and warehousing invites new questions, not least that of the viability of replicating previous success formulae when stretching control and the quality of your people resources. Too slow an expansion invites early imitation by bolder and better-financed rivals.

Expansion driven by opportunities and not by prudent financing has a knife-edge quality, courting disaster and success in equal measure. The Strategic Negotiation Process Model highlights the strengths or weaknesses of a poorly-timed growth plan by identifying the resources required to deliver the Commercial Imperatives, thrown sharply into relief against projected performance in a 5-year horizon of the business plan. Imprudent decisions to add to capacity beyond an organization's cash flow projections (how far should capacity race ahead of the organic expansion of cash flow?) require policy decisions under the operational imperatives for finance, such as: if not organic growth, then how?

In general, organic growth is usually contained within the contractual negotiation experience of the organization if it sticks to its familiar business, because it requires more of the same negotiated factor inputs from markets it understands. When the organization undertakes completely different products in completely different markets, or markets not very closely related to its core business, it risks unfamiliar turbulence.

Newspapers and greetings cards are different products but the customers likely to buy one are also likely to buy the other and they can be sold from the same premises by the same staff. Adding Internet cafes to a newsagent chain adds a different product with not enough overlap either in customers or trained staff to be managed easily.

A conscious and deliberate decision to grow a business should be taken by the owners, in the case of a small business, or the most senior managers in the case of a large business. It is not possible to hide the consequences of growth from the controllers of an organization. Growth makes new demands upon all the organization's resources, if only because growth will deplete the availability of some resources and the managers or users of the depleted resources will react to the changes they experience in the normal supply of what they need. Growth creates its own demands for access to resources – more people, more inputs, more facilities, more time – and when resource demands run up against availability, the strains become apparent in the functions trying to use those resources.

To increase from a one-person to a two-person business doubles the organization's employment. This highlights the risks of growth; everything is dependent on the quality of the additional person. To open new depots in other places, even nearby, dilutes direct managerial attention and weakens its controls, which are appropriate to dealing with a single depot but which are unproven in managing multiple sites.

Growth decisions must be more than good ideas (especially when brought to your attention by sellers or brokers with an interest in selling you the idea); they have to be well thought out and prepared, and the act of preparing should raise challenging questions about capabilities. Growth strategies are as much managerial as financing decisions and they should be made with the most careful attention.

Joint ventures

There was a time when business formation was relatively simple but now the law and related regulations, including taxation liabilities, intrude to the point that without legal expertise it is unlikely that the essentially simple decision of two parties agreeing to cooperate for some purpose would be achievable without high-level legal, taxation and accounting advice and guidance (it certainly would be extremely inadvisable for you to attempt it on your own).

The business plan could envisage that a product is to be taken to a wider market beyond the initial jurisdiction within three years. That strategic decision creates an agenda for future negotiations. New opportunities bring their rewards, but also their burdens. What appears to be a logical development from a strong domestic market for an organization's products, in turn produces a host of questions that complicate what starts out as a straightforward decision. Among these questions is that of how the organization is going to give effect to the decision to market beyond current boundaries. One answer could be to form a joint venture (JV) with another company already located in the target market. This is where strategic negotiators ought to have some exposure to what is involved in a JV and what to look out for.

WHY A JOINT VENTURE?

To take a simple point: any decision to form a JV between two separate companies is bound to raise high-level policy concerns among regulators about the reduction in competition implied in this decision:

- Why don't the two entities remain separate and compete?

- Are the gains to the public good from their JV such that they should override considerations of a reduction in competition?

No firm answers can be given without detailed consideration of the circumstances.

One such consideration operating in favour of a JV might be one between two separate companies domiciled in separate markets which combine to pursue a worthwhile or necessary project that neither could do on its own.

Joint ventures in R & D also are looked on favourably, except, perhaps, in drug medication where the major drug companies are strong enough to conduct independent projects without recourse to partners from among their rivals. Many smaller companies specializing in fine chemicals are sub-contracted by the main drug research firms to mass-produce their products, but these are covered by normal commercial contracts and not JV agreements.

Full-scale JVs face regulatory interventions or at least close scrutiny by the competition authorities. This led to experiments with various forms of alliances among passenger airline firms around the world. These are subject to approval by national authorities, and some notable attempts to form code-sharing alliances were frustrated by being linked to separate issues, such as the degree of freedom accorded to non-US airlines for open-sky routing across the USA, or to the vexed and continuing problem of the redistribution of landing slots at Heathrow, London. The takeover of KLM, the Dutch national carrier, by Air France was dressed up as an alliance to deter intervention by the European competition authorities, though the takeover was backed by each country's government.

Joint ventures are useful vehicles for separate businesses to cooperate in the supply of products or services to markets. Cooperation between organizations within the same country, and sometimes among organizations formed under different laws in different countries, is not unusual, despite the difficulties in forming them and their less-than-startling performance. The successful creation and operation of a joint venture poses unique strategic problems, not the least being: Why a JV and not a wholly owned subsidiary?

The nature of a JV varies from arms-length licences through franchises to a formal legal entity ('NewCo'), jointly owned and operated by the partners. The range of intermediate structures for marketing products and services is extensive and necessarily I have reduced them to a few.

You could consider almost any relationship between two organizations that cooperates in an arrangement as intermediate suppliers as a kind of JV – the outputs of one company are inputs into another company's outputs. In the normal course of business our suppliers are in a kind of JV with us to deliver added value to final customers. However, the JVs we are concerned with are of the kind where there is a relationship with independent organizations (an existing entity, or a NewCo, jointly owned or not) that delivers added value product to final customers.

FORMS OF JOINT VENTURE

The form a JV takes will be influenced by the reason for agreeing to form one. That decision is where we should start from: what problems could be addressed by the formation of a JV that cannot be addressed any other way at least as well? As usual, such a question can only be seriously answered by beginning with the organization's business plan and deriving from this its commercial imperatives. The JV should be justified by its being essential and efficacious for the objectives it is designed to accomplish. But a JV also brings with it burdens that the partners may not wish to carry.

One partner may be expected to provide almost all of the local inputs – people, locations and product – while the other provides a proportion of the capital and makes a contribution to costs. Seems straightforward enough, until the details are negotiated and each realizes that it is unfairly exposed in different ways:

- If party A is providing the local infrastructure of the JV, how is it to be recompensed?

- If party B is contributing to the running costs, how sure is it that these are not open to padding by its partner?

- How are the profits to be divided?

In these circumstances party A might press for Newco to be wholly owned by itself, or for party B to contribute a much larger initial investment. This does not alter the difficulties of party B monitoring its interests in the distantly located JV, closely managed by party A and effectively closed to daily scrutiny by party B.

Early in the negotiations to form the JV, the parties might conclude that a JV is not the best vehicle for what they propose to do together in the distant territory and they could agree to revert to party A setting up a wholly owned Newco, and that party B will enter into normal commercial arrangements to exploit each other's interests in the collaboration.

When the JV is in the territory where both parties have a substantial presence, a Newco could be formed, with each providing it with personnel, locations, technology, IPR and marketing facilities, and it could be run on normal commercial lines of a registered independent company, wholly owned by both parties, and open to close monitoring by the parent partners. JVs of this type can accommodate several partners; for example, Britvic, the fruit juice producer and bottler for several competing breweries and owners of public houses worked well as a JV for many years and as the JV's internal affairs were transparent to the partners, there was little friction between them.

There are certain essential features for negotiating JV Newcos that are worth reviewing. All UK companies (and similar arrangements are found in most countries) are formally registered with the State authorities. This facilitates taxation and compliance with company laws and helps to protect the rights of shareholders who do not participate in the daily management of the company. In the UK two formal documents, the Memorandum of Association and the Articles of Association, are required. The former identifies the name of the company ('Newco' is a working title only until an official name is agreed and registered), outlines what business will be conducted (written as widely as possible), and sets its share capital and its private limited or public limited status. The Articles are about how the internal affairs of the company will be managed, often written as a mixture of boilerplate and bespoke clauses. In the USA, in place of the Memorandum and Articles, a Limited Liability Company (LLC) uses an Operating Agreement, which serves much the same purpose.

SHAREHOLDERS' AGREEMENTS

For a JV, a Shareholders' Agreement is normally negotiated (remember that the shareholders of the JV are limited to the parties that have set it up, though the JV itself should be made a party to the Shareholders' Agreement too). Unlike the Memorandum and Articles, which are registered and in the public domain, a Shareholders' Agreement usually remains (but need not be) confidential to the parties, and its contents may extend to cover a wide range of matters not dealt with in the Memorandum and Articles. Whereas the Memorandum and Articles bind any new shareholders, in the case of the Shareholders' Agreement a new shareholder (for example, party C joins the JV) is not bound by the previous Shareholders' Agreement and a new agreement has to be negotiated or agreed. (A LLC Operating Agreement can bind new shareholders without requiring to be renegotiated.)

Boring as the Memorandum and Articles may be for those impatient with detail, a careful consideration of them is essential to prevent mishaps, such as directors from party A being able to pass board resolutions in the absence of directors from party B or share transfers occurring that (intentionally?) alter the ownership of the JV. A Shareholders' Agreement can be a comfort if it sets out strict rules for such meetings and transfers, but unless these are aligned with the provisions of the Memorandum and Articles, and the parties are aware of their importance, a serious controversy lies dormant until events bring it to the fore, usually at an inconvenient time.

An area of concern in any JV is on the transfer of shares both within the JV company and between a shareholder and third parties outside the JV. For example, where the parties to the JV are individuals and companies, on the death of an individual, the shares of the deceased become part of the estate and third-party beneficiaries would inherit the shares. This may be unacceptable to the JV partners because the beneficiary may sell on the shares to, say, a competitor of the JV, or because the parties to the JV formed the company so that each of them contributed something important to its operations and success, whereas the new outsider is regarded as having nothing to contribute to the JV, except to draw dividends.

By negotiating a pre-emption clause for the Articles and a Shareholder's Agreement, the parties can ensure that the shares of the deceased must be offered to the remaining shareholders (to prevent erosion of the original membership base) and that the beneficiary of the deceased's estate receives the money value of the shares and not the shares themselves (also prevents erosion and so on).

Similarly, if a party to the JV wishes to withdraw from the JV and realize their investment, the Articles and the Shareholder's Agreement could specify that the shares must be offered first to the other parties in the JV and only on a refusal to buy could the shares be transferred to an outsider. If the existing shareholders wish to block the entry of new shareholders, they can club together to buy out the leaver and pre-empt dilution.

Such measures prevent the dilution of the original parties' ownership. But all such measures require to be negotiated when the JV is set up and not afterwards at a distant date in the future when reliance on everybody's goodwill and their continuing commitment to the JV may be tenuous. Member organizations of a JV change personnel over time and new views as to the value of a JV, or pressing financial circumstances, may arise, that make a disposal attractive to one of them.

Of similar importance is the non-competition clause that prevents a party to the JV from competing with the JV. The interests of the JV parties are clear: there is less incentive to invest in a JV company if one or more of the member parties continues competing with it, and, anyway, as the member parties will know about the costs, pricing and plans of the JV, it could give them an unfair competitive advantage if they were to compete with it. However, such a clause could be of concern to the competition authorities if it reduces competition in the territory where the JV operates.

In summary the main points to look for in a JV are:

- In place of a JV NewCo should we form a wholly-owned subsidiary?

- If a JV is chosen what is each member bringing to the party?

- How are the members assured of each other's contributions?

- What should be included in the content of the public Memorandum and Articles of Association (and what excluded)?

- What protections are essential for inclusion in a private Shareholders' Agreement?

- What protection do we need to prevent members from competing with the JV?

- How might we cope with the scrutiny of the JV's intentions and practice by the competition authorities?

- How do we distribute the profits between the members and fund the necessary growth of the JV?

A most useful contribution to the analysis and diagnosis stage in the Process Model can be made by those at least aware of some of the common pitfalls of JV propositions that otherwise look most tempting. Looking for the consequences of an action down track is a fundamental obligation of those who would seek to implement decisions from the business plan three or more years after they were first made or mooted.

Mergers and acquisitions

A merger by any other name should be called an acquisition, for that is the reality, sooner or later, no matter how it is presented before, during or shortly afterwards. When two equal partners merge, the leading personnel of one of them emerge eventually as the leading players of the merged entity; in short they physically take over the merged organization. In few mergers does the equality of the leading players remain tangible for long and, as happens, rarely do people from the two previously independent organizations lose their previous identities and merge into one new one – only post-merger recruits tend to do so.

One of the leading team usually gives up, burns out or steps back to spend more time with their family, encouraged by a golden parachute (a large dollop of cash for their retirement). The only question is how long this takes – a few months or a couple of years (seldom longer). In other cases, the accidents of life

CASE STUDY

Together But Separate

Over 12 years after the Royal Bank of Scotland merged with William & Glynn's Bank, when speaking of middle ranking managers, it was common to hear people described as: 'Jim's a William & Glynn's man' or 'Mary is from RBS', and so on.

After the merger between the Royal College of Science and Technology and the College of Commerce to form the University of Strathclyde in 1964, similar expressions were still used in the 1980s to describe a person as being from the 'Royal College' or from 'Pitt Street', where the College of Commerce had been located.

These incidents indicate the necessity for a long period to pass before the folk memories of the merger dissolve.

re-organize the main players' prospects (age, illness of self or family), as do the manipulations of the more energetic players, less inhibited by considerations of inter-personal ethics than their elders. Previous ethically doubtful behaviour can also trip up strong candidates if discovered and used in time to spoil their party.

Acquisition remains the major strategic route to growth for most companies. Acquisition involves intense negotiation, including pre-negotiation preparation. It is time-consuming and hard work. It takes strong commitment to the strategic goals of the organization to maintain the necessary focus. And in many cases it fails in its objectives, when, sooner or later, the organization tries an acquisition too far (the predator is out-predated by a smarter predator).

But whatever the track record of acquisitions, it remains the most common form of growth. The strategic choice having been made, strategic negotiators are left to get on with it.

The Strategic Negotiation Process Model provides guidelines for ensuring that the negotiation part of the acquisition process does not contribute unintentionally to the failure of the acquisition. Some of the avoidable early fault lines in an acquisition destined to go sour are inherited from errors made during the negotiations; the rest are divided between the mistaken strategic choices which initiated the acquisition before the negotiations began and from faults in the implementation of the plans to add value to the acquirer's business from the acquisition after the negotiations are concluded.

Once the strategic decision is taken to pursue an acquisition, suitable targets can be put into play by the potential acquirer's team. The identified targets can come from a search for a suitable target (sometimes these are obvious), or can emerge from prompting by a merchant bank, accountancy firm or professional go-betweens, searching for a potential buyer for a business on their books. The names of suitable candidates are in constant circulation among businesses, complete with prospectuses, but beware of going after something merely because a competitor is reported to be interested in it.

The question in all discussions about suitable targets becomes: how might this target deliver the Commercial Imperatives that will achieve the objectives in the business plan? In short, does this target fit our plan (and not, you should note: does our plan fit this target!)?

Basic questions include:

- If the business plan is looking to increase output, could the target do so within the cost parameters that make it profitable to add its capacity to our current capacity?

- If the business plan requires penetration of new regions, what would the target contribute to this goal?

- If the business plan sets goals for purchasing downstream/upstream capability in our business sector, how might the target contribute to that end?

- What aspects of the target's operations, including surplus assets, could we dispose of to raise capital for our other operations?

- What technology (broadly defined, and including IPR, patents and copyrights) does the target own that would add value to our operations?

Acquisitions are associated with intensive, even exhaustive, diagnosis in a process known as 'due diligence', usually conducted by professional third-party accountants, lawyers and risk analysts. Due diligence has to have a forensic quality about it because it is about proving positively that the acquisition is what it purports to be and what the acquirer believes it to be, that is, for example:

- Its accounts have no black holes in them, they are a true and fair view of the business, and its claimed turnover and transactions are confirmed by its bankers in writing.

- It has no undisclosed (backed by tight warranties) liabilities to actual or potential litigants, the tax authorities, customers, suppliers, employees, third parties and so on.

- Its assets are owned with clear and proven titles and their valuation is confirmed professionally.

- Its principals' CVs are as represented (checked by employee search and investigation agencies).

- Its board has the power and authority to sell the business.

- What the seller is selling is identical to what the buyer believes it is buying (an all too common negotiating error!).

Due diligence is the 'caveat' part of 'caveat emptor'. It is not a substitute for identifying the imperatives; it moves the decision to proceed with the acquisition to the starting blocks. And the allusion to the start of a race is often a good description of what follows once contact with a potential seller is made. While the initial approaches may seem leisurely in comparison, everything speeds up from the moment that a seller's decision to sell in principle is aligned with a buyer's decision to buy, again in principle, and as always, subject to contract.

The pressure is on psychologically, as the aspirations of each side firm up (the seller contemplating the post-sale enjoyment of the riches to come, and the peace of mind from shedding all responsibilities for the business; the buyer contemplating excitedly the post-purchase environment and how it might affect its existing business), and their aspirations crystallize around how much the seller will get and how much the buyer must pay.

The pressure intensifies if the seller has put the business on the market and invites bids from several buyers. The seller will provide much of the data needed for prospective purchasers to contemplate a bid, but it still has to be checked carefully by the professional advisors of the buyers and detailed searches have to be performed if key information is unclear or missing.

Inevitably some buyers drop out (the target did not fit their plans, or they discover aspects of the target causing them to raise their risk assessments). Those left in the race might be expected to make indicative bids to permit the seller to identify a preferred bidder, or a serious bidder might insist on a period of exclusivity (or lockout) as the only bidder while conducting its negotiations.

The seller will also conduct a form of due diligence into the bona fides of the potential buyers and the focus will be a mixture of factual (the evidence is either factual or not), or negotiable. For example:

- Who they are (are they legit)? (Factual)

- Where are they domiciled (can we litigate if they are from another jurisdiction with some hope of recovering losses)? (Factual)

- What is it they think they are buying? (Negotiable)

- What is their financial status and the security of their covenants (do they have the money)? (Factual)

- What indicative price might they pay? (Negotiable)

- Are there any barriers to their completing the purchase (do they have power and authority to make the deal or are there any complicated consents required from their shareholders, bankers and creditors, or the local version of the Monopolies Commission)? (Factual)

- What warranties and indemnities do we require from them? (Negotiable)

The acquisition will be negotiated between the principals, supported by their professional advisors.

Due diligence specialists search the data and the business environment for threats because surprises usually are bad news. Threats sometimes appear during a negotiation and are expressed explicitly or implicitly during debate, or become obvious in slips of the tongue during debate.

Dominance ploys, such as imposing pre-conditions, rigged agendas and non-negotiable issues, imply that a failure to concede to them threatens termination of the negotiation (though they may be bluffing). Sometimes they appear as shaping ploys, when a negotiator tries to force a decision on something over which the negotiations have stalled. Closing ploys (take it or leave it; or else; now or never; yes, but; quivering quill and the imposition of a time deadline) also imply a threat to conclude negotiations without an agreement.

Are the threats real or bluffs? Hard to tell. Deterrence theory operates on the basis that there is a threat if a party's capability (can they damage us?) is matched by its commitment (are they likely to do so?). On the basis of the assessment of threat perceptions, a party should prepare its defences.

If any party has the capability and is committed to using it, then the threat has to be deterred by demonstrating capability to resist it, and by regular reinforcement of the commitment to use that capability, should the party initiate its threats.

Do these same considerations of deterrence in business apply to threats during negotiations? In part, yes, but (thankfully) the purpose of deterrence is to inhibit a party's willingness to initiate its potential threat and not to provoke a party to implement its threats. Though a business can lose a contract, it is seldom except in the most pressing of circumstances that it will go out of business as a result of the loss of a single contract, and if this is a threat of a real consequence it suggests that the firm is at risk of going out of business anyway.

Most books on due diligence are technical in scope, looking at the data and for evidence of black holes in the accounts or the contracts. What a strategic negotiator needs is due diligence based on good commercial sense, and I recommend that you look through Peter Howson's *Commercial Due Diligence: the key to understanding value in an acquisition* (Gower, 2007). Its scope and hands-on feel for commercial strategy is just what the strategic negotiator needs to evaluate more confidently due diligence reports and to question those who present them, often under time pressure to support or not a proposed acquisition or joint venture partner. It will also help you in briefing the professionals about to undertake due diligence assignments (even to evaluate their suitability) in the areas you consider are critical for a go/no-go decision. Leaving it to the experts is as risky a strategy as doing it yourself to save expense; you will also learn a great deal about what is important in analysing the commercial and operational imperatives of your own business.

Threats often feature in negotiation, originating from implicit or explicit messages sent from one party to the other, and from analysis of vulnerabilities that could be or might be initiated by the other party. Not all parties warn those they deal with that retribution inevitably follows some action on their part. Sometimes a party is warned that action will follow without further warning. For instance a party is told: 'Unless it ceases "passing off" its products as if they are produced by the Acme Corporation, then Acme will initiate legal proceedings without warning.'

Threats that are specified have both strengths and weaknesses. Once they are given with a date, time and place, the clock ticks. The recipient can judge the seriousness of the threat beforehand – can they damage us and will they

---

CASE STUDY

The Power To Inflict Terminal Damage

An example of a severe consequence of ignoring a strategic threat can be seen in the case of a regional tyre distributor (Ajax), which was approached by another distributor (Phoenix) from an adjacent region with a view to it purchasing the Ajax business as a going concern.

Ajax rejected the approach almost out of hand, though it was already ailing from poor commercial performance, and it ignored the nascent threat from Phoenix that it intended to expand into the region. Its purchase of Ajax would give it the opportunity to do so within months rather than two or three years. Ajax's main assets were in the tyre depots it owned, most of which were sited in good locations, close to heavily populated centres across its main operating region (the Home Counties around but not in London). Phoenix withdrew its opening offer (which it considered a basis for negotiation, not an ultimatum) and Ajax unwisely considered the matter to be closed. It did not undertake a threat assessment of Phoenix's intentions or its capabilities (power) to achieve its ends by other means.

Phoenix, however, had done its research and noted the financial performance of Ajax, the locations of its tyre depots, the ill-prepared basic business skills of the Ajax owners and their outdated marketing image. Ajax's owners failed to consider their vulnerabilities fully, nor did they make any efforts to modernize their image. Most depots needed refurbishment, a few needed to be relocated, and its marketing image looked dated and in some cases tatty. In short, Ajax did not take the Phoenix threat seriously.

The situation began to change three months later when, adjacent to one of the Ajax sites, an empty warehouse re-opened as a Phoenix Top Tyres depot in a blaze of local publicity and a wave of special offers (for example, buy-one-get-one-free-type promotions). This was followed quickly by three other Top Tyres depots all opening within a few yards of other Ajax depots and all flying 'nobody beats our prices' banners on their buildings, a theme repeated in the local press and on local radio. Sales at Ajax plummeted whenever Phoenix opened near them and there was no sign of the Phoenix depot opening campaign slackening.

By the time that Ajax realized what was happening, it was too late. Within six months it called in the administrators, who sold Ajax at a debt-clearing price (no premium) to Phoenix, which sold on the sites it did not want to single buyers, as long was they were not in the tyre business. Phoenix took its vulnerabilities seriously.

---

do it (that is, their capability and commitment)? – and while it has time to appear to comply with the demands made upon it. It will also know for certain whether the threat was real or a bluff when the date, time and place for the implementation of the threat pass. The party making the threat also knows that the truth or bluff of their threat will be revealed to the recipient at that moment, which may make them carry out the threat, or some version of it, just to maintain their credibility.

To avoid such a dénouement, if making a threat for some (good) reason, leave the threat unspecific, because vagueness lowers the seriousness of the threat. A threat that there may be serious consequences from taking certain actions carries less weight than specifying that serious consequences will follow and when. But vagueness leaves it to the recipient to imagine the nature of the threatened consequences and their timing. However, if the capability of the threatening party is less specific, it dilutes the threat's impact, added to its dilution of the commitment of the party to an unspecified course of action. True, imagination may produce in the mind an even more serious impact of a threat than a specified but limited threat, and where there are doubts about the form that the threat might take, there is likely to be a lower estimate of the probability of its occurrence.

This also points to the important consideration: for the party making a threat it is not your own estimate of your capability and commitment that counts in deterrence, but the perceptions of the other party as to your capabilities and commitment. One factor that weighs on the other party's mind is your history of making threats. Some negotiators invest considerable resources in raising their credibility as a threat maker. That is why firms pursue small breaches of their copyright and trade names that cost much more than the actual damage to demonstrate their seriousness in suing for more major breaches that others might be tempted to risk. ('Look, if they'll spend £20 000 suing for a breach worth £750, they'll sure as heck sue us for a breach worth £120 000.')

Three growth options

I shall illustrate some aspects of the Strategic Negotiation Process Model for three options that the organization might consider when deciding on a growth path:

- growth by expansion of the organization's activities (organic) from its home base;

- growth by expansion of the organization's activities by locating wholly-owned branch capacity in another region or country;

- growth by acquisition of an existing independent organization in another region or country

The three options are considered together because they are related in scope. Merely shipping product into another region or country is a normal initial expansionary route for an organically growing company. On a small scale it may not even be noticed, except in rising sales figures, and may not need additional resources – the data are inputs into the business plan and not a consequence of it, up to some level of additional sales. However, as distant sales increase in volume and value, the logistics of servicing them will begin to press on existing resources. The need to respond to the opportunity is illustrated in Figure 6.1.

The planners could respond to the reported opportunities for distant sales with acknowledgement in the business plan of the detailed need to manage and fund this additional work.

If we stick purely to the physical requirement for despatch and delivery capacity, and ignore the changes that may be required in the output capacity of the organization to produce whatever is being sold at a distance. In Figure 6.1, the business plan target is summarized as a 30 per cent increase in distant

Business Plan

Increase distant sales by 30%

Commercial Imperative

Improve capacity for distant sales

Operational Imperative

Requirement for shipping facilities:

• People: recruitment; training.

• Facilities: dispatch space; transport; storage; insurance

• Technology: packing; tracking; invoicing; credit control

Negotiation Agenda

• Rewards: remuneration packages

• Contracts: personnel; leases; delivery (outsourced)

• Purchase: packing systems and materials; insurance

Figure 6.1   Increasing distant sales

sales within the planning period. This produces the commercial imperative to assemble the capacity to meet that target, plus others. To achieve the commercial imperative, operational imperatives are required, from which list, Figure 6.1 refers to people, facilities and technology (there could be many others depending on the nature of the product, the distance despatched and the circumstances).

The Negotiation Agenda comprises all the arrangements that must be negotiated to acquire the resources to deliver the commercial imperative(s) that deliver(s) the business plan. Once again the seamless link is emphasized between what the negotiators undertake to agree to with many third parties (and internal members of the organization) and the business plan. Figure 6.1 shows three headings for the Negotiation Agenda (rewards, contracts and purchases), and each set of negotiations is undertaken with different negotiation partners, but in this approach they are all linked strategically.

If we now go to the next stage of growth policy, we assume that the organization has found that the policy of distributing its products to distant markets from its home base exposes inefficiencies and risks which compromise continuing success in its markets unless significant changes are made. It could also be the case that the organization took the decision to set up distant production and distribution branches from near the beginning of the emergence of distant sales. In either case, the same process of aligning its negotiations with its Business Plan is followed, as shown in Figure 6.2.

Although there are obvious differences between expanding home facilities and locating expansion capacity at a distance, there are many similarities in both options. The major difference is that the distant location option is liable to be more expensive than local expansion and the decision is certain to be made at board level because of the risks and investment required.

Leasing rather than purchasing is not necessarily cheaper because there is still a financial commitment for the duration of the lease, requiring top-level approval, and while a purchase option may be expensive in the initial outlay, it may be easier to sell a property if the growth option fails to meet expectations than it would be to break a lease before its review date. There is also the usual problem of the multiplicity of locations that could meet the objective in the Business Plan, at least in the minds of those favouring the different options, and this adds to the time needed to come to a single decision.

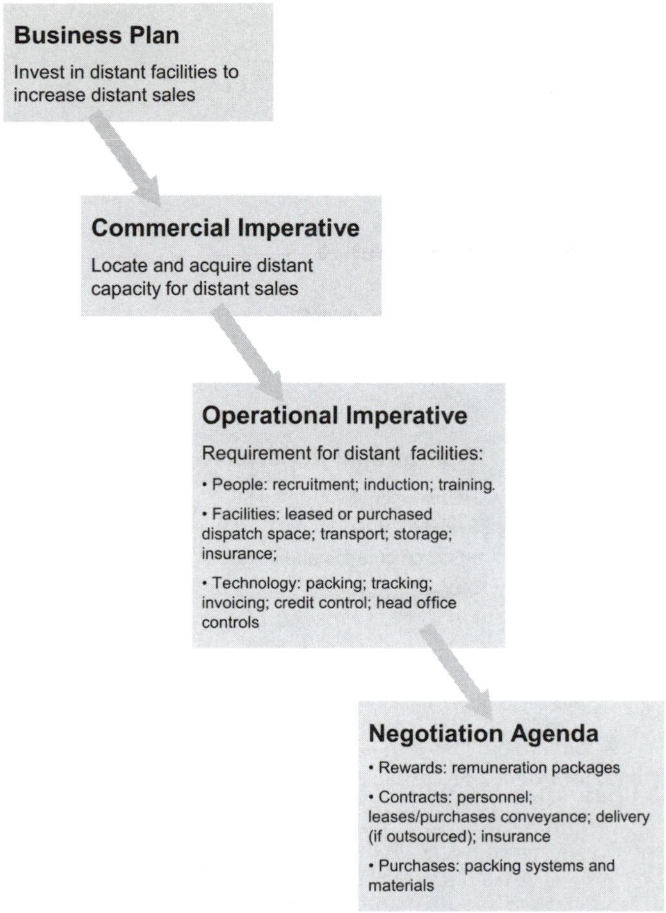

Business Plan

Invest in distant facilities to increase distant sales

Commercial Imperative

Locate and acquire distant capacity for distant sales

Operational Imperative

Requirement for distant facilities:

• People: recruitment; induction; training.

• Facilities: leased or purchased dispatch space; transport; storage; insurance;

• Technology: packing; tracking; invoicing; credit control; head office controls

Negotiation Agenda

• Rewards: remuneration packages

• Contracts: personnel; leases/purchases conveyance; delivery (if outsourced); insurance

• Purchases: packing systems and materials

Figure 6.2 Locating wholly owned distant facilities to increase distant sales

This choice is bound to raise the question of making an acquisition, either searched for or brought to the attention of the organization by an adviser. Acquisitions in the home territory are less complex than acquisitions in a foreign territory but there may not be much choice if they are not perfectly substitutable and the market opportunity requires it.

Acquisition is complex and time consuming whichever route is followed, whether you are buying or selling. Figure 6.3 illustrates a brief summary, greatly simplified, of how a Negotiation Agenda is derived to deliver one objective out of many in the business plan. Instead of five items on the Negotiation Agenda there can be many more – thirty or more main headings are not uncommon – and the documentation alone accounting for several volumes of documents, all of which must be mastered by the negotiators and their professional advisers.

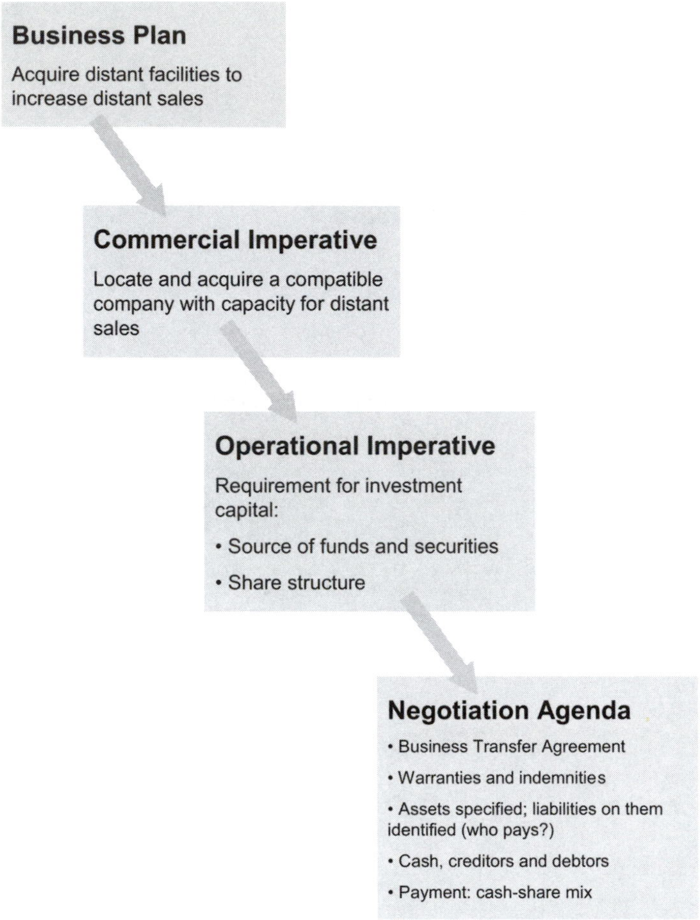

Business Plan

Acquire distant facilities to
increase distant sales

Commercial Imperative

Locate and acquire a compatible
company with capacity for distant
sales

Operational Imperative

Requirement for investment
capital:

• Source of funds and securities

• Share structure

Negotiation Agenda

• Business Transfer Agreement

• Warranties and indemnities

• Assets specified; liabilities on them
identified (who pays?)

• Cash, creditors and debtors

• Payment: cash-share mix

Figure 6.3 Acquiring a company with wholly owned distant facilities to
increase distant sales

When the negotiations conclude with an agreement the paperwork is
completed and the transfer of ownership from the original to the new owners,
the crucial stage of implementation, commences. Acquisitions can go sour from
poor agreements, but poor implementation is also a major cause of failure.
If selling at a distance has its problems, managing at a distance adds more
problems such as adequately staffing distant negotiations.

Activities
for Chapter 6

Activity 6.1

What do you know of the history of your organization, where and when it started, how it developed, what it is doing now that it was not doing earlier in its history (and what it is not doing now that it originally set out to do)?

COMMENTS ON THIS ACTIVITY

You can find out by asking around and looking up the files, or old brochures and catalogues, checking old addresses and reading press clippings – try a Web search to get background on your organization.

Activity 6.2

If your organization has a business plan you should apply to read it at your earliest opportunity – even an old one – to familiarize yourself with its construction and contents.

COMMENTS ON THIS ACTIVITY

There is nothing like reading an old business plan to reveal just how fragile the assumptions of many of them prove to be when what they achieved is measured against what they intended. However, how they were constructed is revealing and this should caution you against the adoption of the weak assumptions that feature in some plans.

Most banks, and the accountancy bodies, offer booklets on the writing of business plans. It is not a difficult activity to undertake. Venture capitalists report that they can often tell the quality of a business plan in the first few paragraphs.

Licensing Negotiations

Introduction

Various options exist for an organization wishing to expand its operations. Amongst these are licensing, agency or franchising (there is a lot of overlap in the negotiations to set up these three options). Each one of them utilizes the managerial and marketing competence of existing organizations through arm's-length relationships. They can be relatively quick routes to market expansion in distant markets, where the organization does not have sufficient expertise to replicate the local successes of operating in its home market.

Manufacturers negotiate with third parties to distribute their products when the costs of setting up and staffing their own distribution and sales services, and learning about distant markets, would be prohibitive or at least significantly more expensive. Shipping products to independent distribution centres which provide regional facilities for final customers to visit and uplift their requirements, may be less costly than staffing a multi-team sales organization to search among dispersed final customers, who may purchase irregularly in small unit lots, to which costs and risks are added to those of disparate distribution facilities. The local red tape involved in setting up the necessary legal company as a vehicle to manage the service is often enough to deter all but the most determined exporter (with deep pockets).

Of course, things may look different if an established exporter which directly exports to overseas markets in its own name acquires another export business in a similar market which exports through local agencies and it is confident that it can make it profitable through establishing, or expanding, its own retail network in the foreign markets. This was what happened, broadly, when Guinness took over Distillers in the 1980s.

In catering supplies, for example, there are about thirty large wholesale distributors in the UK serving thousands of retail units and users. Two sales staff could cover the thirty main distributors in a year, whereas for the company to recruit a direct sales force to visit each of thousands of sales prospects would require as many as a hundred people trained in sales, plus the recruitment of a sales management team. This could add several million pounds to its selling costs and might not get into the company's business plan on cost–benefit grounds.

However, there are circumstances where a different choice may be made: to reconstitute a direct field sales force for retail distribution operations after trying the option of third-party distribution through a local centres approach. Clearly, a company's business strategy determines the content of its Negotiation Agenda.

Licensing agreements are commonly used when entering a new regional or national market, especially in foreign jurisdictions. The quality of a decision to adopt a licensing strategy is not discussed here; if it is in the business plan it is the management's task to implement it, which implementation includes the negotiation of the licences.

If, say, the business plan envisages the headline objective of expanding sales of its products, either nationally or abroad, and this is transformed into SMART (Specific, Manageable, Achievable, Realistic and Time-bound) objectives that within three years licensed sales will account for 40 per cent of turnover (among its other goals), the commercial imperatives part of the plan could include:

- Locate and negotiate with licensees in six named national regions and secure licensees in six foreign countries within three years.

The commercial imperatives produce the operational imperatives of training or recruiting expertise in the selection and management of potential licensees in the target regional or foreign markets.

Your negotiation of licences requires legal support in their drafting if your in-house expertise is unfamiliar with the avoidable pitfalls of poorly drafted licence agreements applicable to the organization's business and products. Negotiation of a licence, however, is not a purely legal matter. The licence embodies your relationship with the licensor and the licence should be drafted to reflect your precise intentions. It ought not to be a case of downloading a pro forma licence and then fitting the relationship to suit its provisions. Negotiable contracts are negotiated and lawyers should be well briefed on your intentions and invited to comment on the practicalities and pitfalls of whatever you assert to be your intentions.

CASE STUDY

Keeping The Brand Built

A decision to choose to distribute through third parties rather than continue to finance a national sales force is not always a clear-cut choice. A main chocolate brand, for example, kept a local direct sales force on the road because it found that relying solely on 30 regional wholesale distributors placed a large slice of its sales into the hands of third parties, all of which also distributed the products of rival chocolate companies.

The dependence of the chocolate company on the regional distributors, without direct contact with its retailer customers, was regarded by some of its senior managers as a strategic vulnerability, a view reinforced by market data showing that the small shops, little kiosks in the street, hotels and cinema chains, and so on, together accounted for a higher proportion of gross sales of branded chocolate bars than the county's seven major supermarket chains, for each of which the company, incidentally, had a dedicated national key account manager, supported by merchandising teams.

The constant pressure to increase profit margins by the purchasing managers of the major supermarket chains, with threats of de-listing the brand if they did not get additional discounts or contributions to their advertising campaigns, and regular threats to introduce new charges for repositioning the brand in the company's stores (eye-level versus floor-level shelf positions, point-of-sale impulse buying racks and so on) were reported by all its negotiators. The store managers' negotiating behaviour underlined the relative vulnerabilities to margins of concentrating on sales through the large supermarket chains and the thirty main local distributors.

It was considered strategically important to counter-balance the large-scale store buyers and their contribution of thin profit margins to the chocolate company, by recruiting direct field-sales staff, also trained in point-of-sale merchandising, to contact the scores of small retail outlets, to promote the chocolate brands and negotiate on tradables (positioning of the brand in front of casual customers, use of colourful display posters and stacking bins and so on) direct with single-owner decision makers within narrow discount boundaries. The heavy national marketing of the chocolate brand in the country's media and through sponsorship of major sporting events helped maintain thicker profit rates from this sector of the market despite the relatively small sales from each retail outlet. Across the country, these smaller outlets accounted for a large and profitable slice of the annual sales of the branded chocolate.

Licence negotiations should focus on the following main negotiable issues (roughly corresponding to the probable order of their discussion). These are:

- degree of exclusivity (if any) accorded to the licensee;

- terms under which licensee obtains the licensor's products;

- territory in which licensee may operate;

- market performance the licensee is expected to achieve (supported by their marketing plan);

- licensee's distribution of rival products (if agreed);

- protection of the licensor's IPR;

- terms under which the licence will be renewed/terminated.

These issues are negotiated and their details are subject to the mutual discretion of the parties. It may not be safe to regard any of the items as of lower importance than others. However, the degree of exclusivity awarded to a licensee influences the expectations of the licensee's performance; for example:

- higher performance standards depend upon the degree of exclusivity;

- extent of territory depends upon higher performance;

- renewal/termination depends upon performance and behaviour;

- distribution of rival products depends upon the degree of exclusivity;

- IPR absolute; no dilution conceded.

Exclusivity

Parties in licence negotiations regularly debate the degree of exclusivity. Licensees prefer the licensor to grant them exclusivity within their defined territory. Their arguments generally run along the lines that if they do not have exclusivity then their marketing expenses benefit rival licensees, who free-ride on their marketing expenditures. This, it is suggested, inhibits the licensee from investing in building the brand, even when no other licensee has been appointed, but because there is always a potential threat of another licensee being appointed, it is a sufficient deterrent to performance if a newcomer could cash in on the first licensee's marketing and brand-building investment without contributing to it.

In a new market with a new licensee, as licensor you prefer to keep your options open until you see what the new licensee achieves and to what extent they fulfil their commitments. Also, the first licensee you transact with may not be the best potential licensee in the territory. Where a licensee is a distributor of many products under licence from other brands, not all of them similar or rival products of each other, its marketing spend may promote the identity of the local distributor and not a particular licensor's brand. They may also distribute rival brands, undermining their assertions that they are committed to building the brand by having exclusivity.

This suggests that the strategic issue for both parties is the extent to which a licensee is permitted to distribute rival products or the extent to which the licensor is permitted to have several licensees in the same territory. In short, is exclusivity to be a one-way or two-way street?

ONE-WAY

This takes one of two forms:

- the licensor awards exclusivity in its own product to the licensee and appoints no other licensees in the territory, but the licensee distributes rival products and substitutes;

- the licensee distributes the licensor's product and not the products of rivals in the territory, but the licensor distributes its product through various other non-exclusive rival licensees.

In the first one-way case, the licensee adds your product to its menu of product offerings and the marketing impact or promotion on behalf of your products is diluted by his marketing spend for rival products, or it is non-existent; in the second case, the licensee reduces his product offerings from your rivals and the licensee's rivals also distribute your product.

Which one-way street applies depends upon the marketing strength of the branded products. In markets with multiple distributors (wholesale or retail) you must make a decision on which strategy is most beneficial. It is not unusual to see examples of both cases in local markets, for example, in branded tools, pumps, small boat engines, replacement windows and vehicle dealerships.

TWO-WAY

This takes one of two forms:

- the licensee distributes rival or substitute brands and you license rival distributors;

- the licensee exclusively distributes your product and not other products in the territory and you do not appoint rival licensees.

The negotiated outcome of the exclusivity issues should be determined by the nature and price of the licensed product relative to substitutes, the expected size of the market and whether the licensee can generate sufficient revenue to justify its restriction to a single branded product. Similarly for you: can you generate sufficient revenue from a single exclusive licensee?

Perfumes, though expensive per unit sale, lend themselves to non-exclusive distribution because customers like to choose among brands in the same location. Department stores may have separate stalls or booths for each brand. Motor vehicles lend themselves to exclusive main dealers, at least on the same site, because marketing and sales costs, and after-sales services are high. Buyers travel to exclusive distributors to see their branded marques. Attempts in the European Union to force vehicle manufacturers to change from exclusive to general dealerships are fiercely resisted at present, though from the customers' point of view it could make the vehicle trade more competitive.

Quality

As a licensor you should set quality standards for licensees and prefer recourse to the termination terms of the licence should the licensee not meet your minimum standards. Complaints, or doubts, about quality inhibit the purchase of products. Without quality standards and clear penalties for breaching them in both sales and after-sales service, including swift remedies to fix problems that emerge from using the product, the brand image of the product could suffer damage, curbing future sales.

Depending on the nature of the product, the maintenance and improvement of quality standards is an important issue. If there are problems with the product, you can expect to hear about them pretty quickly; if there are problems with the licensee's services it takes longer for you to hear about them! The question then becomes what should you do about the complaints?

Complaints about the product require early attention for obvious reasons; complaints about the licensee require a mechanism in the licence for monitoring performance and, should it be necessary, for your intervention. The ultimate sanction for poor quality should be the termination of the license (both ways). Quality itself is non-negotiable, but the frequency of the monitoring, evaluation and remedial interventions is negotiable.

Visits to applicant licensees to inspect their operations, interview staff and assess financial viabilities are usually part of the appointment process, including 'secret shoppers', who test the service anonymously and report. Where the product or service is of a technical nature, specialized training and proof by qualifications and awards obtained may be required. Diamond buyers require good background knowledge of the geology and laws of diamond mining and production, and hands-on practical experience of assessing the value of cut and uncut stones. Similarly, background knowledge is required to work in oil and gas, fine chemicals, vehicle sales, pharmaceuticals, yachting and cruising, real estate, travel agency, IT, radio and TV, education and other businesses.

Credibility in quality audits rapidly diminishes if applicant licensees demonstrate ignorance of the business in which they seek a licence. Conversely, if the licensee needs no knowledge at all, it is not likely to be an income generator, because it is easily copied.

You should search for workable measures of quality, consistent with the customers' satisfaction with the licensee's overall performance. This is not easy because measuring quality is not subject to clear rules and numbers. Consistency is one dimension of quality and, where possible, the measure of acceptable performance should set a minimum standard below which the performance quality is deemed not to be satisfactory, and when remedial action may be invoked.

Another indicator of quality could be the opposite of consistency, as when a service provider does something well beyond what is normally expected within its normal service. Capturing such incidents is not easy and much depends on the effusiveness of the customer's report, though the content of the unexpected service might be quite trivial.

Where direct questionnaires are used, supplementary indirect checks may be necessary too. Some branded hotel chains provide details for customers of how to access the CEO with their complaints, as well as in-hotel voluntary surveys of guest opinions. The Marriott family, for instance, claim to read (and act upon) every complaint received from customers using any of its owned and managed hotels across the world. The details of a licensor's quality checks are negotiable.

Of course, quality is a two-way process: what you deliver to the licensee is as important for the licensee as what they deliver to you in terms of your revenue and your reputation. The same is true for licensees. A well-established brand may not feel that quality assurance is a necessary component of the licence agreement – the brand itself has a real interest in maintaining its reputation because that is what a 'brand' implies; its name is a signal of quality to all its consumers. And so it must remain so, and from a potential licensee's point of view their concerns about the brand's quality may not be on the same level as the licensor's concerns about an unproven licensee's adherence to the brand managers' requirements in respect of quality. But nevertheless, a potential licensee ought to have legitimate concerns about the durability of the brand's quality and of the associated services that go with it.

The licensed branded product may have a world-class reputation – that may be one of the factors attracting the potential licensee to it – but any product or service has associated activities which must be maintained to a high quality standard if the licensee is to succeed in delivering the brand within its territory, and therefore, the licensee's negotiators may wish to have commitments in these respects included in the licence contract. In short, licensees do not want a one-way street approach to quality (theirs only) and a total neglect of the licensor's continued maintenance of the brand's world image for quality.

It is better that the licensor act from the start, rather than leave it to the licensee's negotiators to require it, to embed its quality assurances in all aspects of the brand's delivery to the licensee's territory, updating the brand where necessary, enhancing the brand at least as often as the licensor updates in the home territory, renewing the brand as opportunities to do so arise, undertaking to continue a smooth administrative process in all relations with the licensee, committing to speedy action on and rectification of problems and complaints, and scheduling regular review meetings with the licensee, for instance.

I know of an active licensee of European/US management education services in Shanghai, who surveyed the licensed products/service firms available and chose to seek his licences from the proven top brands to market in China. He showed me the licensors' procedure manuals and the supporting documentation, and it was impressive. He chose to deal with only proven brands for quality reasons and local prestige. He was regularly inspected by licensors and had all of his staff trained in Europe and the USA by the licensors at their headquarters. This passed a subtle message to his staff.

He argued that if they were top brands in the USA, they had to be good to survive in a tough market. He also had two relatively unknown, or at least not highly regarded by me, Western brands. He took a closer interest in their quality regimes and the proofs of their quality than he had with the major brands. He declined to deal with any unknown products. Given that these less-well-known brands were joining his portfolio of top brands, his negotiation line with them was to require that they embedded quality assurance measures in the standards he copied from the main brands. He presented his stance on quality along the lines of: 'The international company I keep cannot tolerate their association with poor quality in any of my products and neither can I, hence I require specific commitments from you in terms of product reliability, administrative support and the speedy resolution of problems.'

I would suggest that a similar stance should be taken on quality with all licensors to ensure that any quality process is a two-way street – what applies to one party must apply to the other, complete with cancellation options and an escalating series of steps to implement measured improvements up to the cancellation option. If they are unwilling to sign something like this, a negotiator should reconsider entering into the intended licence.

Terms

Both parties can be expected to focus on the distribution of the revenue from the operation of the licence. The usual caveat applies: negotiating 60 per cent of not much may be less beneficial to you than 15 per cent of a lot. Your choice of growth strategy, by expanding the business using licensees in distant territories rather than setting up direct distribution under your own control and management, presumably is based on your assessments of the relative risks, costs and benefits of both options.

Among prominent benefits are considerations of the relative risks in starting up a business in the distant territory, the lower costs of working through third parties (who bear the risks and the bulk of the marketing and distribution costs) and the relative speed to market of each option. These factors should play a major part in your preparation of the entry terms and their negotiation with the licensee.

How all the elements of price combine to produce an agreement on terms is as varied as there are licensable products under negotiation. For example, the product could be an established domestic product with known costs and margins, ready for shipping ex-works to a licensee in a distant territory. The costs of producing, insurance and shipping (CIF – Cost, Insurance and Freight) and import duties are known or knowable to the parties. The price may be determined ex-works or ex-works plus delivery to the licensee's premises. Does the licensee pay the ex-works price plus the insurance, shipping and import duty? Which party bears the risks once the product leaves your premises and when does legal title pass – on receipt by the licensee or when the licensee pays your invoice?

The product could be a recently developed new product, technically well ahead of its rivals, for which there are no firm ideas yet of its market price. It could be embodied in a new physical product, manufactured and shipped from your premises, or embodied in a patented design suitable for manufacture in a distant territory under licence, or a mix of each. You should prefer some control of the physical product (it is easy to count physical objects for royalty purposes when it is shipped – so much per unit). But the output of distant licensees is more difficult to assess if they have complete control of production, independent of you (that is, out of sight). In these circumstances, you should prefer a royalty based on total revenues received or receivable by the licensee and not royalties based on some version of net profits. Net profits are notoriously open to (mis)representation.

In film and TV production, net profits, expressing it politely, are often a fiction much argued over by media accountants, who might find ways to charge to a current film's production costs old amortized costs of film sets produced and used decades ago! Net profits in Hollywood are definitely not based on what accounting professionals understand as 'generally accepted accounting principles' (GAAP)! It is not unknown for definitions of acceptable costs to fill many pages of a producer's contract (the producer raises the funds and is accountable for the project and hires the director, actors and film crew, plus all the facilities needed).

While the costs of a licensee's production and marketing of a product are less vague than in film production, there is room for manipulation. Each party attempts to load its costs to increase its claim to a larger share of the revenue. Where the total revenue (TR) from sales of the licensed product are made up of the licensee's costs A, and its share B of TR, plus the licensor's costs D, and its share C of TR, we can write TR as A + B+ C+ D, all of the elements being negotiable (Figure 7.1).

In Figure 7.1, the licensee's total revenue from exploiting the licensor's proprietary knowledge is divided into four categories:

- the licensee's costs of supplying the market with the Chimp Drive (which could include production of the electronic units, or, if they are imported, their acquisition costs at ex-works, or CIF prices, plus their selling costs);

- the licensee's share of total revenue net of costs;

- the licensor's share of total revenue net of costs;

- the licensor's transfer costs (where the licensor exports the products to the licensee their production costs are compensated by their prices).

Total revenue equals A + B + C + D, Total Costs equal A + D, and the profit available for negotiation equals Total Revenue – Total Costs = B + C. If the

TOTAL REVENUE A + B + C + D	Licensee's share A + B	A	Licensee' *supplying* and *selling* costs	Licensee's costs
		B	Licensee's share of the *total revenue* net of own costs and licensor's costs	PROFIT FOR NEGOTIATION B + C
	Licensor's share C + D	C	Licensors' share of the *total revenue* net of own costs and licensee's costs	
		D	Licensor's *transfer* costs	Licensor's costs

Figure 7.1 Negotiating range in a licence agreement

Source: Adapted from Farok J. Contractor (1981), International Technology Licensing: Compensation, Costs and Negotiation (Lexington, Mass.: Lexington Books), pp. 41–6

licensor proposes a distribution that gives him B + C + D he should expect the licensee to counter with a proposal for her to retain A + B + C. Given that the licensor cannot accept a return below D and the licensee cannot accept a return below A, their negotiations will tend to centre on the division of B + C.

Licensors in general will want to recover their *development* and *opportunity costs* as well as their *transfer costs* from the licensee's total revenue. As noted, a licensee will want to eliminate, or at least severely limit, a licensor's claims in respect of development costs, particularly in cases where these were clearly amortized before the licence was granted (design costs in a successful production model or, for example, a long-established cartoon character like Disney's Mickey Mouse). In the licensing of new pharmaceuticals, however, R & D costs can be expected to feature heavily in the licensor's negotiating arguments because the exploitable patent life of the product is relatively short due to the time taken to complete government drug testing procedures and gain authorization to supply the drug to the public.

Claims by the licensor for opportunity costs are likely to come under pressure given their vagueness (who knows what he might have earned if things had been different?). A belief that these costs are large, even if they are not specified exactly, has featured in the decision of some licensors to cancel or lapse their licensing agreements when they have felt that a switch to a direct marketing and distribution arrangement in the territory would be commercially advantageous.

This happened in the cases of Sony in the United States in the 1970s (and led to a court action), United Distillers throughout the 1980s (and led to much resistance in Spain) and to several major vehicle dealerships in 2000–3 in Europe (for example, Mercedes, Ford, and Renault). Because these corporations saw their overall profitability improve dramatically as a result, we can appreciate the cause of dissent among the affected licensees (who lost lucrative operations) and understand why there were tense negotiations over the lapsing of their original agreements.

Hence, while the claim for opportunity costs is based on a sound theoretical principle and can be supported in many cases by reasonably realistic calculations (including simply taking it to be equivalent to the gross profit of the licensee – all things being equal there is no reason to suppose that a licensor cannot at least do as well in the market as a licensee), we should expect that the claim could be challenged as something nebulous by a licensee when large amounts are claimed under this heading by the licensor.

As a licensor you expect licensees to press for the principle that only properly identified *transfer costs* (D) are to be considered. This should lead you to make highly liberal and exaggerated claims for the items you claim should be included in your transfer costs, so as to enlarge your claims to your share (C) of the profit (B + C). Your arguments may be based less on hard facts and more on your quasi-monopolistic status as the owner of the licensed product. If you were successful in doing this you could hope to recoup some contribution towards your debatable, and perhaps successfully challenged, development and opportunity costs from within a larger share of the profits earned in the licensee's markets.

Transfer costs generally consist of two elements: those costs that are confined to the setting up of the licence, and therefore can be expected to diminish over time, and those costs that continue to arise throughout its term. Many licence agreements require the licensee to pay all the licensor's costs in managing the agreement, including the cost of management time and travel to and within the territory, and licensors should aim to include these in the agreement. What is included under this heading and to whom it applies are subject to negotiation. Likewise, it follows that you should be vigilant in scrutinizing what the licensees claim as chargeable costs against their profits (that is costs claimed in A).

In most cases licensees soon know if their direct costs are compensated for by their share of the income from the agreement (they tend to be aware of whether they are making a profit or a loss!) and in the event of their sustaining losses they can be expected to press for cancellation of the agreement if their share of the total revenue does not cover their costs.

Many licence agreements break down or simply lapse because the actual net revenue the parties realize falls far short of their expectations. In some cases, you can try to protect yourself from this sort of failure by requiring that the licensee agree to annual or quarterly revenue targets and also agree to penalties, including a withdrawal of the licence, if they fall short of the targets. Naturally, you attempt to raise the minimum sales the licensee must attain, and the licensee attempts to lower the minimum targets they must meet.

For you, your entry price is constrained by what you think your licensed proprietary knowledge is worth to licensees in future income. While nominally you have an absolute monopoly on your registered patents, trademarks, secret know-how and so on, this is effectively only a quasi-monopoly in the market because of the availability to the licensee of imperfect substitutes from other licensors or from their own resources (cases of absolute market monopolies are rare and where this occurs the ultimate option of doing without the monopoly product is always present).

You should set your entry price by estimating the maximum value to the licensee of exploiting the licence (measured by their estimate of the present value of their future profits from the licence), but must adjust this value downwards if there is a substitute licence available in the market from a rival, or a capability at some price from an in-house substitute. As sellers tend to be more optimistic than buyers we would expect your estimates of the value of the licence to the licensee to be higher than the licensee's own estimates.

Your exit price should be set at the present value of your transfer costs and, where appropriate, the present value of your opportunity costs. Where the opportunity costs are too high (that is the benefits of your supplying the licensee's market direct were greater than your entry price) you should consider whether it is worthwhile continuing with the negotiations, or if the agreement were already in place you should consider lapsing the deal at the first opportunity. For this reason, your proposed agreement should always include a termination date to prevent you being locked into an arrangement that is shown by subsequent events to be unfavourable to you. If local laws prohibit direct entry to the market your exit price reduces to your transfer costs alone.

As people tend to exaggerate their own costs, particularly when they have an interest in doing so, we would expect your estimates of your own costs to be higher than the licensee's estimates. The licensee would determine their entry price on the basis of an estimate of their minimum transfer costs, but would adjust this estimate upwards if you might be tempted to market your product directly if the licence fees were provocatively low (see Figure 7.2).

People estimating other people's costs, particularly when they have an interest in minimizing them, often do so; hence we would expect the licensee's estimates of your transfer costs to be lower than your own estimates.

The licensee's exit price would be set by their own estimates of the present value of their profits from the licence as they would certainly not be prepared to pay more in licence fees than their own profits from exploiting the licence. As buyers are more pessimistic than sellers, they would be likely to set the present value of their future profits from the licence at a level lower than that estimated by you, the licensor.

In summary, I would expect each negotiator to open with a proposal that each should receive the total revenue earned from the licence *net only of their (low) estimates of the costs incurred by the other party in operating the licence.* Out of the net revenue you both receive both of you would meet your own costs and, if this left a profit, you would regard it as a just reward for inventing the proprietary knowledge and they would regard it as a just reward for skilfully exploiting the market. However, in reality, both of you would have to accept less than your entry proposals and share the net profit (total revenue minus actual costs) in some proportion to be decided by your negotiation.

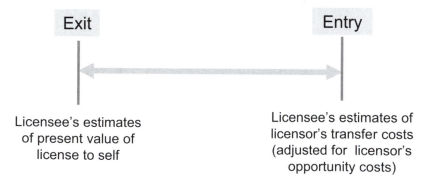

Figure 7.2 Licensee's negotiating range

The entry and exit points for your technology transfer licence are shown in Figure 7.3. Your entry point would be to propose an income from the licence which meets your (optimistic) estimate of the present value of the licensee's future income, constrained, if necessary, by the licensee's other options. The licensee's entry proposal is to pay to you just enough to cover your (pessimistic) estimate of what would cover your transfer costs, constrained, if necessary, by your opportunity costs of foregoing a direct presence in the market, or the possibility of an attractive offer from another potential licensee in the territory. These constitute the negotiating range, but whether they produce a settlement range depends on the values assigned to each point by you both.

The exit point for you is your (pessimistic) high estimate of your likely transfer costs, perhaps padded by an estimate of your opportunity costs from refraining from direct entry into the territory and by possible offers from other potential licensees, all of which draw your exit point to the left in Figure 7.3. The exit point for the licensee is their (pessimistic) estimate of the present value of income from operating the licence, which draws their exit point to the right in Figure 7.3. If your negotiating range is pulled far enough to the left, and the licensee's negotiating range is pulled far enough to the right, a gap between your exit points is inevitable.

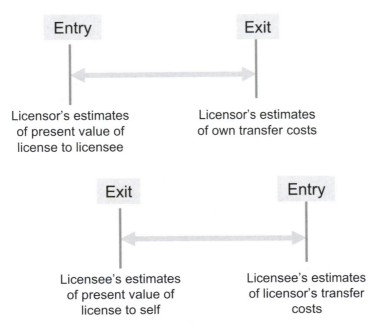

Figure 7.3   Negotiators' entry and exit points

The question for you, the licensor, is whether or not the entry prices of $200 000 from yourself and $60 000 from the licensee (Figure 7.3) represented the extremes of negotiating ranges that overlapped. If they did, you could negotiate a mutually satisfactory agreement; if they did not, either you would have to revise your exit price or seek somebody else as a licensee for the territory. You know your own exit price ($100 000) but you have no idea of the licensee's exit price.

This analytical exercise helps to clarify what is at stake in the negotiation with a potential licensee. It does not solve all the problems faced by you as licensor, and neither could it be expected to do so. Though basically a simple device, Figure 7.3 reveals potential pressures from the negotiators and what is behind their demands and arguments. That alone enables you to address your interests and to take account of the licensee's interests. You now know roughly what you should be looking for and why.

Territory

Territory is either unbounded or bounded. In licensing and joint ventures the defined territory is of high importance and subject to negotiation. Broadly, licensees favour larger (even universal) territories; licensors prefer smaller (even minute territories). The reasons are worth noting: smaller territories can be sold to many licensees but only one territory can be sold to license the whole world; larger territories cut down the proximity of active competition.

Recent contracting practice indicates the extremes of territorial definition:

> *The 'territory' shall mean all countries, bases and locations throughout the world, the universe or otherwise without limitation of boundary including outer space. (Fosbrook and Laing (2001), Media Contracts Handbook, 2nd Edition (London: Sweet & Maxwell), p.74)*

No ambiguity there!

Most territories have boundaries, often defined by countries or groups of countries. From publishing, until recently, the UK definition was bounded by the Commonwealth (54 countries), the USA, continental Europe and Asia. The open border between the USA and Canada (a member of the Commonwealth) produced 'North America', which with NAFTA (North Atlantic Free Trade Area) brought in Mexico, it being difficult to police a free trade area. Since the European Union was formed, laws relating to the single European market preclude separate territories within its boundaries – a licence to supply in one member state is a licence to supply in all member states (now 25 separate countries). The

22 Arabic speaking states form another natural territory, as does China or Japan, and (Latino) Spanish speaking countries in Central and South America and the Caribbean. Brazil forms a large territory (Portuguese speaking). Hence, some territorial definitions are shaped by political or language boundaries.

There is a strategic element in the definitions arising from the implied natural boundaries of a given territory. For example, a licensee or joint venture partner may make a claim to a territorial definition that has a commonsense rationale for the licensee but which could be problematical for you, the licensor.

Suppose a proposed partner, intending to operate within a multi-country geographical area with political, language or other such similarities, makes a claim for exclusivity within the boundaries of the area. It could be a partner located in, say, Mexico, who proposes that the territorial boundaries should be 'Central and South America and the Spanish-speaking islands in the Caribbean'. Reasonable enough? Yes, except when the partner's roll-out programme envisages a start with five named countries within the proposed larger territory (say, Mexico and Chile in year 1, Argentina in year 2 and Uruguay and Peru in year 3), and the remaining countries over the following 5 years. Allowing for a preparatory year after signing the agreement, this programme bars you from supplying the other countries either directly or through other partners. It could be nine years before 'Latin America' is supplied with your products, in the meantime leaving the unsupplied territories wide open to competitive suppliers, which the licensee is not due to supply (and presumably is not in a position to do so) for up to nine years, and you are barred from doing so (even though you may be able to do so right away and you receive enquiries from these parts of the reserved designated territory). You could agree to deliver product to those parts of the territory where the licensee is not operating and pay an agreed nominal royalty to the licensee as if they were supplying product, until such time as they open operations across the whole territory.

Questions that may be asked are: Does this support the licensor's strategy of building a presence for its products in Latin America within an acceptable time period? Is it the best defensive strategy against rival products in the territory? If the contract is signed without consideration of this problem then your Negotiation Agenda works against a commercial imperative needed to deliver your business plan. Better to address these awkward questions from the start.

Claiming the entire natural territory certainly suits a licensee's strategy. Licensees claim that it takes time to build up a market for a product and that there are longer-term benefits from learning from experience within a manageable number of countries before rolling out distribution to the entire multi-country territory. Exclusivity protects a licensee from a competitive supplier of your products free-riding on the marketing expenditures of the licensee and thereby becoming established in neighbouring countries. You face a conflict of interest in such cases. You might also face a problem of credibility when a prospective licensee claims to be able to sell into an entire market (like China) from a tiny operation on the fringes of downtown Shanghai.

Where there are spill-over effects of the licensee's marketing of the products (perhaps, heavy marketing expenditures in regional aircraft magazines or television programmes that cross national borders within the territory), some of these expenditures will benefit rivals producing substitutable products from other territories, and marketing campaigns of other licensees could cause confusion among potential customers who move about in the natural region. The spill-over effects of Internet marketing are global and not easily policed.

From your point of view, granting exclusivity to a territory in which a substantial part will be left fallow for a number of years may not be your optimal strategy. Waiting nearly ten years for full territorial coverage is a slow way to grow a business and leaves it open to pre-emptive early coverage by rivals with competing branded products who spot the potential for their similar products, especially in parts of the territory where the licensee is not yet supplying your product.

This consideration may be disregarded where the local licensee is dominant in both the product sector and the territory. The long-term growth prospects of working with a prominent, financially sound and marketing-savvy regional firm may be too attractive to disregard. It comes down to bargaining power and the relative difficulties of entering the market by some other route, including directly. Negotiating the wording of the termination clauses to cover exigencies that may arise from poor performance of the licensee in the early years of the licence may be required.

Performance

Output measures, usually in terms of sales volume, are fairly standard requirements, though some licenses are also left fairly vague, it being assumed by licensors that because it is in the interest of licensees to achieve sales growth, they will act to do so. This may be naïve, or at least there is an imperfect correlation between interests and outcomes. There are many motives for becoming a licensee and not all of them have to do with serving the licensor's interests in issuing licenses to market their products.

Some distributors may wish a licence for a certain brand to complete their range of rival branded products in stock. Others might wish a licence to pre-empt a rival from building their business around that branded product. If a licensee holds the exclusive rights to a particular brand, or set of brands, it precludes new entrants in his markets. The licensee's exclusivity could work directly against your interests in this case because the current licensee may not invest in vigorously pursuing sales to the same extent as a new entrant or another existing distributor. This could block serious growth of the licensor's products in what may be a promising market.

Now if the licensee in that market has exclusivity and vague, or worse, non-existent performance targets, and you remain locked into the agreement, you could suffer severe setbacks in your plans to grow through licensees. Non-performance becomes an issue where branded products are merely items in a licensee's catalogue. Granting early exclusivity compounds the problem; hence be cautious before agreeing to exclusivity.

Non-performance of specified targets may trigger the termination of the agreement and to avoid termination the licensee will be motivated to perform. The negotiable issues in performance are the quanta of the targets (annual, quarterly and cumulatively) and their rates of growth, usually modest initially and perhaps escalating over time until market share is dominant. In product sales, where the quantities shipped and sold in a specific market can be monitored, you have the data to assess the financial viability of that market. You know your own costs – the price at which you supply the licensee with your products – and you will know the licensee's mark-up, from which you can estimate the licensee's gross and net profits.

It is not unknown for licensors to terminate a licence where a licensee proves the profitability of a particular territory, after it has invested in introducing the product and establishing it as a brand, and the licensor intends to run it directly.

A branded copier company practised this type of take-over for the distribution of its own products whenever its licensees established the brands in their locality or, crucially, failed to exploit their territories fully when the demographics suggested their performance was below what was achievable compared to other similar territories. Hence, before castigating such take-overs as unethical, we must distinguish which was their cause – a licensee being too profitable or not being profitable enough.

Renewal

Licences should be for a set duration. Their renewal should be conditional on performance, but performance can be a slippery concept. It could be that you agree on performance standards based on the pre-licence experience of zero sales in the territory, and any reasonable sales volume target looks tempting. However, from experience of the territory later on, and perhaps the visible achievements of competing firms selling into the territory, what was regarded as satisfactory when the licence targets were agreed could seem to be unchallenging later on. But, the renewal wording, focusing on achieved performance to the targets that were set, prevents using comparative lack of presence in the market as grounds for declining renewal and termination.

True, you can usually pick a fight with a licensee and terminate on other grounds but apart from the doubtful ethics of such conduct there is always the risk of litigation in a foreign jurisdiction, which may be inconvenient if you contemplate remaining in the territory by finding another licensee or by importing direct. The contract's designated jurisdiction authority may not count for much if the jurisdiction in the territory decides to try the case under local laws and to ignore courts in your country.

Potential licensees are likely to examine the renewal terms fairly closely. Their concern will focus on their building a product's presence in the territory only to have you terminate their licence to hand it to someone else who will reap where they never sowed. Both parties need some form of protection: the licensee to protect its investment in building the brand; you to protect your brand from a licensee achieving results that fall well short of potential.

At a minimum, dated periodic reviews of financial performance, including costs, losses and profits, should be included in the renewal clause; exclusivity should only be granted in exchange for tougher quarterly or annual targets; and market share, which takes account of the comparative performance of competitors, should be an admissible criterion for non-renewal.

Master franchises

A master franchise agreement is a step up from the standard franchise or agency agreement that usually applies to a single company. Master franchises tend to

CASE STUDY

Adios, Ex-Amigo

A global drinks company, famous for its global brands, changed its policy of distribution through national licensees, some of them established for several generations in their countries, when it was taken over by a famous and more aggressive global rival practising a direct distribution strategy.

The new corporate managers decided to take distribution in-house and to abandon distribution through long-established local agencies. In some cases, they bought out the local distributors and made them 100 per cent owned subsidiaries, with the former owners hired as the first generation of managers; in others they terminated the licenses and redirected distribution to their existing directly-owned and managed subsidiaries in the same territory.

In at least one case, a failure to agree to a buy-out price led to costly litigation, but the European Union's competition law worked in favour of the global corporation and a settlement was eventually made. The upshot of this strategy was that the directly managed distribution strategy proved to be significantly more profitable in relative and absolute terms compared to the inherited policy of licensing local distributors and setting them performance targets.

be larger in scale and to involve the master franchisee finding, selecting and contracting with many individual and independent sub-franchisees.

They are not suitable for a small licensor business with the notion to franchise its operations globally on the basis of limited success in its home territory. Visiting a foreign country on vacation and seeing opportunities for exporting a business model to that country is no basis for deciding to embark on a franchise programme. Wild and improbable notions of global franchises can cause a failure of the home business.

On the other hand, if a nationally based business is well established, strong financially and approaching saturation in its home base (with perhaps a small international presence in some foreign territories), it may be timely to consider negotiating a master franchise agreement with one or more candidate businesses in certain carefully chosen foreign markets. Be sure, with international travel so prevalent, almost any growing business model will attract enquiries (many of them obviously defective in quality for one reason or another – at Negotiate we receive maybe four or five such requests a year) from ambitious business people seeking an opportunity to export the same idea to their own country.

If the organization's business plan contains the objective of seeking a franchisee in a foreign region (Latin or North America; China; India; the Arab Middle East and so on) there are at least three main commercial imperatives:

CASE STUDY

Too Fast, Too Far

The number of excellent restaurant businesses which have gone on to failure by dabbling in franchising too early is high. For a while it looks good – the single city restaurant with a good business theme proves itself a success and within two years it grows to 30 franchised operations in other cities. It keeps growing for a couple more years and then crashes.

There was nothing wrong with the business theme; except that it did not travel so well, so fast. Adherence to the theme erodes at the edges as the quality of the franchisees and their commitment to the branded theme declines – local attempts to improve on the theme prove costly and local failures from recruiting the wrong people in the wrong locations compromise the brand. Legal arguments about the ex-franchisees' initial investment enter the public domain and the familiar story of expanding too fast and too far, including into foreign countries, undermines backers' and creditors' financial confidence in the franchise.

- The organization is strong enough financially to afford the unavoidable expenses (and absences of key staff) of seeking out, evaluating, meeting and negotiating with prospective partners in foreign lands (this is no fast road to riches).

- The organization conducts the appropriate preparatory work to judge the credibility and workability of the proposed partnership (these imperatives of proper preparation will also be present in international joint venture negotiations).

- The right partner is chosen.

What works commercially in the home country may not work so effectively or at similar costs in a foreign country. This is not something that is purely a reflection of the immaturity of a foreign country's commercial markets, different political structures or economic policies. The European Union provides classic examples of hidden costs that result from government interventions in markets every bit as inhibitive of foreign investment as those of the most anti-commercial interventions of some developing countries.

US and UK firms have been surprised on occasion by just how difficult and expensive it is to carry through commercial decisions that are normal in their home countries when investing in Belgium, The Netherlands, France and Germany. The highly protective labour laws of these countries act as barriers to the sort of flexibilities that are commonplace elsewhere, and the presence of these legal barriers unintentionally boosts unemployment because one way to avoid employment complications is to avoid employing new recruits unless tightly justified.

CASE STUDY

Seas Of Red Ink

Even banks get it wrong (for example, Midland Bank's purchase of Wells Fargo Bank in California), but no business sector is immune. Ferranti's US acquisition bankrupted the UK company, until then financially sound; Marks & Spencer's foray into the US also ended in a sea of red ink; Germany's Daimler-Benz's merger with US Chrysler awaits a final assessment by sceptical fund managers and doubters concerned that the Mercedes brand will lose its edge in quality. Foreign investment into China has not proved to be financially prudent yet, with many withdrawals from projects launched with great optimism when they commenced.

Assuming that these issues have been properly considered, the choice of a master franchise agreement to deliver the objectives of the business plan has certain advantages over other routes. A master franchisee has full authority to recruit sub-franchises within the designated territory. The franchisor stands back from the territory and devolves authority to the master franchisee, who acts as the local franchisor, for all intents and purposes, within the terms of the master franchise agreement.

The benefits of addressing the market in the territory through a master franchise agreement, assuming the franchisor has found a suitable organization for this role include:

- There is only one entity for the franchisor to deal with, and no day-to-day dealings with the sub-franchisees will be necessary – arm's-length contact may be beneficial to protect its longer-term interests.

- Quality standards can be set for the franchisee to apply to all sub-franchisees as a condition for the continuation of the master agreement. This is a critical, and therefore, high priority negotiable issue. Monitoring and dealing with below-par sub-franchisees is a condition for continuing the master agreement, leading ultimately to its termination if it becomes necessary.

- The finance for introducing the franchisor's products into the territory is a responsibility of the master franchisee not the franchisor – this is one of the reasons for choosing this route to this market. Some master franchise agreements do, however, include an initial level of financial contribution from the franchisor in exchange for a shareholding in the master franchise company. This can be seen as a toehold for the franchisor's eventual takeover of the sub-franchisees in the territory, if or when the master franchisee founder seeks to exit the business.

- The master franchisee is chosen because of their commercial contacts and experience in the territory, their knowledge and working familiarity with local business practices, local laws, and banking and finance arrangements. Where these exceed by a significant amount the knowledge obtainable from outside the territory by the franchisor, it could be a safer route to this market than trying to set up local franchisees one at a time. The master franchisee should be able to recruit and retain suitable managers and employees with greater confidence than the outsider franchisor.

- Though franchising always pays lower revenues than a directly managed operation (and this is true for domestic franchising as much as it is for international franchising) the franchisor's net revenues, after deducting its lower costs of managing the master franchisee, should still make it a worthwhile route to a market that would be difficult to enter any other way. The relative franchise fees are negotiable but realism must intrude on expectations. The master franchisee imposes franchise fees on the sub-franchisees and these are unlikely to be much different from the home market franchising fees. But now there are two parties sharing them – the master franchisee and the franchisor – and each party's share is going to be smaller than when only one claims them all.

For the longer term, this tension gives:

- the master franchisee an incentive to search for a means of substituting a replacement product for the franchisor's and building on the chain of sub-franchisees they have established in the territory;

- the franchisor an incentive to consider taking over the master franchise by buying out the master franchise agreement, or via termination of it with or without just cause.

In these unhappy circumstances a lot will depend on the loyalty or otherwise of the sub-franchisees to the two parties and this may inform the quality of the relationships each maintains over the years with them. A termination dispute could also encourage sub-franchisees to seek to improve (that is, lower!) their franchise fees in exchange for their loyalty.

NB: *As always, when it gets down to legal detail you should consult a lawyer qualified in the applicable jurisdiction.*

Activity
for Chapter 7

Activity 7.1

How familiar are you with a licensing or franchise business operation, either as an employee or as a customer?

What products, if any, of your organization potentially are marketable via franchises? How many franchised products do you buy?

COMMENTS ON THIS ACTIVITY

Franchise arrangements can be found in businesses supplying services in car hire, hotels, travel agents, bureaux de change, fast food outlets, taxi services, flower delivery services, laundries, opticians, driving schools, wedding dresses and so on.

PART II
Tools

Bid Strategies for Tenders

CHAPTER

8

Introduction

Major high-value contracts are usually put out to tender to various companies able to undertake them and you have to become familiar with the theory and practice of bid processes if you are to contribute to the analysis of tender procedures and their associated negotiations.

Behind the pure theory of bidding lies the central belief that bidders bid their 'best price' because they believe that competitors also bid their best prices and that the best-priced bidder wins the contract for the work. This way, in theory, the most competitive bidder undertakes the project and the client receives the best value for money.

In practice, the simple rules of the pure theory of the bid become more complex with the passing of time and the exigencies of managing large complex projects, particularly where it is not always known how the specifications should be defined until the R & D work has been completed and the project is well under way. The bidding process tends to increase in complexity because bidders learn to stretch or bend the rules and because clients find it necessary to forestall irritating accusations from rival bidders that successful bidders somehow received unfair or favourable treatment.

The pure theory of the bid assumes that the bid is a firm fixed-price bid, with no hidden or unspecified extras, and that it is an unconditional offer to contract. If accepted, the work and the price are set in stone and cannot be varied. This assumption excludes any room for post-tender negotiation.

In practice, tenders became a means of selecting bidders for 'pre-qualification' to enter into post-bid negotiations. Over time, post-bid negotiations grew in scope and a great deal of communication between the preferred bidders and the client's tender team, or the consultants the client engaged to manage the selection process, took place.

Tendering is an expensive activity; it has become more expensive with the size of projects. In large defence and civil engineering contracts, bidders vie for the status of 'prime contractor' and, if successful, they then repeat the bidding process with competing sub-contractors, and seek portions of the contract value for supplying their particular skills and competencies. The prime contractor manages the entire project including the sub-contractors for the client.

Bid/no bid decisions

The decision to bid for work has important consequences for the bidding firm. Much has been written about the bid/no bid decision. P. D. V. Marsh, a specialist consultant in this field, developed a useful approach to bidding (*Contract Negotiation Handbook*, 2nd Edition, Gower, 1984; 3rd Edition, 2000). I use a version based on Marsh, summarized below in a slightly different format.

Marsh divides the bid/no bid decision into four parts – marketing, production, financial and contractual – and he uses a 200-point scoring system to assess the desirability of a bid decision. I prefer a 100-point range and I ask slightly different questions.

The weighting and scoring of the questions is less important than how you answer them and weigh up their collective impact on the bid/no bid decision. Sometimes the answers will be clear cut; other times they require a judgement call, bearing in mind that the natural proclivity for sales managers is to encourage their staff to chase every order they can. To illustrate the Marsh approach, I apply Table 8.1 to a recent bid/no bid decision made for a Middle East contract.

Taking each question in turn and applying scores from –5 to +5, except for questions 14 and 15, they are arranged as below. The maximum score is 100, and the marketing and financial questions are marked as positive for a bid (high marks out of 5 for each question significantly favour a bid). If the finance and the marketing have low positive or negative scores, this should cause you immediate concerns. Overall, it is better that both of these question sets are positive.

The production and contractual questions are scored from –5 to +5. Significantly negative represents being against a bid for the deal. It is critical that the negative aspects of the deal are identified because if these are neglected, they create rosy-scenario thinking by those overly close to the deal, especially in relatively desperate order droughts. Most negatives are found in these two areas.

Of course, the grading of the contractual negatives does not consider what might be improved in them by negotiation, assuming that negotiation is possible in regulated public contract situations. Negotiation would only proceed if pre-qualification is won and when prior bid/no bid pre-tender decisions are possible in post-qualification situations. It is better to proceed or not proceed to a bid before *hope* conquers *experience* in these matters.

Table 8.1 Bid/No Bid decision (score –5 to +5 points, unless otherwise stated)

Marketing (+)		
1	Is the tender for a core product in the firm's activities?	3
2	Is the tender within the firm's business plan in relation to (1 point each):	
	(a) the territory?	1
	(b) the customer?	1
	(c) the products?	1
	(d) the competitors?	1
	(e) the organization?	1
3	How does the product fit the existing order book and sales budget?	4
4	Is there idle or spare capacity available for this order?	3
5	What is the probability of not receiving other orders just now?	3
		+18/25

Production (–)		
6	Are special materials, staff or capacity required?	–5
7	Are additional materials, staff or capacity, required?	–1
8	What costs are imposed if the tender is not won?	0
9	Is it a special product or from the range?	–5
10	Are there serious product or special requirement risks?	–4
		–15/25

Table 8.1 *Continued*

Financial (+)		
11	Is the expected cash flow sufficiently positive?	4
12	Are there low risks in relation to:	
	(a) cost escalation?	1
	(b) FOREX?	2
	(c) customer's financial performance?	3
13	Is the profit contribution satisfactory?	3
		+13/25

Contractual (−)		
14	Is it a buyer's contract (score −10 to +10)?	0
15	Are there contractual risks foreseen in relation to (score −15 to +15):	
	(a) penalties?	−1
	(b) warranties?	−1
	(c) liquidated damages or consequential loss?	−1
	(d) inspection and testing?	0
	(e) dispute procedures and bias?	−5
	(f) termination for cause or without cause?	0
	(g) performance bonds or guarantees?	0
		−8/25
	TOTAL	+8/100

On the assessment in Table 8.1, the Middle East tender is marginally positive at +8.

The most worrying aspect is the negative score of −5 in anticipation of problems of bias ((e) under 'contractual') against a foreign exporter to the Middle East under local dispute resolution procedures. Exporters with little experience of trading in the region must consider the relative non-independence of the justice system in certain Middle Eastern countries. Everything depends on the local alliances forged with Middle Eastern partners and their track record, indicating a need for some serious staff work by the exporter's back office to review evidence of the reputations and influence of the proposed allies.

Both the marketing and financial questions show positive responses (32/50) at a passably high comfort level. This is counterbalanced by as high a negative score for the special adjustments required to produce the product as specified in the RFP (two scores of 5/5 and one at 4/5). This is a major cause for concern and perhaps the one that would induce a risk-averse management not to bid.

The method indicates the areas of concern that must be discussed and assessed before deciding to bid. In the case example, the firm decided to bid, fully aware of the negative scores and the marginal overall positive bid score of only 8/100.

It also decided to take action to change the scores, not by simply adjusting them with a pencil – a wholly ridiculous action, as it changes nothing of substance. Instead, it examined what could be changed by the intervention of its staff with the staff of the customer on specially identified areas of concern. The idea was to raise the positive scores and lower the negative scores.

Under marketing, two of the three lower scores of 3/5 each come from:

4	Is there idle or spare capacity available for this order?	3
5	What is the probability of not receiving other orders just now?	3

At first glance these questions appear to have negative connotations. Idle capacity is an apparent problem, not an advantage, and a high probability of not receiving other orders is another potentially serious problem, but they are presented here as positive scores because it is the effect of them both on the bid decision that is important and relevant. The existence of idle capacity and the high probability of not receiving other orders actually are positive reasons for bidding, not negative reasons against bidding. Winning the bid and getting a new order would address the problems arising from these two questions by taking up some of the idle capacity and by diminishing the negative impact of not receiving other orders soon.

In similar vein, the high negative scores in production arise from the specialized nature of the four questions relating to special requirements of the order:

6	Are special materials, staff or capacity required?	-5
9	Is it a special product or from the range?	-5
10	Are there serious product or special requirement risks?	-4
		-14

The tender is not for an off-the-shelf product or one easily produced by extending current production runs, or supplied by taking product from unsold stock. It has some special features which always add to costs and complexity in production decisions (special tools, breaking into existing runs of standardized products, higher unit costs until familiarity with the product is established as personnel climb the learning curve, and so on). These account for –14 of the –15 points scored under this heading. It is likely that production staff will be highly sceptical of bidding for this order as their scores account for more than half of the negative scores in the survey. In the post-analysis discussions, you must seriously consider the views of production staff.

In the cases of both marketing and production, functional managers will be looking closely at each question to see what action they could take to change the circumstances that lead the current assessments and in so doing to test the robustness of the assessments. The RFP may constrain them taking any action – it may be too tightly drawn to allow for any working flexibility – in which case the negative assessment will have to stand. Detailed discussions focussing on these questions can be a productive exchange for the bid team.

It is time to discuss briefly typical comments from practical managers when they see numbers assigned to questions like those in Table 8.1. 'Subjective wishful thinking', 'Think of a number and halve or double it depending on the answer you want', 'Not worth the time or the trouble it takes to write them down', and others like them (sometimes not as politely put) that are hurled across the table when you present them with the questions, a flip chart and a pen to comment on the tool.

'OK,' I respond, 'what method do you use?' In most cases the response is usually words like 'experience', 'nous' and that old standby 'you can't make eagles out of ducks'. In other words, they don't know, and their best guess is as good as anybody else's. Of course, the number scale is subjective, but so is any opinion.

The discipline of attempting to give a subjective opinion some sort of number usefully ranks the degree to which a subjective opinion is scaled in the opinion giver's mind. When opinions are given in an unweighted format it is hard to judge anything about them, other than from tone, facial expression and loudness of the speaker. To say there that this course of action is risky could give an entirely false impression. How risky it is can be indicated with a subjective assessment that on a scale of 1 to 10, it is a level of about '8' that tells us something useful, as does describing a risk level as about '2'. Numerical assessments are guides to the subjective estimates of others.

Managers searching for answers are disappointed if they ask for bread and all they get is a stone. Practical advice has to be replicable to be useful and the questions in the bid/no bid decision format are one useful way of structuring discussion. Judgement must still be exercised in allocating scores, but these are a long way from wild guesses, because any quoted score has to be explained to knowledgeable peers and the credibility of the explanation tested by colleagues, which is more than a step up from relying on someone's unexplained (and unexplainable) nous, which may be no more than a claim to have the authority of an eagle when there is a suspicion that they are in fact a duck.

Bid traps

Tenders claim to be the most efficient way to secure value for money and, because bidders know they are in competition with others, they therefore are assumed to bid lower margin over their costs than they enjoy in a normal sales context. A tender is supposed to be an example of one shot only at winning the bid. If bidders miss the purchaser's target (defined as the lowest bid) they know they are out of the game. That is the theory.

Tenders create problems not found in the usual face-to-face situation. Buyers use one shot only as an intimidation tactic. It puts maximum pressure on the supplier to trim prices to the lowest, or close to it, hoping it will be low enough to win the bid. Tenders require bidders to submit sealed bids and the buyer selects the lowest one (or none at all).

Some procurement managers manipulate the bid process by setting traps for the unwary. They may be seeking bids merely to put price pressure on a regular supplier's prices. It is not unknown for finance directors to call for tenders – or just threaten to call for them – for their audit business, which, once the regular audit practice obliges by cutting its audit fee, merely encourages them to continue doing so after each annual audit. Non-executive directors on boards that successfully used the tender threat on their accountants pass the technique onto the financial directors of other company boards they sit on. The tender trap begins springing up all over the place and for many years accountancy firms had no realistic response.

Similar consequences followed the spread of tendering across a growing public sector (testing for probity, not savings – tendering adds to costs) and, inevitably, it spread across the private sector (testing prices against competition) servicing the public sector. As the value of public contracts and private civil projects rose from the mid-1960s onwards, tendering became the norm, but its practical limitations caused changes in the tender process at variance with the pure theory of bidding.

Bid theory and practice

In theory there is a problem with adopting a bid strategy in a tender situation. Blind bid tenders are supposed to be a means by which a buyer forces sellers to bid at their lowest acceptable price for delivering on time a stated quality and quantity of product or service to the buyer's specifications. The buyer opens the sealed bids at a specified time and chooses the lowest price at which a seller is willing to undertake the work. All higher bids are binned. There is no negotiation and no re-bidding. The dirty tender trick, using successive rounds of bidding to reduce bid prices described below is precluded.

In theory, bidders are unable to pad their bid prices because it is a one shot deal and all bids but the lowest are subject to sudden death exclusions by the buyer. The bid price is the only chance to win the contract, so maximum pressure is felt by bidders to bid lowest first time. They cannot sensibly hold back any room for negotiation or re-bidding because there will be no negotiation or re-bidding. Padding, if any, is risky because somebody will submit a lower and, it is presumed, minimal bid.

That's the theory. In practice there is a wide variety of exceptions to the theory. For example, the party specifying the product or service soon discovers that what appears to be a simple commodity (lead pencils, say) requires more than a simple invitation to tender for supplying pencils. There are all kinds of specs for pencils:

- The graphite core (the so-called 'lead') comes in various specifications of hardness and softness (for example HB).

- The wood holding the cores can also be soft or hard.

- The wood can be enamelled in different colours or left as bare wood; it can have a square, round or triangular cross-section.

- It can contain a metal attachment for an eraser (USA) or rubber (UK).

- The pencil can have a long or short shank.

- It can be delivered in varying quantities (from six to a hundred gross).

CASE STUDY

Dirty Trick

A purchasing guru advises procurement managers to manipulate the tender process by what can only be described as a dirty trick. It plays to the gullibility (or desperation) of companies new to the tendering game.

Invitations to tender are sent out to known producers of a tightly definable standard commodity, reducing, if not removing, ambiguities in its specifications. On receipt of the bids, the buyer does not reply to any of them. In a short while, bidders make enquiries (apparently, most of them always do!) but the buyer refuses to give any details of who has bid or any hints of the best bid price received. The callers are told that bids have not yet closed, so if they want to revise their bids they may do so.

This always prompts some revised (lower) bids, and one or two (sensible folk!) to drop out. The cycle is repeated: no response to enquiries about the progress of the bid; only that revised bids are still being accepted.

This goes on for as long as at least one bidder stays in the game. Even then, the same policy is applied of no details plus an invitation to re-bid. When it is clear there is going to be no more re-bidding, the buyer calls the last bidder and accepts their, by now, very low bid.

The assertion of the purchasing guru is that this will produce substantial reductions in the prices of those commodities every firm requires. He regards it as ethical on the grounds that none of the bidders are coerced into re-bidding. They make their bid decisions on whatever basis they wish, including selling below marginal cost if their circumstances suggest that they could earn contribution in this manner.

A firm that plays the game below marginal cost is unlikely to remain in business, which is why the sensible sellers quit the game in the first round.

- It can be sold in mixed lots of hard and soft leads.

- It can have colour capabilities.

- It can have the manufacturer's brand name or the customer's name or brands printed on the shank in black, blue, silver or gold.

- It can be sold loose, in cardboard boxes or in tins.

Once the detailed spec is determined, there may be room for influencing the spec, or some details of the specs may be flexible because they have a lower priority for the customers.

Why do buyers become more complex in their specifications? Ironically, because they want to make the products they buy into bespoke commodities so that they can compare bids from different suppliers selling the same products they have specified! The results are different. They make quasi-commodities (simple products almost the same in design and performance) into tightly specified bespoke products, which reduces competition because few suppliers wish to over-specify their commodity product lines they sell (pencils, oil cans, spanners, coat racks and so on) to the non-bespoke market and avoid special products for individual customers.

This leads to a tendency for tender specifications to become more precise through time and even the simplest of products can become overly specified as buyers try to constrain sellers from working to loose interpretations of the spec, which undermines the quality of what they deliver if they win the bid.

The phenomenon of 'spec escalation' has led to 20-page specifications for oilcans for the US Army, and simple spanners for the US Air force costing thousands of dollars each. Just as buyers tend to tighten the specifications, bidders try to work round them, adding new layers of decision making to the tender process, and high costs, with field trials, sample evaluations and laboratory testing exercises.

Bidders may have to be approved suppliers, which are inspected, approved or rejected, and only those listed as approved receive an invitation to bid for anything, including sub-contractors and sub-sub-contractors. Organizations supplying government departments, major corporations and publicly-funded agencies, must complete the approval processes, and not just to assess the bidders' technical competence, because approval may also be required for their HR and social policies too, and judgements may be made about their financial standing.

Big government is a multi-billion pound spender on procurement and as such exerts a huge influence on the implementation of favoured social policies by requiring all of its suppliers to conform with the government's social policies outlawing discrimination and harassment of all kinds, as well as quality assurance (ISO 9000), minimum wage, hours of work, human rights, freedom of information and other legislation. Certain suppliers may be excluded from bidding for certain work, or they are vulnerable to political lobbying by local firms, because they are foreign owned or otherwise disqualified.

Changes complicate the bidding process. If simple commodities like pencils promote complex specs, what of more complex products like power stations, satellites, fast jets, computer systems and outsourcing contracts? Bidding behaviour has three possible impacts on the process:

- If the product is proprietary to the sellers, the buyer emphasizes the performance required in the specification (what the product must do for the customer), rather than how it does it.

CASE STUDY

Defence Costs

In major defence projects, the main cost contributors fall into three phases:

- R & D (development, testing and evaluation)

- investment (procurement and placing the product into operational use)

- operations (costs of operation of the equipment over a period of years).

Each phase has different implications for contracting, usually with a nominated prime contractor in overall charge of the sub-contractors for the first two phases. The third phase is normally under the control of the defence department, with continuing contractual requirements supplied by specialist firms.

R & D defines the weapon system and its platforms; investment acquires the system, installs it, assembles the levels of stock (spares and replacements), trains the initial users, establishes the chain of command and deploys it with its infrastructure; and operations puts the equipment/platforms into use, or ready for use, plus operational replacements, maintenance and repair capabilities, pay and allowances for the designated users, the training facilities and staff, stocks of consumables, transportation and support.

These, therefore, are big projects, usually costing billions of dollars each. The contracts underpinning them are complex, as are the negotiations and associated activities supporting the winning of the contracts.

- If the seller designs product and builds it for a specific purpose, the buyer expects to have a say in specifying how it performs, as well as in what it does.

- If the product is designed by the buyer, or it is part of a follow-on series of what has been designed and produced by another supplier (as is common in defence orders), the buyer specifies the design and determines how it is made and what the product must do.

The very complexity of such products also introduces another variation in the bid process by opening space for official pre-bid and post-bid discussions between bidders and customers.

Suppliers offer indicative bids, including proof of competence, and customers pre-qualify the bidders invited for detailed discussions on the specifications, the production plans and delivery schedules. Bidders who fail to pre-qualify drop out of contention. The door opens to negotiations on the specifications, on the design and the operational performance of the product and its lifetime costs. The bidding process becomes a means not of discriminating between bidders to award the contract, but a means of separating bidders into those who might be selected and those not to be selected (non-compliant bidders, firms with risky features in their finances and technical capabilities, or with doubts as to their stability).

Once suppliers are judged to be compliant, inclusive of variations, they are invited to submit their final bids by a set date. Once the bids are in, the client may ask for new discussions with selected bidders to explore potential changes in their bids (usually, to lever upwards certain performance characteristics, or to lever downwards prices). The client then selects the winning bidder.

In all but the routine tenders for fairly simple commodity purchases, tendering for contracts moves from sudden-death-type decisions to negotiated tenders for the more complex products and services, albeit preceded by pre-qualification tests to eliminate non-starters. This is a different bidding world from the one-offer-only sudden-death bid where the cheapest bid wins. Where negotiation takes place as part of the bid process, it requires different bid strategies to succeed.

Negotiation helps selection if it clarifies how a bidder would tackle the problem of the client – who has a pre-conceived and specified solution to a need – and the bidder believes from experience they know of a better way to address the client's problem. Negotiation hinders selection if it encourages bidders to pad their bids in the anticipation that their numbers and solutions will be open to negotiation.

Bid strategies

The two basic bid strategies are a choice between sudden death (SD or one-offer-only) and padded bid (PB or first-not-final-offer). A third variant is where the RFP process begins with a 'beauty parade', during which potential bidders are invited to make presentations to the customer's contracting personnel on their general approach to a potential proposal and to exhibit their capabilities and experience in delivering similar products or services. Both sides question each other about the general details of the broad proposal and what, broadly, they can offer. When satisfied that there are sufficient potentially compliant bidders in play to select from, the customer issues a detailed RFP to the pre-qualified bidders on either a SD or PB basis.

Where the bid rules adamantly remain SD there is no choice for bidders but to conform (or, of course, not to bid!). In some public tendering procedures,

---

CASE STUDY

New Policies

The Ministry of Defence instituted new policies during Mrs Thatcher's governments to force down defence procurement costs. These included:

- Transparent negotiations: contractors had to reveal their detailed costs and profit expectations to MOD negotiators so that the MOD could identify cost or price padding.

- After definitive bids were received by the MOD, it circulated them to other defence contractors, including major rivals in the European Union. The information circulated included copies of the rival product designs and their technology (including proprietary IPR), and their bid prices(!) and invited them to bid against their

rivals' bids. One UK defence contractor bitterly complained that its advanced electronic technology in missile design was handed to its main French rival, against which it was actively bidding for other contracts in Europe;

- The MOD instituted a 'best and final' bid round to compel bidders to reduce their definitive bids, or risk being undercut by other bidders. Another defence contractor said a best and final bid policy was acceptable – though the profit rate on bids after transparent negotiations was already slim – but it objected strenuously to a policy with seven best and final rounds in it!

SD is mandatory and penalties for breaching its rules of conduct are dramatic, even draconian. For example, communication by a bidder with the client organization once it issues invitations to tender is expressly forbidden and any attempt to do so results in automatic disqualification.

Questions that might arise in the RFP are handled strictly in the open. The bidder is allowed to ask questions of the RFP but may only do so under an explicit instruction to address all questions in writing to a named person, or face disqualification. Often, this person is a middle-ranking administrator detached from the contract decision process and only consults the contract personnel for answers to bidders' questions. This keeps the contact managers at arm's length from the bidders and prevents collusion, or, as important in public bidding, any appearance of collusion. Questions from a bidder and the client's answers to them are circulated to all bidders, ostensibly to prevent any charges of exclusive communications that may unduly influence the purchaser. It is not unknown for certain questions to spread disinformation about sellers' intentions to other bidders, because the questions asked indicate areas of interest and cause rivals to waste time following up on dead-end lines of approach.

Telephone calls are forbidden (social contact is explicitly prohibited and could cost the employee of the organization that issues the contract their job) and any accidental contact must be reported for the record and for possible investigation. Bidders are warned that any attempt to communicate with a client's employees, either in writing or by conversation (including casual social conversations), will be reported to the contracts manager and could make them liable to disqualification. This last provision blocks off any suspicion that a preferred bidder has been appointed in circumstances detrimental to the interests of other bidders (if they think the RFP is a smokescreen for bid collusion they could be tempted to complain to the civil service ombudsman, or to make their complaints public).

Does communication take place despite these draconian prohibitions? Yes. Evidence? Only anecdotal, for obvious reasons, but there have been occasional whistleblowers from the clients or bidders and in some cases (for example, India) of prosecution of government ministers and officials as a result, with rumours of cases pending in the UK.

A PB strategy allows for an initial bid close enough to be in touch with the client's broad expectations to pre-qualify and to remain a 'compliant bid' (CB). The differences between expectations and the PB become subject to negotiation. There might also be elements marked as having understood-but-wish–to-discuss status, and for which precise bid quanta have not (yet) been stated.

If there is a pre-qualifying stage in the bid process, and a beauty parade, much of the time might be taken up with each side assessing the other for bargaining strengths and weaknesses. Bidders want to assess their bargaining position relative to other players (most of whom will be known to them – only a few well-known prime contractors have big-project capabilities), because this influences the degree of padding worth risking to remain in the game and, for the client, how far to push a bidder on elements of bids which are important to the client, whilst avoiding pushing a serious contender out of the game.

It is not useful to theorize about the appropriate bid strategy for general situations. Many try to do so, only to create plausibly realistic strategies *in theory*. The important consideration of strategy is its practicality. And that depends a great deal on the intelligence available about the other party's capabilities and intentions. In the distributive bargain (zero-sum), each party knows three of the four variables that define the settlement area. The absence of knowledge of the fourth variable (the exit price of the other party) creates a serious lack of information inhibiting some otherwise plausible strategic choices.

In general, we can agree that the negotiating range in an open negotiation will be wider than in a SD tender, and that a PB tender plus negotiation will also have a wider range than a SD tender without room or opportunity for negotiation. A strict SD game narrows the negotiating range most because the bidding range is from the lowest to the highest SD bid price. Of course, both parties prefer to contract close to the other's exit price and, of course, clients prefer to choose the lowest SD price rather than the second lowest bidder's price, and winning bidders would prefer to contract close to the client's exit price, if they knew where it was. But as they do not know what the other party's exit price is, they can only assume that the lowest bidder's price out of a competitive field of serious rivals is the group's exit price for that product. If that price is within the client's acceptable price range, the client will be satisfied – provided the client does not start wondering whether there was a lower bid price that could have been found if it had tested the padding in the winning bid through a best and final bid round (or more than one!).

Clients prefer SD bidding to a negotiation of a single PB tender. But SD tendering has disadvantages, especially in complex contracts, because the client foregoes the opportunity to test the pricing (and priorities) of elements of its RFP with the winning bidder. If it switches to post-bid negotiation, it opens the door to PB once the SD bidders realize that it is no longer SD. Unless, of course, the client has the procurement strength to enforce transparency in the bidders' cost and profit details (as in the procurement policy imposed on defence contractors by the MOD).

Two erroneous bid strategies

Clients entering a new product market with new sourcing arrangements may not be thoroughly conversant with the market and the firms in it. Bidders, conscious of their superior knowledge of their markets and well-endowed with current business, may approach RFPs from new clients with a PB strategy, while the clients have adopted SD.

If clients accept bids on a SD basis – choose the lowest bid, no post-bid negotiation – they forego opportunities to squeeze the padded elements in

CASE STUDY

Television Franchise Bids

For the regular renewal of UK commercial television franchise rights, the existing TV companies bid against new entrants and, subject to proof of its programming merits and compliance with government regulations regarding independence and balanced current affairs airtime, the highest cash bidder wins.

In a recent renewal round, an existing occupant of a regional franchise won the bid because no new entrant made a bid, not even a nominal one. And the winning bid was for the nominal sum of £2000 instead of the millions bid in the other UK regions! How did a TV company manage this? By pre-bid preparation that altered the cash bid rules through knobbling the non-cash pre-qualifying conditions.

Bidders had to produce credible programming plans as part of the pre-qualifying conditions and submit these in sealed packages with their separately sealed cash bids. The programming plans were opened first and, if the regulatory authorities passed the bidders, their price bids were opened next and the franchise awarded to the highest cash bidder.

But to have a credible programme plan, the regulators considered that they needed bidders to supply the names of the directors, the senior staff (executives, producers, actors, artistes, authors, programme makers, news teams, sports teams and presenters), all of the studio and back office staff involved in the proposed bids, and the company's financial backers, along with detailed statements of programming policies.

An incumbent TV company in one of the TV regions set about retaining all of its staff on golden-handcuff contracts that made it financially attractive for its current employees not to sign with anybody else

who might put in a bid for the franchise. The value of the golden handcuffs depended on the commercial value and importance of the person, but everybody got something. They also signed up (with tight confidentiality agreements) well-paid consultants, anybody who had worked for them in the previous few years and who had left for any reason (including a few who had left following the rows common in the frantic TV business), as well as key TV people in other companies in other regions, hired ostensibly to help draft the bid documents on programming, who also signed with tight confidentiality agreements.

Shortly before the bid deadline, there was nobody unsigned of any note or experience in TV production left in the region who could appear with credibility in a rival bid. When it came to bid day, there were no obvious candidate new entrant companies about to bid, unless a total surprise emerged at the last moment, but careful research showed no sign of any defections from the bidders in other regions (TV production is a village in all countries, dominated by broken confidences, two-faced gossip and frantic rumour).

With no real opposition to mount a credible programming plan, the incumbent felt confident that its own plan would pre-qualify its bid. This left the decision to turn on a winning cash bid. The masterstroke – but still a gamble – was to decide to risk a low minimal bid price with no viable competitive bid likely to emerge, and if it did emerge, for it to pass the programming quality test. But how low?

With no credible pre-qualifying competition left in the game, any sum from one pound upwards could be the winning highest cash bid. They decided on a cash bid of only £2000 (though they had several other cash bids ready just in case somebody emerged at the last second) and handed it in to the regulator's staff with only a few moments to spare just before noon on bid day. For once, a bidder beat the auction system, perfectly legally and ethically. They conformed to the bidding rules and their bid was compliant. They won the bid.

the bid price. Bidders make higher profits by default. A better bid strategy for clients lacking experience of a particular market would be post-qualifying bid negotiation. In general, if the value of the purchase is high enough to justify the time and effort of negotiating, then treating all bids as padded bids may be preferable as a strategy to SD.

This section discusses two opening bid strategies recommended by a few consultants in the guru class of advisers on negotiation strategies. That they are plausible is part of the problem of their impracticality. Understanding why they are impractical enlightens you and provides a more practical approach to opening bid strategies.

Some negotiation strategists, transferring dubious advice from general negotiation strategy on the derivation of entry prices, advise bidders to choose an entry price close to the client's exit price.

Figure 8.1 shows that such a strategy means the bidder or seller adopting an entry bid price of p close to the client's exit price b in the bidder's range cs. This strategy is strange because the choice of the entry price in any negotiation should be a price that is credible and defensible in the circumstances. It is strange too in the bid situation, because p is well inside the bidder's/seller's range of cs. Therefore, adopting the strategy of choosing an entry price close to the client's exit price implies that the bidder/seller abandons prices in the range cp!

If the client, assuming it possible, follows the same choice of an entry price in the bid situation as the bidder of opening close to the bidder's entry price p, the strategy requires an entry price close to the bidder's exit price of s at p', well inside the buyer's/client's range, ab, and thereby abandoning prices in the range ap'. Effectively, the strategy advises negotiators to narrow their normal negotiating ranges from ac to sb.

Surely, reply advocates of opening close to the client's exit price, this is a half-plausible suggestion because it conforms to the experience of tender

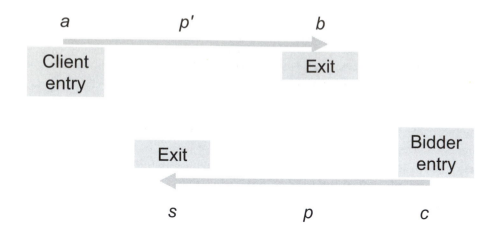

Figure 8.1   Entry strategy opening close to client's exit price

situations? Tenders, they assert, tend to narrow the negotiating range, which is why firms use the tender system! That is true, for SD bidders, who are likely to open nearer to their exit price than to their free negotiation entry price. Each experienced party can make an estimate of the likely cost of a product which one of them makes and the other intends to use. But, as neither the bidder nor the client, nor the parties in general negotiation, know the other's exit prices, advising them to open with entry prices close to the other party's unknown (and unknowable) exit prices in practice is disingenuous. It is a theoretical strategy which for most purposes is inoperable. I asked one of the advocates of this strategy how he knew the other's exit price and he replied: 'I did not say that it was easy,' a wholly flippant reply.

Those who advocate the strategy advise negotiators to open bidding close to the other's exit price and not at the exit price, which would raise eyebrows at the implied precision of their strategy. And anyway, how close is close?

Among trainers of negotiators, the name of Dr Chester Karrass is well known. He headed the largest negotiation skills training company in the USA and, probably, the largest in the world too. He had considerable senior procurement experience in the US aerospace business and at age 42 left Hughes Aircraft to study negotiation behaviour for his PhD. Once he completed his PhD in 1968, he realized he was onto a gold mine. He developed a (unique, at that time) negotiation skills seminar, 'Effective Negotiation', which he heavily advertised in aircraft in-flight magazines and won the attention of thousands of business managers the world over in his target market, eager for help in improving their negotiation skills.

One of the enduring recommendations of Dr Karrass was the advice that negotiators should always follow the strategy of 'aim high' in determining their entry demands or offers. If selling, enter with a high price; if buying, enter with a low price – the shock-them-with-your-opening-offer strategy. This clearly has implications for negotiators when preparing a bid for RFPs, or when responding with 'indicative bids' (quite common in mergers or acquisition negotiations, or in the purchase of a large block of shares in a company).

I shall explore the Karrass aim-high advice and you should reconsider my comments above when assessing the advice to open close to the other party's exit price. Both the open-close-to-the-buyer's-exit-price and the Karrass aim-high strategies have flaws in them and may not be workable in practice. If so, what is the better way to decide on an entry price?

First, I examine the evidence that Dr Karrass used (Chester Karrass (1970), *The Negotiating Game* (New York: Thomas Y. Crowell)) to support his popular aim-high assertion.

One hundred and twenty negotiators met to work through the experiment. They were characterized as skilled or unskilled negotiators by two of their managers familiar with their negotiating abilities, and were paired into negotiating sets. They were briefed on the experiment and given either a plaintiff or defence attorney's kit containing details of the case and other information of a private nature. The case concerned a claim by the plaintiff that a prescription drug had caused eye damage, which the defendant drug company disputed. These details were studied for 30 minutes. The pairs then negotiated for 60 minutes.

If agreement was not reached in 60 minutes the outcome was classed as a 'deadlock'. All agreements were analysed to compare results across the 60 pairs and the negotiators were classed as either 'winners' or 'losers' depending on the degree to which the damages outcome favoured the plaintiff or the defendant. The extent to which the negotiators won or lost was also ranked and related to the skilled or unskilled categories pre-allocated to them.

In addition, for some of the experiments the case notes and references to precedents were altered to introduce a relative power dimension and thus also attempted to capture the effects of power as a variable on skilled and unskilled negotiation performances. The claim was for US$2 million. A few of the unskilled negotiators were also coached to explore the differences, if any, skill levels made to the outcomes.

Karrass claimed that the results showed that:

- People with higher aspiration levels won higher awards than people with lower aspiration levels.

- Skilled negotiators with higher aspiration levels did better regardless of their relative power.

- Large initial demands improved the probability of success.

These seem pretty clear-cut results. No wonder Karrass recommended an aim-high strategy!

Yet there are two problems with the conclusion. The first is that the evidence is not conclusive. Other results from the experiments suggest the exercise of a degree, at least, of caution in asserting that the aim-high strategy is appropriate. For example, his report of the results include this statement:

- Very high, unexpected initial demands tended to lead to success rather than failure or deadlock.

This introduces the spectre of deadlock, always a worrying outcome in negotiation, though it also downplays it as a frequent outcome in this case. However, other conclusions from the experiments also relate high aspirations with some probability of deadlock and together they raise questions about the unqualified validity of an aim-high strategy:

- Persons with extremely high aspirations who possess power succeed phenomenally *if they do not deadlock*.

- Obstinate persons *deadlock more frequently* than conciliatory persons.

- When one or both negotiators have extremely high aspirations the *probability of deadlock is higher* than if neither person has high aspirations (emphases added).

Another problem with the conclusions is quite worrying:

- Unskilled negotiators improved when they had power, skilled negotiators did not.

Power, a variable introduced to some of the experiments, had a disproportionate effect on unskilled negotiators, raising their performance quite dramatically. It is as if the awareness of their relative power had a greater positive effect on their assertiveness than the advice to aim high – apparently they did not need the advice to aim high if they felt more powerful than the other party. And skilled negotiators actually lowered their aspiration levels if they felt the power balance was strongly in their favour, unless the other negotiator was overly aggressive, in which case they raised their aspiration levels.

Karrass does not report on the net effect of losing or deadlocking across the whole group. For the aim-high strategy to be dominant over any other strategy it would have to produce a higher total value from its successful outcomes, net of the deadlocked cases, that was greater than the total value of a greater number of successful outcomes from the lower aspiration level cases (with fewer incidents of deadlock).

But its fundamental flaw is common to quite a lot of expert advice on negotiation:

- It requires a degree of discretion ('high' to one person may not be 'high' enough to another).

- Advice of this kind is not replicable.

People applying the advice to aim high may choose such a wide range of interpretations of the meaning of 'high' that the advice is insufficiently precise. In banking, interest rates are counted in basis points, or one hundredth of a per cent. For some situations, six basis points is a high number; in others, 20 basis points is quite low. What is the guidance value of aim high in these situations? It is just too vague.

And that is the problem with zero-sum negotiating. The advice is not replicable by others and it always requires some special feature not always present in all or most situations. Sure, the situation is always decisive, but situations vary and advice that is only replicable in special circumstances is next to useless if you are required to use the advice in situations that do not include the special circumstances.

What entry price strategy, then, is replicable and workable in most situations? My answer is to pay close attention to the determination of your entry price (one that is credible and defensible), which has the benefit of being under your control, unlike the other party's entry price and their unknowable exit prices, and, of course, that Avis counter-staff don't know the difference between an IBM speaker's card and a staff card.

CASE STUDY

Implausible Advice

A well-known negotiation guru in the United States (not Chester Karrass) included an extreme example of plausibly sounding advice, which was so blatantly inappropriate that it was amazing that audiences did not comment, though they probably were happy to be entertained by him.

His most blatant impractical advice was headed 'How to Get a 40 per cent Discount off Avis' (the global car rental company). He explained how he had been a speaker at an IBM function and had been given a lapel badge complete with his photo with IBM in large type on it ('in case I forgot who I was' – cue laughter!). So, when he went to an Avis rental desk, casually he laid his IBM 'identity' badge next to his credit card. The

red-coated Avis desk clerk saw IBM on the badge, assumed he was an IBM employee, and promptly discounted his car rental charge by 40 per cent.

Simple? Yes. Was it advice that could be replicated? No.

How could you try this ploy (assuming you were inclined to commit a passive but clear fraud under quasi-false pretences) unless you too had been a guest speaker at IBM and had kept your photo ID card?

A good story – presented brilliantly – but not replicable by listeners. As advice for negotiators it was dead in the water; likewise, with advice to open close to the other party's exit price, or to aim high.

Entry-price padded-bid strategies

Negotiating a simple product's price poses certain problems for the parties, of which not knowing the other party's exit price is only one. The more complex the product, and the more its sale or purchase impacts on the affairs of other negotiators, the more the problems associated with the transaction have to be considered when the parties make their entry offers to commence the negotiation dance in a sequence of traded movements within their negotiation range.

Factors that might be considered in deriving an entry price include:

- The capacity of the seller's available workshop and machinery for the proposed order book if the bid is successful, and the impact of a lost bid on the company. Substantial spare capacity in a firm or in the sector suggests a softening rather than a hardening of entry prices.

- Winning a bid has the side-effect of depriving a vulnerable competitor of needed work to keep it in business. Therefore, the presence of a financially vulnerable company, or one determined to enter the market, could mean an unusual softening of all competitors' entry or bid prices, leaving the stronger bidders with an additional quandary when choosing their entry prices. None of

CASE STUDY

Trade-Offs

A major concern of a UK company specializing in the manufacture and installation of deep-sea underwater cable systems in a bid for some small-scale but scarce work was that it needed the work to keep one of its manufacturing plants ticking over for six months. There were five companies in the world which could undertake such a project and on average only three projects a year came up for tender, leaving the average failed bidders with insufficient work for up to six months to run their plants close to a break-even half capacity. This put pressure on the tender team.

Related to this consideration was the fact that the company needed a minimum volume of work to maintain existing capacity, and to retain its skilled workforce, support its R & D activities, and its sales, marketing and tendering teams.

In a high-technology business, expensive R & D is unavoidable if the company is to remain a player over the next three years. In the undersea cable firm, R & D had developed 'redundancy' in its seabed repeaters, considered crucial for the competitive reduction in downtime from the current norm of below 20 seconds towards 10 seconds. Access to this winning technology, and an ability to offer it packaged with the cabling for the small contract, took much of the pressure off the tender team in determining its entry price in almost a direct trade-off of the much-valued reduction in maximum downtime to 10 seconds for a similar price that they had bid successfully for the previous contract that met the 20 seconds target.

CASE STUDY

Low Bid Too Far

A Japanese construction company's bid for a hospital building contract in the Middle East came in at a surprisingly low price that would, in the opinion of rival firms, not cover its labour costs. In the post-qualifying negotiations, none of the other bidders were willing to match the preferred bidder's prices or get close to them.

They pointed out the government's vulnerabilities through the usual informal channels and warned of the consequences

of new entrants destabilizing established markets. When the Japanese company, as predicted, went bankrupt and the government approached the losing bidders for one of them to take over and complete the hospital building contract, they all refused, preferring to make clear to other potential clients in the region the dangers of exploiting predatory pricing from new entrants or near bankrupt bidders, and to other suppliers who might consider making wild bids in future.

CASE STUDY

Low Price, Low Quality

A major UK firm in the transport industry sought bids from five major training companies specializing in securing improvements in customer services (for which the purchaser had an appalling public record) for its 90 000 employees. It split the bid up into its seven regional organizations and asked bidders to indicate for which region or regions they wished to bid.

One large global training company regarded the regional areas as of insufficient size to warrant only winning one or a few bids because the revenue stream from bids that competed with smaller local suppliers would not support its normal profit targets. Its analysis of likely rivals, most of them small players with small turnovers, suggested they could make individual regions profitable from low entry prices, but few if any of them were likely to bid for the whole national contract. On this basis it decided to bid for all the regions on offer and to manage the programme as a single national project.

While the profit rate (4.76 per cent) would have to be smaller for each bid price to defeat local suppliers and win each region's separate bid contests, its absolute total profit across the seven regions would be satisfactory (about £1.05 million on a £22.05 million turnover). It also considered that winning this prestigious bid would lead to other more profitable contracts with other large employers.

In the event, its bid was unsuccessful because the national transport client was unconvinced the bidder could manage such a large quality improvement programme, not withstanding its low entry price, and subsequent PB offers.

them knows what to expect from a new entrant, or how to counter desperation survival pricing.

- The prospect of new, follow-on business from the client, or other similar clients around the region, acts to temper overly high bids even from settled bidders.

The contractual risks of managing a successful negotiation should not be ignored. At some estimated level they would tend to restrain downward movements in the entry price. Risks tend to harden moves against a lower entry price and to restrain casual acceptance of compliant clauses required by the client's RFP such as:

- demands for tight warranties and indemnifications;
- imposition of penalties for delivery and erection on site;
- performance bonds, especially where irrevocable and unconditional and subject to drawdown at the absolute discretion of the client (sometimes an invitation to corruption or theft);

- high retention percentages;

- volatile costs for elements of inputs to the product;

- loose *force majeure* (excusable delay) criteria allowed;

- unusual performance specifications or technological design risks;

- reliance on third parties for elements of the programme;

- termination without-cause provisions, or one-sided termination for-cause provisions;

- unstable foreign exchange rates, or non-convertible currency;

- risk of late introduction of a requirement for a counter-trade transaction;

- non-independent judiciary system and the governing law in the other party's jurisdiction;

- security risks – transport to or from sites located in high threat areas;

- political risks – government agencies not subject to rule of law, for example.

Activity
for Chapter 8

Activity 8.1

Why is choosing an entry price close to the client's exit price difficult to apply in practice?

COMMENTS ON THIS ACTIVITY

If the other party's exit price is not known it is hit or miss whether a chosen entry price is close to the client's exit price. So, to choose an entry price close to an unknown, and probably unknowable, exit price exposes the dubious quality of the advice!

Requests for Proposals

CHAPTER

9

Introduction

In a tender process, potential clients invite supplier companies to study a document called a 'request for proposal', or RFP, detailing what they require, and if they wish to tender for the project they must respond positively by a specified date and time that they can meet the technical specifications, and also state their indicative commercial terms, including an indicative price.

The RFP sometimes asks for an outline on how they would undertake the work and in some cases, such as consultancy, this produces (unwisely) a detailed account of what the consultancy would do to solve whatever problem for which the client is seeking help. The risk in the consultancy providing too much detail on how to undertake the project is that this constitutes free revelation of its intellectual property rights and know-how. Some firms compare consultancy replies to RFPs and then opt to do the project themselves, using the freely offered insights from the top consultancy firms. The other risk is in being too vague: it creates the impression that they are not competent enough to undertake the project at all, or at least not as competent as rival consultancies, which are less vague. Getting the balance between transparency and opaqueness is an art form. Many consultancies employ people who prove to be outstanding at replying to RFPs and winning the bids, even if they would make less than excellent consultants.

Underselling their services is another risk for a consultancy firm making indicative price bids. Subsequently raising an indicative bid price is not easy after they win the bid and wish that they had bid higher. Some firms, desperate to win the bid, offer an extremely low indicative price, in the (sometimes forlorn) hope they can recover their costs by a proliferation of 'variation orders' every time the client changes its mind on what it wants. Unless the client has a well-established record of regular design changes, this strategy is not advised, and in all cases negotiators are advised to check carefully the clauses relating to variation orders.

Response problems

The response documents used in tendering can follow a format set by the client not the bidder and the bidder is required to use the client's form. The technical and contractual specifications have two columns printed down the right-hand margin, one headed 'compliant' and the other 'non-compliant'. Against each item the bidder is instructed to tick (or check) one of the columns to indicate whether it can or cannot meet the client's specifications. Tender officials from the client prefer to see all the ticks in the compliant column and few, or preferably none, in the non-compliant column.

At meetings between the bidder's tender managers (the people in charge of administrating the tender process) and their production staff (the people who will deliver the product if the tender is successful), things can become heated if there are too many, or even any, ticks in the non-compliant column. The fear of the bidder's tender managers is that ticks in the wrong column might provoke the client's tender staff to declare the bidder non-compliant and on these grounds reject the bid without further consideration. As tender managers are judged by the contracts they win, they do not like being thwarted by fussy technical colleagues who compromise winnable bids by posting what they regard as minor deviations from the RFP's specifications. If what is unimportant to others is very important to you, there is vast room for heated rows in these circumstances.

Clients use the compliant/non-compliant format for good reason: it tends to force bidders, no matter how reluctantly, to agree to comply with the stated specifications and within their bid price and thereby forces them to carry any extra costs of doing so within their indicative price.

One of the reason for clients using a bidding process is to put maximum pressure on suppliers – indeed, virtually to intimidate them – into bidding their lowest price for the work in the belief that the threat of sudden death from lower bids from competitors forces the bidders to sharpen their pencils and to bid low final prices for the stated specifications.

Once clients allow non-compliant exceptions, they open the door to negotiation. As important, if the psychological restraints of blind competitive bidding, which aims to curb suppliers from price padding, are relaxed, the effect may be (such news often leaks out) to reduce the disciplinary effects of bidders not knowing what other bidders will bid. Bid pressure is exacerbated when bidders only get one shot (sudden death) at winning a bid.

In practice, some specifications are difficult to price from the start. Unusual architectural features (difficult shapes, unusual materials, untried water-sealing surfaces, heavy weights of glass shapes hanging at unusual angles, striking designs of unusually shaped and suspended stairs or ceilings, and so on) may worry a bidder's pricing team if the technology to build them is not well known.

The architect's drawings may be too general for accurate pricing. Artistic imagination and life's limitations are not always identical – compare the original lines and shapes, and price, of the Sydney Opera House with the building that was built (or use the Scottish Parliament as an example). These factors create a need for negotiators to have some means of signalling a degree of non-compliance without being charged with submitting a non-compliant bid, especially before being given a chance to explore or negotiate alternative design options.

The bidding problems of suppliers trying to cost for various uncertainties when working at the frontiers of existing technology are mirrored by the problems for customers trying to assess the costs of procurement and choose between different bids. The tighter are the specifications of the products they invite suppliers to bid for, the higher the front-end design costs imposed on the customer, not the supplier – it is the customer's spec, not the supplier's.

Ironically, customers tend to increase the complexity of their specifications because they want to turn the bespoke products they buy into commodities, so that they can compare bids from different suppliers selling the products they have specified! The results are different. They make quasi-commodities (simple products almost the same in design and performance) into tightly specified bespoke products, which also reduces competition because few suppliers wish to over-specify the commodity product lines they make and sell (pencils, oil cans, spanners, coat racks and so on) to certain customers, often the government, which are no longer suitable for the non-bespoke market!

Customer attempts to specify simple office commodities, like pencils or slightly more complex commodities like watering cans, too tightly leads to over-specified products with many pages of densely packed detail, and cost estimates to match. Dependence on government orders may not be a good strategy.

CASE STUDY

Non-Compliance

In a bid for a contract to supply heavy all-terrain 'up-country' vehicles for a Department of Defence, the bidder, specializing in the design and manufacture of such vehicles, felt unable to comply with four items in the RFP:

- 5-year technical warranties on the vehicles' engines, which required the design and testing of special air filters to deal with desert conditions and semi-submersible waterproofing for rainforest conditions;

- high penalty clauses on late delivery of any vehicles, with which the supplier had concerns about the higher than normal risks of delays due to R & D uncertainties about the air filters;

- the price of the vehicles and their spares which did not allow for the R & D uncertainties;

- the consequential loss provisions, which are seldom acceptable to suppliers – the bidder preferred a low liquidated damages clause.

To signal non-compliance without early disqualification, the supplier did not tick either column but wrote against each of the above clauses in its response to the RFP: 'understood, wish to discuss'. It succeeded in getting to the next stage of the bidding process.

Post-RFP negotiations

Except in public tendering regimes, where absolutely all contact between the supplier and the customer is conducted at arms length and not across a table with both parties present, it is normal and expected that suppliers and customers will have at least one meeting.

This can take the form of a suppliers' conference, which brings to the same room at the same time a number of potential suppliers to hear a presentation from the customer's procurement team on what they are looking for and how they will conduct the selection process, during which some of the suppliers present may ask questions. Suppliers tend to be inhibited from asking questions, other than those for general clarification, in case they provide rivals with gratuitous intelligence. Where there is a known or suspected 'preferred bidder' present – an informal status accorded on grounds of the bidder's recent performance as a main supplier to the customer, or an actual status announced by the customer at the conference – the body language and general demeanour of the preferred bidder's team is carefully scanned by rivals for clues as to their confidence and their chances of holding onto their status.

Suppliers who respond to the RFP issued at suppliers' conferences seek subsequent meetings with the customer's selection team, providing that their responses indicate a possibility (or desirability on the customer's part!) of an agreement. This is where the post-RFP negotiations begin in earnest and where the extent to which your response to the RFP, including its selective padding, could prove significant, as long as the negotiator remembers that padding creates room for trading and not unilateral conceding!

Identifying the other party's relative ranking (priorities) of negotiable issues becomes important in the contact phases of the negotiation. The terms of the deal are inter-dependent and not separate items to be agreed individually. In large contracts price cannot be divorced from risks. A nominally large price accompanied by severe risks of expensive penalties and liquidated damages may be a worse deal than a lower price with lower risks of manageable penalties and liquidated damages. Hence, avoid negotiating on a separate item-by-item basis ('nothing is agreed until everything is agreed'). Faced with a demand that you must reduce the overall price of the project if they are to continue with the meeting (a dominance ploy), you do not need to comply with an offer of an isolated concession ('OK'), or resign yourself to the termination of the negotiations. You can open consideration of expensive (to you) items in the specification as a means of reducing your prices provided there are compensating moves elsewhere. Listening is not identical to agreeing.

In negotiation, you always have a choice of how to frame your responses. In this case, your measured response could be: 'Provided that we can agree to a reduction in your proposed penalties for late delivery, then we will be prepared to consider the overall project price.' You answer the domination ploy without isolating the price issue by offering an unspecific trade on the penalty issue. Conditional trading is not an option; it is an imperative. It is a tool for micro-strategy discussions within the team too.

The RFP itself constitutes a proposal from the customer and, by virtue of post-conference meetings, the customer puts the RFP into negotiation. With both the RFP and the supplier's response on the table for negotiation, cross-linking between the issues guided by the preparatory assignment of priorities to all of the issues ought to be an acceptable basis for conducting your negotiation towards an agreement.

Strategic choice of bid targets

Businesses would waste a great deal of money if they tendered for every RFP they receive. Tendering is not cheap for large contract operations. Some defence contracts can easily cost millions of pounds just to respond to the RFP, before the bidder orders materials, prepares workshop drawings or cuts metal. Bidders have to be selective about what they tender for, which means they should have a method of deciding between the RFPs they should respond to and those they should not.

At any one moment in a tendering process, competing firms approach the bidding phase from different situations and pressures. A competitor with, say, a full order book of successful tenders approaches a bid differently from another competitor, which has reduced, say, its capacity recently because of successive failures to win new tenders. Additional pressures are felt if its existing projects are close to completion, leaving it without profitable or any work in the pipeline.

Commercial rivals soon find out who won and who lost recently available business. They may hint or spread rumours of the financial vulnerability of losers to deter clients from letting their contracts to dangerously low bidders, who allegedly might go out of business before delivering their products (known as spreading 'fear, uncertainty and doubt' or the FUD factor). Clients too, aware of which bidders are in trouble and willing to take risks, could impose tighter warranty terms and draconian indemnities on them as a condition of awarding them contracts (known as 'thumping them with the fist that feeds them').

Two rivals could have full order books and both could be working at capacity, but one of them may be working less profitably than the other, due perhaps to having bid too low in a recent tender, or because of the unforeseen design and rework expenditures required to meet the client's specifications. The firm in difficulty might be very keen to win a tender to increase its profit rate. The so-called 'level playing field' often isn't, and the disadvantages of a bidder in a tendering situation may have nothing to do with the behaviour of rivals or the client. Players bring their own problems to the bid process.

Bidders and the process method

Bidders should identify their objectives from their business plan. The need to win a minimum amount of new business is a commercial imperative when existing contracts are completed and spare capacity emerges in people and other resources.

At a minimum, the amount of new business a bidder must win to remain in equilibrium roughly relates to its output capacity. This number specifies

---

CASE STUDY

Benign Collusion

An internal fitter and finisher of office buildings was extremely busy with current contracts for several architects. It won its competitive contracts largely on the high quality of its work, finished them on time and within budget. One of its larger customers put out a RFP for a medium-sized contract worth about £1 million. There was no way the fitter's firm could refrain from responding because the firm of architects seeking bids was a major source of work for them – they had several fitting contracts worth £7 million each on the go from this architect. The fitter did not want to antagonize such a good customer.

Simply putting up its prices may not be enough because one of the firm's architects had revealed, in casual conversation during progress discussions on another site, that his firm was desperate to have the job started by the end of the current quarter and completed by the end of the next quarter.

Unable to manage such a project to these time constraints, and because he did not know what price his rivals would bid for the work, he did not know by how much of a mark-up he had to bid to deter the architect from choosing their bid.

After much thought, the MD decided on an unusual approach to the boss of a rival firm at a social gathering. He revealed to his opposite number in the rival firm that he did not want to bid for the work but would have to for reasons his rival would

understand. If his rival would reveal his true bid price he would reveal his likely bid price and ensure that his price was sufficiently higher than his rival's (whatever that amounted to) for the rival to win the bid with a lower (but profitable) offer.

His rival hesitated to reveal such commercially sensitive information to his longstanding rival, but did so eventually after the MD, to show his good faith, revealed what he thought the RFP was worth in costs of overheads, fitters' wages, materials and profit. This price was close to the price the rival's estimators had pencilled in for their firm's bid. The MD then added twenty eight per cent to stated price and said that this would be the bid price he would submit in response to the architect's RFP. After further discussions the two MDs shook hands on their deal.

His rival won the contract. Afterwards they went back to competitive blind, non-collusive bidding.

NB: An editor commented on the illegal nature of this behaviour. Yes, it is, but that is not the point of the example, which is to show how real-world negotiation dilemmas are resolved in practice. Neither the architect nor the client was cheated; the architect got the same price that the MD would have bid in the tender. The MD did not want the job for his firm and he deliberately over-bid. His illegal collusion established what not to bid and the margin to over-bid, leaving nobody worse off.

---

its sales target for the quarter or the year. A firm's market share is a clue to its required successful bid ratio (its market share compared to its RFP responses divided by its number of successful bids). If a firm has 10 per cent of the market for its standard products, then it will not do better normally than one successful bid for every ten it submits; if it has 30 per cent of the market, it will not do better normally than one successful bid for every three it submits, and so on.

Sales directors who expect their sales staff to sell to every prospect using their sheer charisma and dedication have unrealistic expectations. Some sales managers belong to the sell-snow-to-Eskimos school of sales fantasy, which is a sales manager's fast route to demoralizing good sales people. Fruitless exhortation to exceed the sales ratio derived from market share is unhelpful. There is little worse for sales people than chasing unrealistic sales targets set by unrealistic sales managers.

The annual sales of a company times its bidding success ratio is a rough target indicator of the minimum total value of business they should tender for per year, all other factors considered. Hence if the sales value for the year to fill your production capacity is £15 million and the current bid success ratio is one in ten, then the value of the RFPs they should respond to is about £150 million worth a year. If you bid for much less than this amount, with no improvement in your success rate, then you may fall short of your required annual sales target and suffer from over-capacity; if you overbid and win more than your capacity you have the reverse problem of overstretching your capacity – customers suffer delays to the completion of their projects, and you risk penalties.

You can reduce the total you bid for by increasing your success ratio, perhaps by targeting more selectively those bids that you are likely to win. If you could raise your success ratio to 1 in 3, your total bid target would fall from £150 million to £45 million to fill the same annual capacity. It would also save on tendering costs and perhaps on staff costs too. One of the problems of being more selective is that bids you are likely to win are not received in a steady sequence and the temptation to bid for what turns up may prove irresistible.

Consider the perennial problem for the lone consultant who decides that their target quarterly income is to be £15 000 (the amount matters less than the principle) if they are to keep what they describe as an acceptable work-life balance. Let us assume that they reach £5000 in the first month and £5000 in the second week of the second month. They are on target with two weeks to spare in the second month and a third month to go to the end of the quarter.

What do they do if a consultancy assignment is offered to them in week three of the second month worth £2000? Do they undertake it or turn it down? If they undertake it, they will move ahead in revenue and time targets. They will have earned £12 000 out of their £15 000 target for the first quarter.

Suppose they take the £2000 assignment and rationalize to themselves that they can take time off before the end of the quarter. But if by the middle of the third month they have received no enquiries about their availability for an assignment, they are now short by £3000 from their quarterly target. They face the prospect of having to take enough work to generate £18 000 for the second quarter to be on target for their annual £60 000 target. If they generate £15 000 for the second quarter, they are still £3000 behind their target, so the problem is repeated until they clear it.

But they are not out of the woods if they exceed their quarterly target from a highly paid assignment which takes them to £25 000 for the second quarter. They are now well ahead in revenue but have to consider what happens if work dries up in the third quarter. They come under pressure to undertake work as it is offered in case they receive no assignments for several weeks or months. They disturb their work-life balance.

Of course, managing to improve the RFP hit rate is no simple matter, as many a sales director knows. There is much more than a sales force to be paid for and managed. Expensive tendering staff analyse the RFPs by:

- assessing the project's engineering, construction or design difficulties against the firm's capabilities;

- estimating all costs involved in delivering the final project to the client, including design, manufacture, assembly, delivery to site, fabrication, commissioning and acceptance;

- conducting detailed market research on the customer's bona fides and financial status (due diligence);

- assessing the political risks of the territory they operate in, or through which the product must travel;

- exploration of the physical site to check for access problems, hidden geological features;

- checking on applicable local laws and planning regulations for doing business;

- analysis of the political security situation, risk assessment and estimation of likely contingencies;

- drafting the legal terms and conditions to protect the supplier's interests;

- managing potential sub-contractors;

- financing the transaction;

- negotiating the contract.

These staff costs can amount to millions of pounds on a large project before a contract is signed. The costs of undertaking this necessary work carefully can also run into large sums even in small projects (as can undertaking the task carelessly).

The cost of tendering raises the interesting question, debated by contractors and government agencies over the years: who pays the costs of an organization's failed bids? If there were 5 bidders and it costs £1 million to produce a credible bid, then £4 million has been spent without earning a penny.

There is no guarantee that a tender will succeed. Careful selection of tendering priorities is easier to theorize about than to practise. There is a well-known romance affecting (some) staff to varying degrees from their long association with a proposed project during the evaluation process. Even the most unlikely of projects can attract champions in an organization, not so much from its inherent characteristics, as from other circumstances, not always openly disclosed, such as the:

- plant needs the work;

- client is otherwise important to the organization;

- politics are important for some reason;

- prestige factors predominate;

- chairperson's need 'to win';

- government has asked the organization to oblige for 'reasons of State';

- organization desperately needs the income;

- assertion that it will do down serious competitive rivals to snatch it from their grasp (rivals may bid high so as not to win the bid).

Not winning sufficient bids suggests a need to downsize the tendering teams, but breaking up an expensive team of expert tendering specialists is easier than putting it together again. The alternative is to maintain a less than successful team by leaving it idle for long periods.

CASE STUDY

Which Bid Strategy?

A high-tech defence firm specialized in radar and guidance systems for combat aircraft and for naval vessels armed with missiles (its unofficial motto was: we make 'hit-tiles not miss-iles'!).

The scale of defence orders from European governments is such that tendering costs per project are always in the multi-million pounds range. The bid hit rate is very high, because of national defence politics, but the bidding process enforced by the Ministry of Defence (MOD) is prolonged, subject to continual technical evaluation and revision, on-going and regular (expensive) changes in the design specifications, and continual rewrites of the bid estimates. There is no possible way in which the MOD would behave differently in these matters given its monopsonist powers as the sole buyer and as sole approver of overseas sales of defence equipment.

The defence firm faced a real problem. Its radar and weapons guidance systems were the most advanced in the world and its two main platforms for the systems were supersonic combat aircraft and naval combat ships (submarines, frigates and aircraft carriers). While the technology was similar, the systems developed for each main mode (air and sea) were different. Beyond the basic science in the systems, separate design teams, R & D resources and manufacturing plants were required and the evolution of the systems was now such that the maintenance of both resource streams was crippling profitability because the phasing of new orders bore no relation to the firm's required capacity utilization for profitable revenue generation (that is, marginal cost less than marginal revenue). The MOD, historically, was uncooperative and would do nothing about contractors' suggestions that it should phase its

tendering and ordering systems to suit its suppliers ('hungry suppliers are tamer suppliers').

This created a serious strategic problem for the defence firm. It could not sustain two separate design, R & D and manufacturing organizations for advanced combat radar and missile guidance systems for two different platforms, without regard to the revenue streams generated by the sole customer's future ordering programmes. With the MOD, its future ordering programmes were at best opaque and normally shrouded in secrecy (the Cold War had a few more years still to run).

The defence firm calculated it could sustain one and a quarter separate organizations (one working at full strength, the other at under half strength) if it knew which weapons platform (aircraft or ships) was likely to predominate in production over the next ten years (nobody at that time foresaw the end of the Cold War and the sudden collapse of Soviet and European communism). These strategic questions, and the attendant commercial imperatives, were the subject of several meetings of the directors and the heads of sections comprising the separate teams. To some of these meetings, experts from outside the firm were occasionally invited.

At one such open meeting, a visiting specialist in defence procurement with excellent contacts delivered a short paper on the future procurement programmes of the MOD. The consultant's paper detailed the platforms planned in a long procurement pipeline for the next fifteen years. The most striking feature of the list was the predominance of investment in naval vessels (surface and submarine), compared to the single programme of a replacement combat aircraft for the air force.

At the time, a new combat aircraft dominated press publicity and public discussion about defence. Very little was mentioned about the naval programmes. Yet the naval programmes together were many billions of pounds greater in total value compared to the one and a half billion pound combat aircraft order (the lifetime costs of maintenance, retro-fits and upgrades were scheduled to carry on well into the future). The expert asserted that no new combat aircraft designs were under consideration at the MOD.

More importantly, the phasing of the expenditures on the two platforms was biased towards naval procurement for the immediate future and the next five to ten years after that, because the bulk of the tendering for the combat aircraft and its guidance and missile components was completed, while the naval programme was yet to get fully underway. Some large elements of new frigate orders (60 per cent of the cost of which consisted of electronic components) were about to be released soon as RFPs; an aircraft carrier with cruise missiles was agreed in principle but not yet defined or designed, and new hunter-killer submarines were planned but not nearly ready for RFPs.

Later, at internal meetings, the directors and the senior managers accepted that if the contents of the expert's paper were reliable (which they were), they could safely reduce and stand down the aircraft R & D and tendering teams, immediately concentrate on R & D for naval orders and switch the released resources to form much enlarged naval design and production teams.

This strategic shift in priorities proved highly successful in the coming years as the anticipated stream of RFPs for new naval electronic defence equipment was released by the MOD. Bids were made for major naval contracts but not for air force contracts, except those re-orders of existing equipment designs, for which tooling and manufacturing capacity was in place or mothballed and available with minimal set-up costs.

The MOD teams engaged in naval procurement were responsive to the competitive bids from the defence supplier and were not influenced by the separate procurement teams conducting the much smaller procurement orders for the few aircraft programmes in progress. With such a concentration of RFPs, bid responses, bid negotiations and production programmes, where the bids were successful, strong negotiating relationships between the MOD and the defence contractor's teams were built up throughout the next ten years. All this followed from identifying the correct bid strategy from the beginning.

Activities
for Chapter 9

Activity 9.1

Has your organization ever been close to running out of work below capacity? What effect did it have on your bid selection? Did it make it more selective or less?

COMMENTS ON THIS ACTIVITY

The prospect of an empty manufacturing plant, or an idle (and expensive) design team, normally concentrates the minds of those responsible for winning new orders. Companies in this position are keen to win RFPs, even at low profit rates, to keep them in business or to keep their key teams together, and they tend to expand the number of tenders they bid for, even by canvassing for low-value RFPs at special prices.

Activity 9.2

If you were in the position where you did not want to bid for a particular RFP because you had too much work on and the RFP was not likely to be profitable enough for your targets, and should you win it, you would overload your already full schedules, what might you do if you believed that not bidding for the RFP could jeopardize your relationship with the client?

COMMENTS ON THIS ACTIVITY

Not bidding at all is sometimes a desirable but impractical option. Regular clients expect regular suppliers to respond to RFPs and can react negatively to suppliers who cherry-pick RFPs to suit their own convenience. However, bidding carries the possibility of winning the contract and where this result carries risks for the supplier – the work is outside their expertise, is disruptive of available capacity, is too small an order for significant profit contribution or is not worth the trouble it causes – the dilemma of bid/no bid is perhaps best answered by a deliberately uncompetitive high-priced bid.

Activity 9.3

What would you do if your consultancy work was done well ahead of your planned annual work load? Take work as it is offered or take time out from consulting as soon as a monthly, quarterly or annual target is reached? What happens if work dries up on your return to look for consultancy assignments?

COMMENTS ON THIS ACTIVITY

The variability of consultancy work makes it difficult for single consultants operating on their own to maintain the work-life balance they sometimes seek, especially when they have left a high-pressure job for what they see as a less pressured role as an independent consultant. If you intend to sell your scarce expertise to whoever will buy it for the time you wish to make available, you may find it more difficult than you imagined. Even if you reach capacity, most likely you feel compelled to keep going; in your non-availability, disappointed clients search for substitutes, among which are consultants from the big four consultancy firms (who tend to search for lone consultants with marketable expertise to employ them in their area of expertise, not covered by the consultancy).

The big consultancy firms face the same dilemma because of the variability in their workloads, which they solve by moving consultants about the country, often in teams, for short spells in an effort to cope with the feast or famine in assignments. If you join one of these firms as a consultant, you soon find yourself back in a high-pressure job, except you are on the move more than you planned for. Turnover in consultants, independent or with the big four, is high for these reasons.

PART III
Applications

Analysis and Diagnosis 1

CHAPTER

10

Introduction

I introduce some practical tools for analysis and diagnosis to improve the preparation of the Negotiation Agenda and its negotiation. They can be used:

- in complex negotiations with multiple issues at stake where the debate phase is likely to be filled with arguments for and against competing options and influenced by intrusive events;

- in competitive negotiations in which more than one player is negotiating with a client for a high-level project and there are differences of preference within the client's team for and against the proposals reaching the table;

- where there are uncertainties (and erroneous certainties!) of the balance of power present within the negotiating team about whether to reject or accept the latest proposals;

- where there are multiple stakeholders in play.

Managing a strategic negotiation is largely about preparation before ,and reassessing earlier preparation (from feedback and review) during, the negotiation sessions. The simple tools discussed in this module clarify and develop the necessary tactical adjustments to existing thoughts about process, personnel and policies that will deliver the organization's strategic objectives.

Force field analysis

The force field diagram is a simple doodle (of the back-of-an-envelope kind) presentable in varying degrees of complexity, depending on what is at stake. It is easy to comprehend and to construct, and it is a powerful tool for visualizing the forces present in a negotiation (not all of them at the negotiating table) that help or hinder the achievement of the Negotiation Agenda and the implementation of what is agreed.

Force field diagrams originated in Kurt Lewin's *Field Theory in Social Science* (1951) and they have gone through many developments and adaptations as management educators and practitioners disseminated them in management courses. Originally designed for use as an organizational change model, they are used nowadays for similar purposes because major negotiations change aspects of the status quo. They may also be used in problem solving exercises when preferences are in conflict.

The force field diagram rests on the simple idea that at any one moment there are forces operating on a decision, some of which drive for positive changes in the status quo and some of which maintain the status quo. To the extent that the restrainers cancel the drivers, the status quo prevails, but if the drivers overcome the restrainers, the situation changes towards the desired objectives of the drivers, though not necessarily all the way. Not all the attempts to change a status quo succeed; sometimes many steps are required to achieve all the objectives of those favouring change.

Assume that you are a negotiator trying to effect a change. Using a force field diagram, you identify the forces present in the decision-making situation and divide them into forces for (drivers) and forces against (restrainers), and assess the relative strengths that each force has on the decision. You may note on

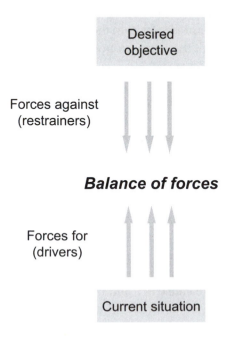

Figure 10.1   Force field diagram

the diagram, by the usual simplifying designations of 'H' (high), 'M' (medium) and 'L' (low), the degrees of importance of some forces over others.

Those forces designated as highly important attract the most attention (assuming they can be strengthened or weakened), although a typical error in negotiation and influence is to attend mainly to those forces easily neutralized or driven backwards, irrespective of the significance of doing so. For example, we tend to spend more time talking to those already on our side, or expanding on themes with which we feel more confident, and tend to avoid difficult people who do not (yet) agree with us. We also avoid discussing strong themes that oppose what we want to achieve. When both sides engage in this behaviour, we get a 'dialogue of the deaf', tetchy exchanges and, sometimes, personal abuse.

For each force in the field, you need to develop specific strategies to weaken or strengthen those that are important, the presence or absence of which is consistent with the achievement of your objectives. This calls for the exercise of good judgement, for you must not only discriminate by the degree of importance of the force as a determinant of the outcome, but also by its sponsors' susceptibility to the influence of argument and the prospects of persuading them with a suitable exchange sufficient to gain their agreement. Modification in your and the contending parties' objectives will probably be required, there being no such thing as a free lunch

Figure 10.2 expands the generic force field diagram by adding the three categories of people, arguments and events. The people arrows identify the key players on each side of the negotiation. We should always remember that organizations do not negotiate: it's the people in them who do. Identifying the other players and discussing privately how they approach the issues, their influence on their team's commitment for or against the issues at stake and how they evolve their preferences, is important intelligence gathering and should not be neglected. To assume that nothing changes in the other team during a negotiation is pure folly; it is likely that our side's team responds to the dynamics of the negotiation with uneven and uncoordinated changes in its perspectives and preferences, and it is fair to assume this is true for the other team too.

I do not subscribe to personality profiling of individuals during negotiation. All people have personalities and all people negotiate and frankly much of what passes for the personality profiling of negotiators is unconvincing, with a fair dose of consultant-speak running through it. The arguments or themes chosen by negotiators to present and re-present their case indicate clearly by

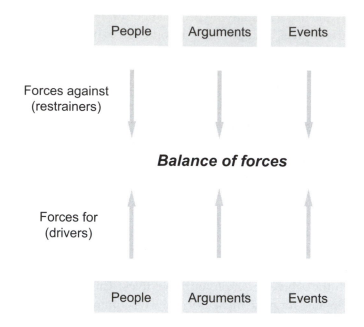

Figure 10.2   Force field diagram: additional categories

what criteria they judge the weight of the case for or against a proposition as the argument unfolds. There is no need to make imprecise and unreliable assessments of their personalities to predict how they are influenced by ideas – just listen to what they say in the negotiation exchanges.

The arguments arrows identify the arguments or themes used by the negotiators. Needless perhaps to say, arguments do not mean furious rows between the players, though rows are not precluded; they refer to the cases people make and not the tones in which they express themselves. You should think of them as something like the arguments of a mathematical function. The arguments of negotiation encompass a rich field of disaggregated meanings as you exchange cases for and against ideas and propositions, exchange arguments about facts and exchange opinions, views, predictions and assertions.

The events arrows refers to those events, historic, recent or possible which impact on the debate and proposal phases of the negotiation. Events can change the arguments used and dislodge or bolster the support of some of the people on either side of the force field. The balance of an argument may shift if some unanticipated event occurs during the negotiations. For example, a collapse of trans-Pacific freight rates during negotiations to order a fleet of container ships from Korea, or news of the outbreak of war close to oil pipelines delivering

---

CASE STUDY

Unexpected Event

Negotiations to purchase an interest in a business trading in China were interrupted by reports in the Chinese newspapers that the CEO of the Chinese company had been arrested on charges of attempting to bribe a local bank manager into making him a loan (HK$20 million). When the local press confirmed details of the arrest, the charges and the ex-CEO's first court appearance, negotiations were adjourned (politely).

---

crude out of Kazakhstan during negotiations to close excess refining capacity in France, are events bound to affect outcomes.

The execution of a negotiating strategy depends on the shifting dispositions of the players in the face of surprise events. Most likely, you do not control the impact of events on any of the forces for or against your strategic objectives. You can only seek to influence their impacts while you cope with whatever they bring to bear on you. How the players are disposed to your objectives at any one moment is influenced by the relative strengths of the arguments made for or against your or their objectives. People, including you, are also influenced by the views expressed by other people not at the negotiating table, who express their views away from the table and beyond your rebuttals, and others, who may be competitors, or hostile commentators in the media, prowling around looking for an opening to intervene.

You certainly need to become aware of the arguments against your proposals and the cases supporting them, and must not (dare not) confine your attention merely to the merits of your proposals as you see them. If you are to weaken the case against your proposals, it usually takes more than a rehearsal of the arguments that support your case and, almost certainly, it takes more than spirited attacks on the individuals on the other side who oppose you in varying degrees.

When UK Prime Minister Macmillan was asked, just before he retired from politics, what he feared most in his political management of government, he replied, poignantly: 'Events, dear boy, events,' which was a point made somewhat more poetically, though no less poignantly, by Robert Burns in his lines about the 'best laid schemes o' mice an' men' going astray, or the lament of the person battered by a string of bad news: 'it's just one damn thing after another'.

To ignore the influence of *events* on your strategic negotiation objectives would be a serious mistake, all the more so when those events are surprise intrusions on your 'best laid schemes'.

The force field diagram, though simple in concept, has great scope for enrichment through the inclusion of new detail and its rearrangement. Remember it is a doodle, not a work of art, and can be redrawn at will on a white board or flip chart as many times as you like – but always make sure you wipe the board or shred your charts when finished with them. Carelessness could make your doodle into an event!

Constructing a force field diagram provides a structure by which you sift through a mass of disparate detail to separate the important from the trivial. Prioritizing the importance of the forces for and against your desired objectives, and assessing the relative difficulties of strengthening or weakening some of them, should produce activity agendas that progress the negotiations. To achieve such objectives requires strategies for your negotiation and related activities.

One caveat, worth noting just here, is that experience suggests that it is often easier to weaken the other side's pressure than it is to strengthen your own. This creates problems for you of maintaining your balance if the objective you seek is bitterly contested. You should not want to appear to be overly negative when attempting to weaken the other side's pressure to maintain the status quo and you should curb your frustration when tempted to personalize the disputed issues.

Expanded force field

Gerald Atkinson's two books on negotiation, *The Effective Negotiator*, 1975 (Newbury: Negotiating Systems Publications) and *Negotiate the Best Deal: techniques that really work*, 1990 (Cambridge: Director Books/Simon & Schuster) are riddled with the kind of sound advice that practical negotiators recognize as worth heeding. In this section and the next, I shall present amended derivations of Atkinson's basic models as expanded force fields, because I have found them useful in practical applications when dealing with complex cases.

Atkinson called his ingenious and enriched expansion of the original force field diagram an 'expectation test'. He started from the basic premise that negotiators bring to the table their expectations. They also, implicitly at least, have to deal with the expectations of the other party. Indeed, the opening debate phases of the face-to-face contact between the parties can be described as being about structuring the expectations of the other side. By this Atkinson means lowering the other side's expectations, or, as he puts it memorably (after Charles Dickens), 'turning [their] great expectations into little ones'!

I usually illustrate expectations by using the diagram in Figure 10.3, which shows the relationship between your perceptions of the other party's power over you to be inversely related to your expectations of the outcome. This links neatly to what we know of the role of manipulative streetwise ploys in negotiation debates.

The stronger you perceive the other party to be relative to you, the lower your expectations of the outcome in your favour, and vice versa. In other words, if you perceive them to have high power over you, then you have low expectations of the outcome being in your favour. Likewise for the reverse; if your perception of their power over you is low, then your expectations of the outcome in your favour will be high. In general then, your perception of their power over you influences your expectations of the outcome.

In this context, it is helpful to remember that all manipulative ploys, as advocated by streetwise negotiators, aim to weaken your expectations by manipulating your perception of the power balance between you. If you believe they do not need what you are offering in a trade, you are unlikely to feel as confident as you would be if you believed they desperately needed it. By hiding their degree of desperation – indeed, feigning that they are almost uninterested

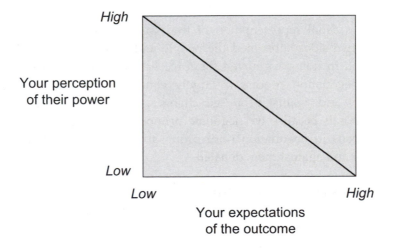

Figure 10.3   Perception of power/expectations relationship

in the deal – manipulators believe they can induce a lower price from you than would otherwise be open to them.

There are other more sophisticated influences on your expectations besides crude manipulative ploys. The expanded force field examines the expectations that are present – yours and theirs – and suggests that you should think about how they might be handled in and before the negotiation.

If we define the interests of negotiators, as they see them, as their 'hopes, fears and concerns', then their expectations of the negotiated outcome relate to the extent to which various proposals, stated in terms of negotiable issues and positions within ranges, address their interests. They always have the option of not agreeing to any proposal that does not deliver enough of their interests in the circumstances to justify their assent. Concurrently, during the negotiation exchanges, events and other pressures may intrude and cause them to modify their earlier rejection of certain proposals, as they originally stood, and change a no into a maybe, and, perhaps, eventually into a yes.

In the negotiation of changes to and defence of the status quo, which covers all negotiated outcomes whether a change is agreed or not, the persons driving the change are characterized by their hopes exceeding their fears, because though both emotions are present, the former exceed the latter, and the persons restraining the change are characterized by their fears exceeding their hopes. This is precisely how Kurt Lewin's force field visualized the balance of forces between drivers and restrainers, and why it has proved to be so useful in practice.

Atkinson's visual representation of the issues present in a negotiation between the two sides subsumed the people and events categories into the arguments and in doing so moved the force field onto new and interesting territory. A negotiation process is largely conducted by the exchange of arguments for and against proposed changes. Fundamentally, negotiation is about proposals because we negotiate proposals, not arguments. Indeed, nothing happens in negotiation until proposals are counterpoised and the arguments for and against them debated.

Figure 10.4 shows an expanded force field, with the wording altered slightly to conform to the 'Four Phases' approach in which all negotiations are conceived of as universal processes, incorporating the phases (in any order) of prepare, debate, propose and bargain (see Kennedy 1997, *Kennedy on Negotiation*, Gower). The top half of the diagram is a mirror image of the other side's assessment of their expectations of your choices. The force field diagram illustrates the two sides' stances and expectations, related to a balance of forces, now read as the 'negotiation movement area'. The diagram focuses on our own party's preparation (steps 1 to 5 and 7); debate (step 6); propose and bargain (negotiation movement area); the same could be done for the other party, if sufficient data were available. In practice, if there is enough time taken to prepare our own case, that leaves insufficient to do other than try to anticipate some areas in the other side's case. I find it better to concentrate the

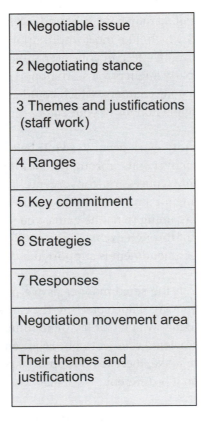

Figure 10.4   Expanded force field

Notes: Issues mean negotiable issues, or wants; Stances are short statements of your principle behind an issue; Themes are what you are going to say and develop on the negotiable issues ; Justifications demonstrate the validity of your views on the issues; for example, a justification for a substantive issue of a price change could be that an increase in input prices justifies the price increase; Staff work supports your stances, especially the research for facts, statistical and other evidence to support your themes; Ranges cover the positions you adopt on an issue; for example, expressed as your entry and exit prices; Key commitments reinforce your stances, including the negotiating ranges, and are best served by carefully honed short sentences or phrases from team discussions that capture the essence of what you are trying to achieve by your proposals.

negotiating team's attention on preparing the staff work for their own case. Once they become familiar with preparation and as they engage with the other party, they naturally become adept at making similar force fields for the other party.

In your preparation you should think about their likely stances on the substantive issues and their justifications, and how you might handle them. It is better to undertake this work in advance because trying to improvise across the table in the midst of a negotiation relies too much on your verbal agility (which some of you but not all may have in abundance, while the rest of us try to muddle through), and which, like most impromptu speech, leads to gaffes and unintended disclosures. In effect, in your preparation you look for possible arguments that the other party might propose in support of their stances and how you would respond with your counters, which could also include considering modifications to your original notions of your stances and justifications.

Undertaking preparatory work generates your better responses, including your offers of traded movements through conditional bargains. Traded movements do not include 'concession convergence' (they move, you move, with neither of you moving for a particular reason other than playing a haggle game), as in zero-sum bargaining (what he gains, you lose). Negotiation is the management of movement through exchanging conditional propositions, and crucially each proposal or amendment is supported by speech contributions.

We do not negotiate in the same manner as we play in a card game, in which our silent statements are made solely by the cards we play, or the bets we lay, and in which sequence we play or lay them (think of bridge, solo whist or poker). Apart from occasional calls as to our requirements from the banker or dealer, or the plays we make, there is no room for speech during a playing session. But in negotiation it is different.

Our speech contributions make all the difference to the perceptions of the other party at each and every moment of a negotiation session, as the other party's speech contributions affect us too. And this is true whether our speech contributions, including our answers to their questions, make good sense or nonsense, or anything in between. Even our tone and manner can affect their perceptions and their reactions can affect ours.

The advantages of using an expanded force field diagram is that it compels you to focus on other issues beside the ones you normally think of – mainly your own – and to think as well about the issues and the arguments supporting them that we believe the other party is likely to bring up. It prepares you for the likely justifications or arguments they might use in support of their proposals. By thinking beyond your wants, represented by a number or the wording of a contract clause, you prepare answers to that most common question: 'How do you justify that number/wording?'

In effect, the expanded force field exercise prepares you for the debate phases of negotiation, proportionally the longest of the face-to-face sessions. (I believe debate accounts for about 80 per cent of the negotiating time it takes to arrive at a determination of a negotiated outcome.) It is the most productive way to use the short time available for preparation at any level of complexity, but at the higher level it is an absolutely essential tool for analysis and diagnosis.

By thinking ahead of your better responses to their justifications of their numbers and wording, you approach preparation in search of what Atkinson calls 'rich themes', that is, powerful parts of the persuasion process during the debate and proposing phases. The better themes are always linked to your strategic objectives, if only in your own mind, and serve the dual purpose of adding credibility to your statements and of keeping your objectives in mind during the negotiation.

The expanded force field diagram brings the pro- and contra-arguments visually into direct confrontation. It does not tell you what you do not already know, but it reminds you of the significance of things you do know and what you may have to deal with without notice across the table. The usual and varied unprepared answers put forward in such circumstances may not be the most effective responses to challenges from other negotiators.

I worked for some months with 200 of a bank's corporate relationship managers along these lines by asking them to report on the common arguments they heard from their corporate customers in response to different bank proposals. This produced quite a list, many of them familiar to everybody present. The outstanding feature of this exercise was the wide variation in the credibility of the reported individual responses used by the relationship managers when they responded to their customer in their negotiations. Many of the (weak) responses fully explained their lack of success, and incidentally their unhappiness with negotiating specific bank policies.

The first step to putting right this problem was to task them in small groups to develop written responses and counters, and to select from them those thought most likely to be effective because of their credibility to experienced managers. The expanded force field formalizes such useful work and, when tackled by a negotiating team together, it generates greater fluency in their debate behaviours and their impact across the negotiating table. Undertaking this exercise regularly before major negotiations has a dramatic effect on the negotiators' performance.

The expanded force field diagram can be used when there are multiple issues for negotiation. Selecting the most important from a proposed contract could still produce ten of them in the average business negotiation (and many volumes more in really large high-value negotiations). To illustrate an application of an expanded force field, I shall take a single negotiable issue in a major competitive negotiation (competitive with rivals not the client!) to describe the method.

CASE STUDY

Rail Bidders

Take a controversial negotiable contract such as buying total management services from an existing national supplier with considerable long-term experience in the industry versus buying the same from a foreign supplier reputed to have a high degree of competence which compares favourably with the competing bidder in the same industry in the buyer's country.

Suppose we consider the management of a large urban rail passenger transport service, managed separately from the main national rail network. The RFP calls for a complete takeover of the urban rail system, track and trains, and its daily management, including an investment programme over the lifetime of the contract, presently set at 10 years, to upgrade track, stations and signalling systems.

Deciding on a contract with a national or foreign supplier is the first major decision around which all the other issues revolve. But the decision also depends on the details of the total packages each bidder offers to the Transport Commission charged with processing the RFPs. However, to go into

such detail here to illustrate the application of the method would provoke you into despair of ever making practical use of the techniques! I shall, therefore, tackle a single issue only, as this brings out enough of the method in outline for you to understand how to apply it to multiple issues in complex cases, remembering that the amount of effort spent in preparation for any negotiation should be commensurate with the value to you of the transaction.

First, I shall consider an important element of major headline contracts that may be ignored until realization seeps in that a bid was lost for want of elementary attention to the facts of complex-bidding life, where the potential rewards are high enough (for example, the survival of a bidder as a major player in the industry) for the bid negotiations to be decided by other than the pure merits of the bid.

It is important that you recognize that not everything in a negotiation, including major strategic issues like national or local versus foreign or distant, is decided from the arguments presented to the people present at the negotiation table. True, those present are charged with conducting and concluding the negotiations but, as major negotiations take time to reach a conclusion, and the participants are involved in other managerial or directorial activities besides negotiation, including meetings with interested parties away from and at arms' length from the negotiations, there is a constant transfer of information from the negotiation and into the negotiation reflecting various sorts of outside influences on the participants.

The scope for outside intervention increases as the importance of the negotiation is recognized by those not at the negotiation table, especially where emotions or politics are involved, as they tend to be the longer the negotiation lasts. Among these outside influences it is difficult to disregard that of the government officials and politicians. A conclusion from realizing the importance of these types of pressures on the negotiators from outside of the negotiations is to prepare to exert influence on those others besides the people present or close to the table.

Let us assume that two competing organizations are short listed to undertake the urban rail management project, subject to negotiating the contract. Call one organization 'Virgo Rail' (the national one) and the other 'Grande Vitesse' (the foreign one). I shall represent Virgo in this exercise and my task is to put Virgo into serious contention for the contract on the merits of its bid and turn the client away from favouring Grande Vitesse's bid without giving proper consideration to Virgo. You might call this a level-playing-field operation.

However, to complicate matters, let us also assume that within the client's team, for various reasons, there is a body of opinion that favours Grande Vitesse, not the least because of perceptions of the relatively poor historical record of

Virgo in the management of the national network. Grande Vitesse is less well known because the rail network it manages is abroad. Therefore, members of the client's negotiating team have not been subjected to regular press reports of this or that problem in various parts of the foreign territory where Grande Vitesse operates, at least not to the extent that they have been informed about Virgo's operations by the home media, pressure groups and local politicians. It is possible that the preferences of some members of the Commission's team may be biased by lack of adequate comparable data.

The strategic goal of this portion of the negotiation is to neutralize, or reverse if possible, predilections in the client's team in favour of Grande Vitesse based on incomplete information. If successful, this opens the way to comprehensive good faith negotiations of Virgo's proposals, rather than Virgo merely playing the other-player role under the bidding rules, while the client privately already accepts in its mind Grande Vitesse's proposals and discounts Virgo's.

In anticipation of the client's unchallenged perception that Grande Vitesse has a better record than Virgo in managing its national rail system, implying that Virgo will not do as good a job as Grande Vitesse in the Urban network, the Virgo team should prepare a careful rebuttal, should it be necessary if this subject is raised by members of the client's team, or made in public comment about the negotiations released by anti-Virgo elements close to the client. It is prepared as background material to the bid documents and develops data on the comparative safety and performance records of the two bidders. This requires detailed staff work to collect, analyse and present the relevant data (to be held on file, with prepared short summaries distributed to the negotiators) and to examine sources of hostile data as they are introduced into the public debate, including material fed to the media from whomsoever, with a view to rebuttal as the occasion arises.

Suppose that Virgo believes that the client's negotiators are asserting a stance that requires Virgo to accept that its comparative record on managing its rail system is not as good as Grande Vitesse's record of managing their rail system. Acceptance of such a belief by Virgo (which it may not have enough information to evaluate), should it be engendered by the client, would make it easier for the client to disregard or downplay the credibility of Virgo's bid and clear the way for the client's secret preferred bidder. Those on the client's team who are uninformed may simply accept what their anti-Virgo colleagues assert and, in the absence of a positive response from Virgo, may switch to opposing Virgo on a false basis.

To remain in contention, Virgo has to do serious staff work because critics of Virgo are likely to have compiled supporting evidence to back up their claims. Virgo staff, therefore, should collect comparative data on Grande Vitesse's record on safety, the usual rail performance indicators (punctuality, cleanliness, proportion of new stock, annual investment in track, state of industrial relations, employment productivity ratios, overall profitability, extent of state subsidies and so on), and the comparability of the extent of network, passenger and freight statistics, the transport mix in its home country, experience of managing networks in a foreign country, media stories about its leading personalities, boardroom stability, source of funds and so on. Such due diligence is undertaken when acquiring a business or contemplating a long-term relationship, and should be seriously conducted when competing for major business contracts against known rivals.

The object is to have detailed knowledge of Grande Vitesse (and any other bidders)

available as background material, perhaps for use in a parallel media campaign to reach the client's people who watch TV, read the press and subscribe to press clipping agency services. A media campaign requires command of accurate data, especially to formulate rebuttals of streams of anti-Virgo press stories, emanating from allegedly independent sources.

One thing to note in such campaigns is that the more subtle the dissemination of the favourable comparative data, the more in fact it is perceived as being arm's length from Virgo, and the more effective it is in causing doubts among the client's team about the significance of past negative information about Virgo. Left unchallenged, the client's belief that there is a significant gap in performance and quality between the two rail companies could lose Virgo its bid before negotiations have moved onto the positive advantages of the Virgo bid, and therefore Virgo must prepare and perhaps use an off-table strategy that aims to close the client's belief that there is a gap, detrimental to Virgo, in the bidders' performance and quality in a key area.

Conversely, to ignore what may well be dirty tricks on behalf of competitors ('we are above such trivia', and so on) is the kind of folly that undoes the most strenuous efforts to present Virgo's best proposals on the substantive negotiable issues. The two strategies – negotiate across the table and prepare a capability to influence the client behind it – are complementary. Incidentally, catching a competitor engaged in dirty tricks campaigns has proven to be significant in recent disputes between competitors in the airline business; hence it is vitally important that you insist on carefully monitoring what your rebuttal team is up to all of the time.

I shall now apply the expanded force field diagram to a negotiating issue – that of establishing the need for realistic fees, plus profit sharing – commonly found in the letting of private sector management contracts of public sector organizations. These could be in industries like rail networks, or in management of oil fields, extraction mining, supply of major platforms in the defence sector, or various public private partnerships (PPP).

Possible steps in compiling an expanded force field for the need for realistic management fees, plus profit sharing in the rail network case are shown in Figure 10.5.

The amount of management fees and the sharing of profits are two of many negotiable issues in such negotiations. There could be other forms of rewarding the chosen operator if these proved inadequate or divisive. Our interest here is in illustrating the method, not in advising on actual negotiations.

From each negotiable issue we derive our negotiation stance or what we want to achieve from the negotiation. In this case it could be something like: We require realistic fees from the client to reward

1 Virgo negotiable issue	Management fees plus profit sharing
2 Negotiating stance	Require realistic fees from client to reward risks of operating the system and to meet traffic targets
3 Themes and justifications	(a) Fees must be realistic to reward effort (b) Reductions in operating costs should be shared as an incentive, not be a one-way penalty for past built-in inefficiencies (c) Investment generating more and safer traffic should be rewarded (d) Certainties in fees assist in longer term planning (e) Profit sharing in favour of Virgo allows for earlier payback of investments (f) Management fees fund the drive to meet ambitious traffic targets
4 Ranges	(g) Fees calculated as a percentage or as an absolute amount (staff work to verify) (h) Profit shares: Entry: 80-20; Exit: 50-50 (unless fees raised)
5 Key commitment	Fees are essential to achieve the ambitious traffic targets safely
6 Strategies	1. Publicity and media coverage of how the current incentives to existing management contribute to poor performance 2. Play (a), (g), (c) and (f) as opening themes and bait, as the benefits of realistic fees 3. Play (b), (d), (e) and (h) as appropriate when moving to the details and the data
7 Responses	1. Curtailing fees inhibits meeting the client's traffic targets and endangers safety 2. Backlog of investment projects must be cleared before haggling over fees 3. Need to make profits to share them 4. Improved performance is the client's, very public reward 5. We cannot skimp on safety costs

Figure 10.5 Expanded force field applied to a Virgo negotiable issue

Virgo's risks of operating the system to meet the client's traffic targets. The quanta of traffic targets are another negotiable issue heading; hence, I have not placed the percentage or quantity on this stance, though in the real world there would be a quantified target or formula for deriving it over a specified period of time.

How the stance is to be achieved will take up the rest of the tool's entries. The next four entries – themes and justifications (which support the stance); ranges; the key commitment (which reinforces it in a short sentence statement); and strategies – are best generated in the team collectively (people who negotiate together should always prepare together – no exceptions).

At all stages, staff work is required, by which is meant detailed analysis and presentation of the data highlighting the issue, its background and past performance. Staff work is absolutely essential and a negotiating team needs support from this source of data. Specific factual data always beats broad unsupported generalizations.

The last entry detailing your planned responses to the themes presented by the other side is an extremely important contributor to the conduct of the negotiations, especially when supported by data from staff work. My examples are purely illustrative and would certainly be improved upon by team discussions among those about to negotiate.

In the above scenario I have linked a move by the client's negotiators to curtail Virgo's ambitions for a high management fee to details of the effect of this on the client's traffic targets and (higher risks) to the safety issue, always an important and sensitive issue in a railway network. I have backed this with 'we cannot skimp on safety costs'. Raising safety in association with fees is a risky move politically, if it provokes thoughts of a linkage between profits and safety.

Item 3 is a lead-in statement for an argument over the appropriate profit level; we can only share what we create and, with item 2, it suggests postponing a haggle over fees, while a backlog in investment projects is cleared (in the interests of both Virgo and the client), earning for the client its public reward from improved performances.

It is not the intention of this example to suggest that a mechanical regurgitation of the detailed arguments derived from the expanded force field is necessary or sufficient for its successful use in the negotiation. Systematic preparation is no substitute for live debate and sensitive presentation of the arguments that use the data. In the absence of detailed preparation of the type involved in the expanded force field, the performance of the negotiators at this level of detail, and throughout the likely duration in these kinds of negotiation, soon reveals the inadequacies of an ad hoc approach.

CASE STUDY

Corporate Borrowing

Another example of the application of an expanded force field in preparatory analysis is given in Figure 10.6, in this case of a bank negotiating a loan with a corporate borrower where the arrangement fee could be the negotiable issue. This fee covers the cost of the bank's staff undertaking credit analysis and the sanctioning of the loan, the credit status risk of the borrower and risks involved in the circumstances of the corporate customer.

Agreeing on an arrangement fee would be only one of many other issues involved, such as the amount of the loan, when and how it is to be drawn down and for what purposes, the interest rate, the repayment period of capital and interest, the security backing the loan and any other conditions attached to the transaction.

1 Bank's negotiable issue	Arrangement fee
2 Negotiating stance	Customers must contribute to the extra costs of analysing a borrowing request and for making a prudent assessment of the risk because loss-making banks cannot lend
3 Themes and justifications	(a) Loan interest pays the cost of money and not the costs of analysis and risk assessment and higher level sanction by bank staff (b) The larger the loan the larger the risk, and higher risks require more extensive checking by more senior analysts
4 Ranges	Determine entry percentage, then decrease in absolute amounts, not by percentage points
5 Key commitment	Profitable banks can safely make loans
6 Strategies to achieve stance	1. Publicity and media coverage of the costs of safe lending 2. Data on the costs and risks of safe lending decisions (staff work).
7 Responses	Without arrangement fees the bank loses money; loss-making banks cannot lend to borrowers

Figure 10.6 Expanded force field applied to a bank's negotiation with a corporate borrower

Activities
for Chapter 10

Activity 10.1

To what extent can you identify the people in a work situation who are in favour of a policy or organizational change from the status quo and those who are opposed to the change proposals?

COMMENTS ON THIS ACTIVITY

To change a situation, drivers must overcome restrainers. Those who wish to change the situation work to strengthen the drivers and weaken the restrainers; those who oppose the change work to strengthen the restrainers and weaken the drivers. Figure 10.1 shows a generic force field diagram. The bottom of the diagram represents the current situation; the top of the diagram represents the situation desired by those supporting the driving forces. The space in between represents the gap that either has to be overcome by the people supporting the change, or which the people opposing the change by supporting the status quo have to defend. In that space, the drivers and the restrainers operate.

Activity 10.2

What do you think would be the impact on a negotiation over warranty and indemnity clauses required by a rail authority from a train company, if news reached the negotiators that one of the company's trains had been derailed that morning in what looked like excessive speeding on a designated slow bend in the line?

COMMENTS ON THIS ACTIVITY

Almost certainly such news would sharpen the focus of the parties on the wording of the warranty clauses, probably in favour of tightening the warranty and increasing the indemnifications required by the Rail Authority.

Activity 10.3

DRAWING A FORCE FIELD DIAGRAM

Read the information below and see how it can be used to sketch a force field representation of the drivers for and the restrainers against change in a current situation.

Ahmed was in charge of invoicing orders for prescription drugs to mail order customers and was concerned that his reliance on manual processing via the postal services and bank cheques (which have to await three days before payment is credited to the company's accounts and the goods despatched) inhibited the growth of business. He proposed that the company install a bank card payment system to enable customers to place their orders and receive their goods by return of post.

He was sure that turnover would grow immediately a bank card payment service was introduced, especially for foreign customers who would no longer need to use the cumbersome system of arranging for certified cheques in foreign currency for each purchase. Moreover, the company would receive payment immediately it deposited the bank card details via its bank's terminal and this would improve the company's cash flow.

Sontag, the accounts and finance officer of the company, opposed Ahmed's proposal. It would be expensive to operate until the number of clients using the system was above 1000 a month; she would have to hire additional staff and train them; automated credit card payments were not compatible with her manual systems and would require a new bank account for secure processing; there was the risk of bank card fraud and, anyway, she and her department were 'too busy just now to take on something so new'.

Ahmed was not deterred by the negative response of Sontag – 'She always opposes anything new, which she did not suggest first' – and he looked around for allies. His boss, Fraser Du Pont, was interested but said it should be cleared first by Sontag. The auditors were relaxed about the security issues because 'bank card payments were well established internationally'. The managing director, Henri, was enthusiastic about improving monthly cash flow, but the personnel manager was suspicious about adding new responsibilities to an already overstretched department.

The best way to learn is to try it for yourself, even if you make a mess of it the first time, because in making mistakes and correcting them you clarify the signs of confusion in your mind about what you are trying to do. Therefore, as an exercise, without of course looking at Figure 10.7 (you learn little by trying to read your way through a practical tool), use a sheet of paper to draw a force field diagram that illustrates how the people, the arguments and possible events could affect the balance of pro- and anti-change attitudes in Ahmed's company. Now compare your sketch of Ahmed's force field with mine.

COMMENTS ON THIS ACTIVITY

Did you spot the need to put Fraser Du Pont on both sides of the force field?

He approved of Ahmed's proposal but insisted on Sontag having a veto: therefore, he appears on both sides.

Did you make entries in the events column?

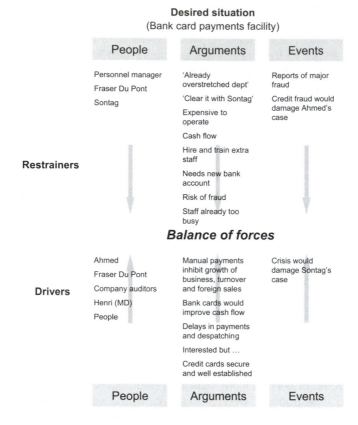

Figure 10.7   Ahmed's force field solution

These were not mentioned explicitly in the case material above, but they are surely the kind of unanticipated events that could swing the outcome one way or the other, and for your own specific circumstances you should be able to identify the type of events, which if they occurred, would influence the outcome, positively or negatively, and part of most arguments about changing anything often involves each party raising the risks of certain events occurring, or taking advantage of any events that occur during the course of the debate that assist their case or embarrass the other party's.

In the bank card dispute you would expect Sontag to search for reports of major credit problems with fraud and circulate them to the policy makers; you would also expect Ahmed to use the cash flow position to highlight (and exaggerate) the risks of cash flow problems emerging unless they do something along the lines he suggests.

Not all events in negotiation happen at the table; some events can turn a problem one way or the other to one of the solutions. With the MD, Ahmed's boss, Fraser Du Pont, and the company auditors strongly influenced by cash flow, but less so by the organizational issues ('too busy' and so on) raised by Sontag and personnel, they would be highly sensitive to problems with cash flow and threats of fraud that could swing the decision either way.

Activity 10.4

Recall when last you felt you were the weaker party in a negotiation (or indeed the stronger party).

COMMENTS ON THIS ACTIVITY

What was it about the situation that made you feel weaker? Was it the:

- *environment – very plush, unfamiliar surroundings?*
- *apparent confidence of the other party – body language, speech?*
- *history of the relationship – their reputation for tough demands?*
- *pressures you were under – time, needs, deadlines?*
- *feeling that they were indifferent to the outcome?*
- *knowledge that you did not have a strong case?*

In the event how did it go? Did you do as poorly as you anticipated or did you surprise yourself and do better than you imagined?

Activity 10.5

Take a regular negotiation subject from your line of work and select one of the negotiable issues. Complete the expanded force field of the selected issue in a table as in Figures 10.5 and 10.6.

COMMENTS ON THIS ACTIVITY

You should be able to identify a negotiable issue from a regular negotiation. Negotiable issues form the agenda for the meeting.

From the negotiable issue you next derive the negotiation stance. This states what you want from the issue and can be thought of as the principle involved in obtaining it in the manner that you want it. At the crudest, for example, 'buyers must pay the sellers an acceptable price', or 'we expect to be paid for the work we have carried out', and so on. Questions still remain, however. For instance, being paid does not specify how much or when. It simply states that there is no question of whether you are paid or not.

Themes and justifications, in the simple case above, are about how much you are paid. Your justifications can be plural; though always follow the rule that three strong justifications beat ten weak ones that have diminishing degrees of credibility. When compromised in this manner, the other party will ignore the stronger of your justifications to concentrate on attacking the weaker.

Negotiators think in ranges, not fixed positions, and under ranges you should identify the appropriate range for what you are negotiating. In banking, 15 basis points (each bp is worth $1/100^{th}$ of a percentage point) can come to a lot of money, well worth negotiating about. In a recent case I dealt with, 15 bp was worth £600 000. In a multi-million civil construction, a £600 000 cost overrun may not be much – in oil exploration a £200 000 cost overrun could be within the discretion of the rig manager. For the activity, identify your organization's entry and exit points and if relevant identify any critical aspects of how you would move within the range.

The key commitment reinforces your negotiating stance on the issue. In Figure 10.7, borrowers must pay for the bank's costs in arranging the loan – why?, 'Because only profitable banks can make loans safely.' Think of the key commitments as the because explanations that answer why 'questions?

Strategies are about how the stances, themes, justifications and key commitments are to be deployed in pursuit of the negotiation objectives and may include across-the-table behaviours as well as off-the-table and outside the face-to-face meetings.

In the activity, identify your organization's entry and exit points and if relevant identify those critical trade-offs for how you might move within the ranges.

The last row of Exhibits 10.6 and 10.7 is for collecting possible responses to anticipated counters from the other party to your stances, ranges and key commitments.

Analysis and Diagnosis 2

CHAPTER 1

Power in proposals

Power is always an illusive concept in negotiation and in relationships. This never stops negotiators from referring to it. Sometimes power is expressed by personal maxims:

> *'Whoever's buying has more power than the person selling.'*
>
> *'She'll blink before I do.'*
>
> *'He's the only game in town.'*
>
> *'I hold all the cards.'*
>
> *'We'll see who has the deepest pockets.'*
>
> *'Time is on my side.'*
>
> *'She's bluffing.'*

A replicable tool for assessing power has to have certain characteristics. Among these it should improve on hunches, wild guesses and intuition. Another is that the steps in the process are definable and, finally, the assessment criteria should be replicable by colleagues who can add their judgements on the credibility of your conclusions. One such tool applied to power develops an idea from economist, Neil Chamberlin (*Collective Bargaining*, 1951 (New York: McGraw-Hill), p. 220). The tool meets the three criteria above.

Power was conceived as a ratio that related the costs of disagreeing with another party's proposals compared to the costs of agreeing with it. This corresponds to everyday experience. If you accept a seller's proposal, the price you pay is the obvious cost of agreeing to buy; if you reject a seller's proposal the cost of disagreeing is whatever it costs you in doing without that which they were offering to sell to you, which includes what it costs to buy from somebody else.

Gerald Atkinson considered this definition of the ratio too restrictive in its original form because in the simple buy/sell case the ratio is confined to the *costs of disagreement* compared to the *costs of agreement*. It is clear, however, that negotiators rank not just their tangible monetary costs but also the non-tangible but nevertheless real disadvantages they feel from comparing two or more situations in disagreeing or agreeing, or more accurately, rejecting or accepting somebody's proposal, because in negotiation we are not simply agreeing or disagreeing – it is possible for a negotiator to be in some measure of agreement or disagreement with a proposal which, for other reasons, they contemplate rejecting or accepting.

It is not the state of agreement/disagreement alone that counts. In fact, that state could be irrelevant to the behavioural moves either negotiator makes. What counts is whether a party rejects or accepts a proposal, for rejection or acceptance is the only real measure of their behaviour and, unlike agreement or disagreement behaviour, rejecting or accepting is observable while their state or degree of agreement or disagreement is not; we can only hear what they claim or assert but we cannot test it.

Accordingly, Atkinson produced his power balance ratio, as in Figure 11.1

This introduced a ratio unrestricted by notions of tangible costs only, into a workable tool for assessing the power balance in negotiation. It focussed on the ratio of disadvantages from each action of rejection or acceptance, neatly capturing the reality of an aspect of negotiation behaviour. There are disadvantages in accepting or rejecting anything different from our own preferred position within our range of acceptable positions (our entry point); if they say 'Yes' to our entry position, we are stuck with the 'winner's curse' – we wish we had opened more favourably to ourselves; if they say 'No' to a proposal within our range, we may have to modify its terms to get a deal, or accept deadlock; whichever outcome prevails, we face continuing the

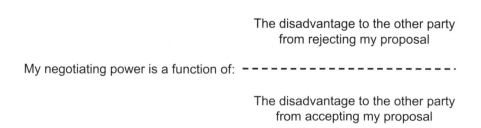

Figure 11.1   Power balance ratio

current negotiation or starting over with someone else, with its consequent disadvantages. Both options have time costs and could perhaps result in a worse deal.

Atkinson's method uses simple arithmetic to derive a feeling for the weighting of the power ratio and it can be summarized as follows:

- State the proposal that you wish to test with as much detail as you would be required to specify in the negotiations (condition and offer terms).

- List the disadvantages to the other party, both above the line (disadvantages of their rejecting) and below the line (disadvantages of their accepting), as they would see them arising in your proposal.

- Using a scale of 1–10, *rate* each disadvantage where 1 = minor disadvantage and 10 = major disadvantage from their rejecting or accepting your proposal.

- *Weight* each disadvantage in the other party's eyes for the probability that this disadvantage would have to be borne on the usual probability scale of 0.0 to 1.0, where: 0.0 is impossible and 1.0 is certain and all probabilities in between are possible in an ascending order.

- Now multiply each disadvantage *rating* by the likelihood of its occurring, the *weighting*, to give a *total* for each disadvantage and add them to produce a total for the elements above the line and for the elements below the line.

- If the disadvantages to them of their rejection exceed the disadvantages to them of acceptance, then you have power over them in your proposal because circumstances incline them to accept it.

- If the disadvantages to them of their rejection are less than the disadvantages to them of acceptance, then you do not have power over them in your proposal because circumstances incline them to reject it.

The power ratio assumes that negotiators prefer to avoid harmful outcomes (that is, disadvantages) to themselves and assumes that there are disadvantages for them in either rejecting or accepting a proposal, because in negotiation we do not (usually) get exactly what we want (our entry proposal) and getting less than we want has disadvantages, which is why we prefer our entry proposal. However, the choice between rejecting or accepting is the balance of these disadvantages; the closer to our entry proposal the other side proposes, the fewer the disadvantages compared to a proposal that offers an almost miniscule amount of what we asked for.

Where the ratio of disadvantages is in the order of 3:1 in favour of rejection, we have little or no power over them in our proposal because they would lose more by accepting it, therefore they would be inclined to reject it; where the ratio of disadvantages is in the order of 3:1 in favour of acceptance we have power over them in our proposal because they would lose more by rejecting it, therefore they would be inclined to accept it.

In the first case of 'no power' we should review the terms of our offer to lower its disadvantages for them; in the second case of 'excessive power' of our offer we should assess if we are offering too much in the offer part of our proposal and are not asking for enough in our conditions.

As the negotiations progress across numerous issues, the balance of disadvantages will change (we trade things that we value less for things that we value more) for both parties. The best deal we can get may just be acceptable because the disadvantages of rejection just outweigh the disadvantages of acceptance, but we are only marginally satisfied. If they do not do enough to tip that balance, we may be compelled to fail to agree and seek opportunities elsewhere. On the other hand (happy days!) the deal on offer may be such that it would be folly to reject it – the disadvantages of rejection may outweigh by a large margin the disadvantages of acceptance – and we may have to restrain ourselves from hugging the other party in an excess of happy enthusiasm. However, back to reality, the outcome is likely to be somewhere closer to the marginally satisfied than of the kind where we strive to remain dignified!

Subjectivism

Before developing a worked example, we should discuss the criticism raised against attempting to measure the power balance using numerical assessments. Negotiators generally are practical people; few are given to theories about negotiation, intellectually qualified as they may be as negotiators. It is not a question of ability; more a question of scepticism, born from considerable experience that has accumulated without benefit of conceptualizing about what they were doing. Hence, not surprisingly, on occasion I have found resistance from hardened professionals to using numerical power ratios.

The most obvious charge against the method is that it is open to manipulation to get the result that you want. Of course it is, but strategic negotiation is not for the stupid. Adjusting the allocated numbers to confirm what you wish to believe is sheer quackery and a waste of time. Play that futile game and it is safe for you to go back to the black box concept of power, into which nobody ever peers, and hide your subjectivism in your assertions about your own and the other party's strengths and weaknesses.

Subjective judgements from such sources are more likely to produce errors than is attempting to assess them through a disciplined method. The act of listing the likely disadvantages felt by the other side promotes valuable discussion in the team and, significantly, it produces attempts to weight this or that influence by statements like: 'this factor is more important than that' or 'that consequence is less likely than that to happen.' The power balance arithmetic adds to the discussion a clean and logical method to aid what goes on in negotiation teams, often implicitly, and as often without much thought about what they are doing. The arithmetical power balance gives the process a clearer expression of the teams' beliefs and of any differences within the team.

The subsequent discussion, once the ratio table has been assembled and calculated, offers certain tasks to the negotiating team should they wish to use them. For one thing, they can derive strategies to improve the determinants of power, that is, to change the current balance of disadvantages in favour of increasing the power balance in the team's favour and ultimately press the other side into accepting the current offer, or one close to it.

Activity directed at changing the components of the power balance as perceived by the other party is perfectly legitimate because it addresses identified barriers to the other side's acceptance of the offer as it has been presented so far. The problem does not always lie in the nature of the offer; an aspect of the offer that has not been properly presented or adjusted can just as easily cause the offer to be too disadvantageous to the other party, either above or below the line, or both. Persons using unspecified subjective feelings do not even begin to see the power balance in this constructive way, mainly because maxim-led subjectivism is not concerned with the other party's reasons for hesitating to accept or consider a current proposal, or their outright rejection of it. They are only interested in using power to enforce the acceptance of their proposals.

The overall strategy of using a power balance ratio is to identify activities that increase the disadvantages of rejecting the offer and reduce the disadvantages of accepting it. Not by altering the arithmetic but by developing stances, explanations and clarifications of what is in the balance as it stands or by changes to the composition of what is on offer in a proposal. This strategy is best illustrated by a worked example.

Power balance ratio: worked example

Consider a construction contract in an overseas country where the client (negotiating the contract for the overseas government) has proposed a heavy warranty condition to the prime contractor that the systems installed on site will be 'defect free' in its ordinary meaning for five years and 'latent defect free' for an additional five years, or ten years in all. The contractor has counter-proposed that the systems be 'defect free' for three years and 'latent defect free' for two years, or five years in all. The contractor wants to assess the balance of power in the disadvantages of rejection/acceptance of its proposal (we shall ignore all the other issues for simplicity). Table 11.1 shows the analysis.

I chose a single negotiable issue out of many that may be on the table (nothing is agreed until everything is agreed) and I am treating it in isolation for illustrative purposes. In practice, you should undertake a power balance analysis across several of the crucial issues, though in the early stages of the negotiation it may be that you appear to have far more areas of disagreement and contention, and prospects may not look good for an early or any resolution. It often looks this way to inexperienced negotiators, much as it did in Lord Nelson's opinion at the battle of Copenhagen in 1801, when he said: 'The Danish defences look formidable to children of war, but I think I can master them.' Experience teaches that the picture generally looks bleaker when you begin than it looks later on. Patience is supposed to be one of the virtues and it is certainly recommended if you negotiate regularly.

Analysis from the power balance ratio is only a first step. The information you collect and include in the exhibit becomes the basis of your strategizing to change the balance of disadvantages acting as obstacles to an agreement (and note once again, this does not mean changing the arithmetic to produce the result you want!). This means your tackling the subjective inhibitions of the other party. In this case, the consultants make the technical and commercial assessment of the total package offered by the competing bidders and make recommendations to their clients, the government's ministers, on the basis of which the government ministry makes the political decision to go ahead or not.

Table 11.1   Power balance ratio for warranty condition

Disadvantages of rejection		Importance rating,(r) (1–10)	Probability weighting (w) (0.0–1.0)	Total (r × w)
1	Possible 'deal breaker'	3	0.2	0.6
2	Hassle of switching contractors	7	0.2	1.4
3	Competence of agents in doubt (demand too stiff?)	3	0.4	1.2
4	Delays to installation of new systems	7	0.5	3.5
5	Poor investment image for the country	5	0.4	2.0
6	Minister's loss of a win	8	0.3	2.4
7	Loss of World Bank loans	5	0.6	3.0
8	Few early advantages	6	0.7	4.2
				18.3

Disadvantage of acceptance				
A	Competence of agents in doubt (too soft a demand?)	3	0.8	2.4
B	Giving in to foreign firm	5	0.8	4.0
C	Wrong signal to other foreign contractors	8	0.7	5.6
D	Risk of early defects	8	0.5	4.0
E	Government loss of face	5	0.3	1.5
				17.5

If your power assessment is honest and reasonably correct (it won't be if you cheat yourself!) then the only way you can change what it tells you is by acting to do something that alters the rejection/acceptance balance. At present the balance is 18.3 for the disadvantages of rejection and 17.5 for the disadvantages of acceptance, a power balance ratio of 18.3/17.5 = 1.046, which is too narrow a margin for you to conclude that they will favour acceptance in favour of rejection. But remember the rule-of-thumb advice that the relative disadvantages are not to be treated as unambiguous one way or the other unless the ratio is much greater, somewhere around about 3:1.

Again, for the sake of illustration, let us assume that this balance on this single negotiable issue is symbolic of all the balances on all the issues and that we can use it to demonstrate how the negotiators could strategize to shift the balance decisively in favour of acceptance. How would we set about this task?

We want to increase the perception of the disadvantages of rejecting our proposal and lower the perceived disadvantages of accepting our proposal. For this to occur we have to select targets from both sides of the line and act to reduce the disadvantages of acceptance and increase the disadvantages of rejection.

Because we would only be engaged in such a strategy near the middle and end game of the negotiation, on the disadvantage of the top line item becoming a 'deal breaker' in their perceptions, we may decide to take larger risks of this issue becoming an actual deal breaker, though it has a low total (weighted rating) of 0.6 from it not being regarded either as too important (3) or having high probability (0.2). If we are going to increase their perceptions of it being a deal breaker we ask ourselves: What can we do to raise its importance in their minds and increase its likelihood of happening?

Deal breakers in themselves are not very important when there is viable competition around, anxious to occupy the seats we might vacate in the negotiation for the large-value contract on offer. However, this is not a case of them implying to switch a purchase decision by opening a competitor's brochures and ordering two of them for delivery next week. Negotiation at this level of business complexity involves considerable time, expense and effort committed to bringing about the end game in a successful closure.

Whatever economists say about bygones being bygones in theory, in the world of business deals, switching from one failed set of negotiations to a new set of negotiations, which could also fail, imposes considerable uncertainty about the costs in time, expense and effort that might be involved eventually. When expensive lawyers stop the clock on one deal, they start (with alacrity) on a new deal – that's how they make their living – while the opposite emotions probably predominate in the minds of negotiators and their staff team when a negotiation looks likely to fail and the uncertain prospects of starting over loom.

Hence, developing themes along the lines of all the past efforts going to waste, and perhaps having to be repeated, by linking prospects of a deadlock over unusual demands for long warranties ('beyond the norm for our business') to the sheer hassle (and it is a hassle) of starting over with another contractor ('who most likely will advance a proposal similar to ours') and also drawing attention to the effects of such a deadlock on the delays to the installation of the new systems, would be some of the suggestions raised in these circumstances, as might the visible failure of our negotiations encouraging a rival firm to be that more ambitious to take advantage of the diminution of competition.

Your themes can also be supported by sub-themes related to the impact of a public failure on the investment image of the country, such as:

- The deadlock has been caused by 'expensive, though worthy, consultants who have unintentionally created this situation by trying to impose unusually high demands on warranties' and 'who earn their fees however long it takes and however long you have to wait for the completion of the new project';

- The deadlock 'is a loss not a win for the Minister' and 'will disappoint those impressed by his public enthusiasm for the project as expressed at our initial meetings'.

If the deal breaker themes in the minds of the client's consultants across the table raise the importance and the probability of the outcomes indicated, its value could be raised from 0.6.

The hassle factor of finding another contractor could raise the weighted total above 1.4 if staff work on the hassle factor showed credible data on just how long this could take under existing public procurement rules. Doubts about the efficacy of pursuing too stiff a demand on warranty and thereby jeopardizing the deal undermine the image of the competence of the consulting agents.

By working down the list of disadvantages from rejection of the proposal, including the Minister's loss of a win (highly important at 8, but not high in probability until you get to work on the 0.3) and the inevitable delays to installation of new systems (already estimated to be important at 7 but with a probability of 0.5), the weighted total could rise enough to cause the client to review their non-acceptance of the proposals and focus on how to make them more amenable.

In examining the disadvantages below the line should the client accept the deal, you should develop themes to lower the identified disadvantages. It is not a question of too tough or too soft, but of common sense. For example, the consultants would not be doing their job if they did not push at the normal frontiers on issues, but good practice must prevail on warranties. It is not about giving in because both sides have moved on all kinds of issues – that is what negotiation is about – and the final deal is the better for the give and take from each of us.

The outcome you wish to plant in the minds of the client is one that sends the right signals to all foreign contractors: 'If you want to do business with the government of Ogoland, come prepared to have your proposals scrutinized carefully and your numbers tested.' Here staff work to check on how often the client has enforced warranties on contractors might be helpful (and if they have been bad, you should be asking 'why?' questions urgently and may need to revise your current stance).

From the expanded force field tool you should see the connection between the power balance analyses and the strategies that follow from them. These determine your tactical behaviours at the negotiating table and elsewhere, especially in those activities happening outside the face-to-face negotiations. Both sets of tools give you an enormous amount of detail from your preparation time, which raises your command of the detail to a degree probably unmatched by your opposite number, but then, perhaps not, because you do not know what effort they are putting into their preparation. Remember, out-preparing the other party is one activity in negotiation where you may ethically seek an advantage over them – each party is free to spend as much time and resources on their preparation as they feel appropriate.

In practice, complex deals involve many negotiable issues and you could still have as many as eight to twelve important issues and the same again on tradables of lesser importance. You might set aside the less important issues and concentrate and complete your theme revisions on the important ones first, but this is not a rigid principle. The task of your team is to reassess properly the power balance of your proposals, though beware, what is an unimportant issue to you often has the habit of becoming more important in the negotiation exchanges because of its unanticipated importance to the other party. Because you undertake this preparatory work in the absence of the other party, it may not matter a great deal in what order you undertake the analysis, given the small number usually under discussion.

Your assessments of the power balance, written on flip charts around the planning room, for what you regard as your entry proposals to address the most important issues could produce a summary row of power balance ratios as shown in Table 11.2.

For example, if their disadvantages from rejecting your proposal add to a weighted total of 6.72 and their disadvantages from accepting your proposal add to a weighted total of 16.3, the balance of power is in their favour, marginally (you do not have power over them with your current proposal because they lose more by accepting it than by rejecting it) and the power balance ratio is equal to 0.4 (6.72/16.3), equivalent to 2.5:1 in their favour. To be wholly in their favour it would be necessary for the disadvantages from accepting your proposal to be in the order of 20.16, so that the power balance ratio was 0.33 (6.72/20.16), which is 3:1 in favour unambiguously of their rejection.

Table 11.2   Power balance ratios for proposals for several major issues

	Negotiable issues							
	1	*2*	*3*	*4*	*5*	*6*	*7*	*8*
Power balance ratios	0.3	4.6	1.1	0.2	0.04	0.6	3.4	3.0
Accept		A					A	A
Reject	R			R	R			
Neutral			N			N		

NB: The ratios are expressed as single numbers by dividing the number above the line by the number below the line.

If their disadvantages from rejecting your proposal add to a weighted total of 16.3 and their disadvantages from accepting your proposal add to a weighted total of 4.79, the balance of power is in your favour (you do have power over them with your current proposal because they lose more by rejecting it than by accepting it) and the power balance ratio is greater than 3:1.

In Table 11.2 your proposals as they stand on negotiable issues 2, 7 and 8 suggest that they might be inclined to view them favourably (the power ratios equal or exceed 3:1). On negotiable issues 1, 4, and 5 the power ratios are close to 3:1 (power ratio less than 0.33) in their favour (they have weighted reasons to reject your current proposals) and on issues 3 and 6 they have close to equal weighting and it could go either way as your current proposals stand and the power balance is neutral.

This mixture of power and lack of it across the negotiable issues is not unusual or unexpected at the start of a negotiation, or for some time afterwards. Progress across the board could be delayed by an obstinate disagreement between the parties on one or two major issues of great importance to both parties.

The information in Table 11.2 summarizes the state of play and shows there is a lot of work to do to reach agreement across the eight issues. Movement on some issues may be achieved by trading movement on other issues, so that the net effect for the negotiator is a satisfactory compensating balance for making an agreement that is less than satisfactory on one issue because agreement on another issue (or issues) is considered to compensate for disappointing their expectations and enduring the disadvantages of a negotiated position somewhat short of their aspirations. Exploring, probing and signalling possible flexibilities and movements in the normal interactions across the table achieve such trade-offs – they are rarely subject to a carefully calculated utility calculus.

As the content of your proposals (and theirs) changes, the power balance ratios will change too, and they will change from proposals linking trade-offs between them. Identifying where you can expect acceptance or rejection of your proposals provides information on the potential issues suitable for trade-offs, always remembering to trade things which you value less to gain things that you value more.

McKinsey's multi-stakeholders model

Most simple negotiations involve two parties with both present at the negotiating table or connected by telephone or email. They are beholden to themselves or to their organizations and not to third parties. Most complex negotiations involve multi-parties who have an interest in the outcome and who may be at the table simultaneously or sequentially, or may be represented by someone at the table, or (as stakeholders) they may exert private or public influence on the negotiators from outside of the negotiations.

Negotiations between utility companies and the industry regulator also have other players at or around the negotiations, including the ultimate customers of their services and inevitably politicians of varying affiliations. These stakeholders exert direct or indirect influence on the negotiators and because they do their influence should be taken into account when formulating negotiating strategies and considering proposals.

The problem for strategists in these complex circumstances is that it is difficult to assess the importance and the relevance of all the influences present during the negotiations. Noise does not always correlate with clout. Nor do all the forces have equal influence, especially where serious changes are under discussion. 'Clout' in this sense does not always submit to merit or worthiness. Indeed, sometimes the party deemed to be most suited to make a decision or to have their decision protected may be overridden by other parties acting in coalition and from what they regard as higher motives. What may have been the accepted and unchallenged traditional view for many years may be swept aside or radically modified because the other players respond to new ideas about the purposes of the activity and the responsibilities of the organization.

In an attempt to model this type of situation, McKinsey's, a global strategy consultancy, worked on a practical model for multi-party negotiations. To illustrate their work, I shall adapt a set of readily understood tools to help decision makers originated by two McKinsey consultants, Tera Allas and Nikos Georgiades, who devised a method for analysing complex negotiations among multi-party and multiple stakeholders ('New Tools for Negotiators', *McKinsey Quarterly*, no 2, May 2001). It is an excellent start in what for long enough has been an empty landscape. Recent published developments of the McKinsey model initiated by other consultants, based on the initial work of Tera Allas and Nikos Georgiades, are proving to be fruitful and I expect that the approach will spread into strategic management practice in due course.

Using the categories of 'position', 'salience' and 'clout' (defined later), devised by Design Insights Incorporated (specialists in computer simulations of political and negotiation processes), Allas and Georgiades applied them to model the behaviours of multiple parties in negotiation.

The ACPOS case study illustrates the McKinsey model using an (hypothetical) example from an issue in public policy related to policing. The original Allas and Georgiades' illustrative application devised a strategy for a public utility's negotiation with several parties, including the industry regulator. They reported excellent results in identifying and clarifying strategic goals for their clients' negotiators.

The best way to test the efficacy of a proposed tool for strategic negotiation is by applying it to an issue with which you are familiar, which is what I have done in what follows. If it works reasonably well in such a different context, then it suggests that the tool has some value. It summarizes a lot of information that reveals strategic relationships in a manner I have not seen practicable in other attempts by other methods.

The application of the Allas and Georgiades model illustrated here – the procedures for inquiring into complaints about police indiscipline – is hypothetical, though the issues involved in such a reform are very real. Hence, I should emphasize that the ACPOS case study is a fictional and not a factual exercise, and any attributions I make for the purposes of the exercise to the alleged views of stakeholders should not be taken as representative of the views of the actual stakeholders.

First, I shall define the three terms used by Allas and Georgiades:

1. 'Position' is what the stakeholders want on a particular issue, such as one of the extremes or something in between.

2. 'Salience' is the comparative importance of an issue for a stakeholder.

3. 'Clout' is how much power the stakeholder has compared to other stakeholders to influence the decision on each issue.

For each term they assigned a number from 0 to 100 to represent the stakeholder's place relative to other stakeholders.

How might we apply these ideas?

Let me take a hypothetical negotiation between the Police Services and the Executive, loosely related to a small country like Scotland, as outlined in the ACPOS case study, where policing is conducted in eight local regions and not through a nationally administered single force. Let us assume that there are four main negotiable issues on a negotiation agenda, emanating from the Executive:

1. the total budget allocation divided among the eight regional forces;

2. changes in the force structure to improve national coordination of policing;

3. allocation of certain traditional policy duties to external agencies (escorting prisoners, protection services at the courts, traffic policing including parking, and forensic services);

4. an independent complaints procedure separated from the eight police forces.

In practice, we would apply the tool to all four issues and assess our strategy across the issues. For illustrative purposes, I shall confine our application to a single issue, namely that of proposals to amend the current internally managed complaints procedure in favour of an independent complaints procedure (item 4). Its relation to the other three issues will be referred to briefly later, but essentially the same procedure would be conducted for all of the issues

CASE STUDY

ACPOS And The Scottish Executive

Senior police officers at the levels of Chief Constable and Assistant Chief Constable, the two highest posts in the UK Police Service, meet in the Association of Chief Police Officers in Scotland (ACPOS) to negotiate with the Scottish Executive (Government) for their annual budgets; these negotiations include detailed examination of their planned expenditures. There are multiple stakeholders with interests in the outcome of the negotiations, some because the expenditure plans address or fail to address closely felt (by them) deficiencies in policing and some because the more police budgets grow, the less growth there is for the government's non-police budgets (budgeting is often seen as a pure zero-sum exercise).

A partial list of the stakeholders associated with (though not necessarily present at), or interested in, the police budget negotiations includes:

- Scottish Government Ministers and senior civil servants from various departments (Justice, Treasury);

- Chief Constables and Assistant Chief Constables (ACPOS);

- Local Government authorities covering the eight police force areas in Scotland (where the police budget is spent on policing);

- Members of the Scottish Parliament (MSPs) and Members of the UK parliament (MPs) whose constituencies are policed;

- Local Councillors in whose wards the police budget is spent (or not);

- Scottish political parties with representatives across Scotland;

- Police trade unions and associations whose members are police officers of all ranks outside ACPOS;

- Officers of the Courts, the Law Society, and firms of solicitors and lawyers;

- Government departments and agencies (also known as 'quangos'), such as:

    - Visit Scotland, which have an interest in foreign perceptions of crime and policing, and bodies such as Age Concern, The Refugee Council, and so on;

    - National Health Service and Ambulance services which deal with the consequences of crime;

    - Scottish Prison Service;

    - Social Services, Education and Road Safety;

    - Fire Service;

    - Drug abuse agencies;

    - Immigration;

    - Customs and Excise;

- Pressure groups interested in policing and resources (civil liberties, local traders, business organizations, single interest groups, churches, mosques, synagogues, temples, community groups, ethnic and religious organizations);

- Voters, whose views are polled regularly to assess satisfaction/ dissatisfaction with policing as currently resourced and to assess public attitudes to crime and the threat of crime;

- The media, which report on daily crime incidents, annual trends in crime and standards of policing, and which influence public perceptions and opinions.

Most of these influences cannot be mapped into an arithmetical relationship because they are too diffuse and often pull or push in different and contradictory directions over time. The best we can do is to map those that are closest to or at the table.

At the table:

- Scottish Government Ministers and senior civil servants from various departments (Justice, Treasury);

- Chief Constables and Assistant Chief Constables (ACPOS).

Closest to the table:

- Police trade unions and associations whose members are police officers of all ranks who work within the budget constraints set by those at the table;

- Government agencies (including the quangos);

- COSLA (Local government authorities) covering the eight police force areas in Scotland (where the police budget is spent on policing);

- The Law Society, Dean of Advocates, Officers of the

Courts (Judges, Sheriffs, Procurator Fiscals).

Indirect influences in declining order of importance by closeness to the parties at the table:

- Local Councillors in whose wards the police budget is spent (or not);

- Members of the Scottish Parliament (MSPs) and Members of the UK parliament (MPs) whose constituencies are policed;

- Scottish political parties with representatives across Scotland;

- The media which report on daily crime incidents, annual trends in crime and standards of policing, and which influence public perceptions and opinions;

- Pressure groups interested in policing and resources (civil liberties, local traders, business organizations, single interest groups, churches and mosques, synagogues, temples, community groups, ethnic and religious organizations, organizers of sporting and other events);

- Voters.

Successful contenders for the highest offices in the police service have to be familiar with all the above influences on their professional work.

which would produce interesting relationships among the parties otherwise likely to be obscured for want of a means to bring them into the open. For this exposition I have simplified what is a most complex situation, and I remind you it is all totally fictional.

The issue of the independent complaints procedure lends itself to two extreme positions, namely, no change in the current complaints procedures (continue to deal internally with all complaints) and a total change in the procedure to have complaints dealt with independently of the police service. Figure 11.2 shows each main stakeholder's stance on the issue of the independent complaints procedure.

Table 11.3 Issue: independent complaints procedure

Stakeholders	Key characteristics		
	Position	Salience	Clout
ACPOS	0	95	65
Executive	100	80	100
Justice Ministry	35	40	50
Treasury	0	40	70
Police Federation	0	60	20
Law Society	70	50	15
COSLA	15	20	25

The numbers in the columns are the assessed scores out of 100 for each characteristic for each stakeholder. The negotiators in the team arrive at the (subjective) scores following detailed discussions by persons familiar with the stakeholders and their views on each category. As before, the discussions add structure to pure subjectivism as the team members refine their estimates as a result of the exchange of views.

Zero scores (for example, ACPOS, Treasury and the Police Federation) for *position* represents their absolute opposition to any change in the current procedures. For ACPOS and the Police Federation, opposition to change is an issue of principle. They argue that the best authorities on allegations of improper conduct are serving police officers and not outsiders who know little about the exigencies of the service, the mendacity of certain individuals where policing is concerned and the incidence of selective memory syndrome. They do not regard themselves as casual players or onlookers in these matters.

The Police Federation links proposed changes to the current arrangements closely to the morale of serving police officers (its members), which is confirmed by opinion surveys across the forces. The Police Federation, however, suffers from the issue of having relatively high salience (60) for them, but relatively low clout (20) compared to ACPOS (95 and 65, respectively). They remain relatively impotent to influence the negotiators, not being at the table, though their position against reform is widely known to the negotiators from ACPOS and the Executive and account of their views is taken to some degree.

The Treasury is opposed to a change because changing existing procedures tends to have (always expensive) financial implications and this particular change has not been budgeted for in the government's forward spending plans. The Treasury's viewpoint tends to carry weight in inter-departmental decision making.

A score of 100 (the Executive) indicates the proposal for reform originates at the highest level politically. The Executive wants to set up a completely independent complaints procedure, reflecting the views of Ministers, some of whose constituents have been vocal over recent years about the time taken for the police to complete their enquiries into each other's conduct and their alleged failure to find in favour of complainants, except rarely. This has become a political issue recently, and not just among Opposition MSPs. It is argued by critics that the time taken to decide on complaints represents an institutional reluctance to pursue even serious complaints of inappropriate behaviour and the usually negative outcomes show a bias in favour of the police protecting their own over justice for the complainants.

For the Justice Ministry, the score of 35 suggests that it is in favour of some modest reforms well short of total separation of the complaints process from the control of the police service. The Justice Ministry, by its nature, works closely with the police authorities and is well informed on the morale and personnel problems that could be caused by a total separation of the complaints procedure from serving officers. This has to be set alongside public cynicism over the occasional cases of miscarriages of justice, as highlighted in the media whenever there is a decision not to prosecute or discipline those who are perceived to be delinquent police officers.

The Law Society, acting as a surrogate for the legal system, is scored at 70 because it broadly favours fairly major reforms but does not go all the way with the Executive; its low score of 15 on the clout characteristic reflects its lack of influence over the other players, particularly the Executive, which tends to view the Law Society's members, all lawyers, as having a financial interest in creating new legal structures, because of the associated legal fees for themselves. The Executive and many MSPs tend to discount some part of the Law Society's advocacy on issues close to their financial interests.

COSLA (Convention of Scottish Local Authorities) has a relatively low *position* score of 15 (and relatively low scores for salience and clout on this issue) and this reflects the politically divided nature of an organization divided on party lines, and its relatively conservative (small 'c') net disposition towards reforms of existing institutions.

[I remind you that this is a fictional and not a factual exercise, and any attributions I make for the purposes of the exercise should not be taken as representative of any particular stakeholders.]

Figure 11.2 takes the analysis to the next stage, that of the 'outcome continuum', which graphs each stakeholder's relative dispositions for and against the reform proposals.

ACPOS, the Treasury and the Police Federation are opposed to any reforms to the existing police complaints procedures and are at the no-change extreme, with the Executive (Scottish Government), because they favour maximum change, at the opposite extreme.

In between these extremes are COSLA, Justice and the Law Society. The average of all the participants pulls down the momentum for maximum reform from 100 to 31.4. This distribution suggests that on a straight one-party-one-vote, without bargaining, that there would be some degree of reform passed, but not as much as the Executive wants or as little as ACPOS prefers.

Even at such an early stage in the negotiation preparation, ACPOS strategists should realize that they may have to alter their current strategy of a stubborn no-change approach to the Executive's reforms. Certainly the message illustrated in Figure 11.2 is clear: reform in the system of investigating police complaints procedures is definitely gathering momentum and likely to move up the political agenda. Once the Executive begins considering proposals for reform in a high-profile issue like complaints against the police – perhaps kept

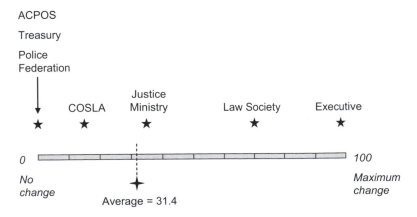

Figure 11.2 Expected average outcome: pure compromise vote, no bargaining

alive by some recent event (never underestimate the importance of *events* to strategy) – a do-nothing stance is inappropriate (unless an event swings public opinion dramatically in favour of the police, though public opinion is fickle).

In the absence of such a fortuitous event, senior police officers should begin to realize that the ACPOS policy of no change at all may not be their best response for much longer. When the pressure for change hardens politically, mitigation of its effects may be a more prudent response than not accepting any change at all because the Executive's influence on promotions within and to ACPOS could gradually swing the composition of ACPOS in favour of accepting draconian reforms, whereas a strategy of controlled mitigation of the reforms could slow down change to a manageable level (that is, within the perceptions of ACPOS). This conclusion leaves negotiation to mitigate the Executive's reforms ('death by a thousand exceptions') as part of a negotiated package of all four issues on the agenda to arrive at a viable alternative rather than a total change.

To confirm this conclusion or revise it, ACPOS strategists construct what Allas and Georgiades call a 'stability analysis' of the police complaints procedure issue (Figure 11.3).

This matrix is based on mapping the distance of a stakeholder from the average (31.4) and the combined scores for salience and clout. Initially at least, ACPOS and the Executive are likely to be unhappy with a straight compromise on the single issue of police complaints procedures and would probably prefer to continue disagreeing to proposals on the issue, even deadlocking on it. The Executive, of course, could resort to legislation to force ACPOS to accept the proposals, but this would run counter to a government's predilection for gaining support for major reforms on a negotiated and voluntary basis. ACPOS would prefer not to confront the Executive on a single issue when it has the other important issues to negotiate. In that context, a traded exchange might become possible, with the Executive challenging the modified outcome as insufficient and ACPOS reluctantly agreeing to support the compromise outcome on grounds of damage limitation.

The four boxes of the stability analysis matrix show the disposition of the stakeholders for the police complaints issue. The two left-hand boxes separate the Police Federation and the Law Society (unhappy with their limited power to influence the outcome) from the Justice Ministry and COSLA (neither of which have enough power to influence the outcome, nor are they highly concerned enough about it, though near to the average).

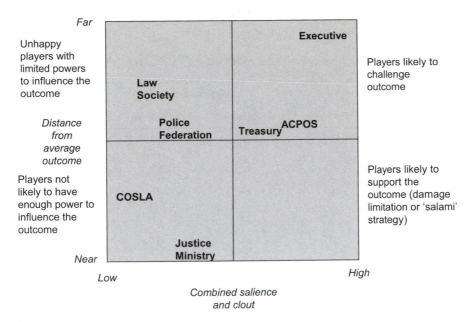

Figure 11.3 Stability analysis for the police complaints issue

The right-hand upper box contains the Executive and ACPOS, the two main players, and greatest in distance from the average, and both sharply divided on the principle of reforms, plus the Treasury, all of which have high salience and clout. These players are likely to challenge the proposals; unfortunately for a decision, they are strongly divided on the proposal.

One conclusion the ACPOS strategists can draw is that they need allies if they are to mobilize them to mitigate the impact of the reforms proposed by the Executive. It is already clear that a package across the four issues should be negotiated and Figure 11.3 shows the disposition of the players towards the four issues. It might be helpful for the ACPOS team to draw force field diagrams to summarize the cases for and against each proposal to confirm what they assume is the balance between them.

Looking at the tabulation of the stakeholders from the ACPOS point of view as potential allies, opponents and those of uncertain allegiance in Table 11.4, ACPOS could be reasonably certain that every player at or near the negotiating table, except the Executive, was on its side in its opposition to, for example a proposal to form a national police force because a national police force was contrary to the way the police had always been organized in Britain and opposition was borne of tradition and deep suspicion of such a radical innovation in British policing. Tradition in such long-standing matters carries great weight in decision-making.

Table 11.4   Stakeholder classification (from ACPOS's perspective)

Stakeholders	Negotiable issues			
	Budgets	National force	Outsourcing	Complaints reform
Executive	opponent	?	opponent	opponent
Justice Ministry	ally	ally	ally	opponent
Treasury	opponent	ally	?	ally
Police Federation	ally	ally	ally	ally
Law Society	?	ally	?	opponent
COSLA	?	ally	ally	opponent

Key: ally ↻   *opponent* ⟳   *uncertain* **?**

A similar situation almost applied on outsourcing of specific police functions. COSLA, dominated by a political party sympathetic to and affiliated to trade unions active in the public sector, tends to oppose all outsourcing of any public functions and it had been resisting the Executive over this issue for years when it proposed some modest outsourcing for local government functions. This made COSLA a natural ally of the police service on two issues and the Police Federation remained a staunch, though junior, ally on all four issues.

The Justice Ministry was a potential ally on three issues (budgets, national force and outsourcing) out of four. The question would become in the matter of trade-offs across the four proposals: how much does ACPOS have to accommodate to the Justice Ministry on some reform of the complaints procedures to secure its support for what ACPOS wants, resisting outsourcing, opposing a national police force and on its budgets?

On budgets, only the Police Federation and the Justice Ministry were likely to support ACPOS. Government departments tend to support bigger budgets for their constituent parts and this encourages log-rolling alliances ('if you support our budget, we'll support yours') among them against the Treasury and the Executive.

With the Executive and the Treasury identified as opponents of ACPOS on its budget and COSLA and the Law Society uncertain (depending on the items within the budget issue) ACPOS was most likely to be on its own on this issue because the Executive could ignore the Police Federation (barring any unexpected events pointing to a deficiency in police funds).

Finally, ACPOS needs to assess which of the players would make the most useful allies, because only allies with serious *clout* really make a difference when negotiations became difficult. Allas and Georgiades divide players into three types of ally (followers, shapers and influencers) on a 'negotiation landscape' matrix (see Figure 11.4) using the two relevant dimensions of *salience* and *clout* to determine their status:

- *followers*:   allies with little or no clout;

- *shapers*:   who care about the issues and can influence the outcome; they may be allies or opponents;

- *influencers*:   who are not concerned with the outcome but can influence it and who can be extremely useful as allies on the issue.

A negotiation landscape for the reform of the complaints procedure shows some interesting features that could be missed in complex multi-party preparation without using these relatively simple analytical tools.

At a glance, ACPOS is going to have to make an effort to win the support of both the Justice Ministry and the Treasury. It should do this by following a strategy of raising the *salience* of the reform of the complaints procedure for both these players (using the expanded force field diagram to check their assumptions). If successful, this strategy would have the effect of moving two players with *clout*, Justice and the Treasury, from the bottom right influencers quadrant upwards into the shapers quadrant where they can influence the outcome because they care more about it now.

If the Justice Ministry and the Treasury support ACPOS in its efforts to limit the Executive proposals for total change in the procedures to something less draconian, perhaps transitional and spread over a number of years, then the Executive's reforms may be mitigated to a sufficient degree to designate the outcome as a success for ACPOS. Politicians, it should always be remembered, usually respond positively to making some progress in their aims when total progress is not possible, to avoid gaining nothing or being classed as extremists.

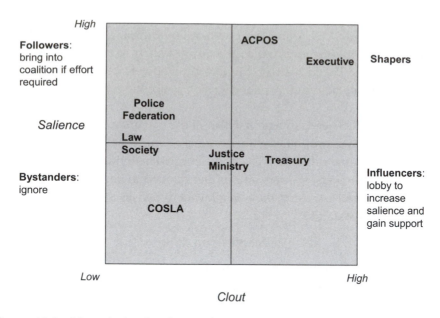

Figure 11.4   Negotiation landscape for the reform of complaints procedures

A modicum of staff work will be required by ACPOS personnel to identify themes and justifications from the expanded force field diagram that would appeal to the negotiators from the Executive, and the influencers from the Justice Ministry and the Treasury. The fact that ACPOS is aiming to slow down the reforms should keep the Police Federation – a follower – on board as an ally too. There will always remain the problem of the extremists for and against the reform proposals in both camps. A side task is to reduce their number and to lower their influence. The negotiation landscape identifies which players need attention and which can safely be ignored.

The negotiation landscape and the preparatory analyses preceding it handle a fair amount of complex data about the players. Both ACPOS and the Executive, the shapers in the negotiation on the reform of the complaints procedure are, of course, the mutual opponents too. ACPOS's allies were the Treasury and the Police Federation, but the Federation had little *clout* and for the Treasury the issue had little *salience*. COSLA was mildly interested but the issue did not have much *salience* (20) for it, and the Justice Ministry was closer to the average position on police complaints reform, but the issue had low salience (40). For ACPOS there was a strategic need to raise the salience of the issue among some of its allies and potential allies, a need clearly brought out by the negotiation landscape matrix.

There is more work to do because negotiation involves trading and exchange, as well as justifications and responses in the debates. The plan is shown in Figure 11.5 where we consider the relative *salience* of the negotiable issues for the Executive and ACPOS. Neither party, except rarely, gains everything it wants in a negotiation. There will have to be movement between them on some issues in exchange for the other party's movements on other issues. Though the method is illustrated by referring to only four main issues, in practice under each main issue there would be many sub-issues, all the terms of which would be tradable.

The top right quadrant shows that both parties regard the complaints procedures and budgets of high salience, or importance, with complaints procedures of the highest importance, reflecting the opposite extreme positions each takes over proposals for reforms in this area. Budgets are always contentious between operating units and budget holders, the former tending to want more resources, the latter tending to prefer their operations people to exhibit frugality rather than prodigality.

Complaints reform is definitely on the agenda and linked to budgets through the inevitable additional expense of the creation of new statutory outside bodies independent of the police service. Treasury is already opposed to the reform (on grounds of the additional expense, not on grounds of it being unnecessary) and the prospects of lobbying the Treasury to support a less expensive compromise

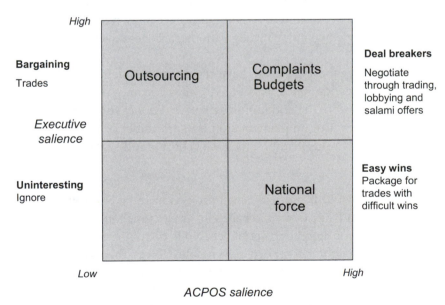

Figure 11.5   Salience relationship analysis: ACPOS v Executive

rather than a total reform looks promising. The more credibly that total reform can be diluted, the warmer the support that can be expected from the Treasury, which can lobby the Executive and the UK Government for a more cautious approach to reform rather than a total transformation in one step (highlighting the expense and serious controversy with the police force from an expanded force field analysis).

ACPOS negotiators should be looking at justifying a modest reform by giving the Treasury credible arguments for their influencing campaigns within the Executive and the UK Ggovernment. Showing a willingness to consider reform could break a drift to 'principled' confrontation and the imposition of the Executive's extreme stance on this issue, if political pressure really builds in this area (events?).

Budgets are always contentious but these battles occur within a narrow range in all organizations. This year's budget is related in some restricted way to last year's plus 'x per cent', and it is subject to the usual horse trading or haggling at the margin of the budgeted amounts proposed for each of the seven police forces.

The top-left hand and the bottom-right hand quadrants show an interesting feature. Outsourcing of some police functions is important to the Executive and less so for ACPOS, while the proposal to amalgamate the separate police forces is important to ACPOS, but of low importance to the Executive (mainly because it is not a likely event). Both the outsourcing of certain functions within the separate forces on a separate basis and of certain functions common to all of them opens the possibility of mixing and matching various packages covering both issues.

Where two negotiating parties have cross-matched degrees of importance to two or more agenda items, negotiated trades becomes a strong possibility. In the cases of outsourcing and forming a national police force, there are fertile grounds for segmenting implementation into a number of measures short of full integration by multiple mini trades, well short of full-scale implementation of either policy.

Outsourcing could begin with small projects in some back-office functions (civilianization and outsourced databases), or in functions such as parking attendants, neighbourhood anti-social behaviour patrols, escort services and so on. Instead of a straight merger of all seven police forces, there could be mergers arranged between contiguous forces where public habits of movement (work, social life) suggest common policing across jurisdictional boundaries, combined with the merger of certain highly specialized functions into national agencies (drug offences, anti-terrorism, criminal databases for fingerprints and DNA sampling, and so on). Flexibilities like these also have an impact on the (normal) stand-offs over budgets and on the extent of reforms to the complaints process.

Using this kind of diagrammatic analysis (Allas and Georgiadis report applications of the model via computer graphics), negotiators are able to pick up relationships and opportunities among disparate multi-parties that are not obvious; and this provides insights into possible strategies to escape from deal breaking confrontations when agenda items contain conflicting proposals that are judged highly salient by the parties who have clout.

Summary

Where there are multiple stakeholders in and close to the negotiations, the Allas & Georgiades' (McKinsey) graphical models can assist a team's preparatory analyses.

The Allas & Georgiades' tools develop strategies to produce negotiated outcomes that are palatable to the parties. They help to separate the parties into allies and opponents of the main negotiable issues. The three key characteristics are a party's *position* (preferred outcome) on an issue; the *salience* (relative importance) of the issue (high, medium or low) and the *clout* (power) enabling the party to influence the other players on that issue. Its does all this using six relatively simple diagrams:

- summary of the parties' stances on position, importance and power

- average outcome without bargaining

- stability analysis of an issue

- stakeholder classification (ally or opponent)

- negotiation landscape of parties

- relationship analysis.

The summary stance diagram scores the three key characteristics of position, isue importance and power using scores out of 100 points for each characteristic for each stakeholder. Where the parties are at the extreme ends of a stance, they score either 100 (everything changes) or 0 (nothing changes) and the other parties prepared to accept some change or nearly all the proposed change score points between 0 and 100.

The outcome continuum shows the outcome of a straight vote using the average of a pure compromise with no bargaining. As negotiators expect to bargain, the outcome continuum acts as a base measurement for calculating how far the parties are from the average outcome relative to a high or low combined relative importance of the issue for them. The stability analysis describes whether the parties would be likely to challenge a voted outcome and make it unstable or accept it.

Stakeholder classification identifies across the main issues whether each party is likely to be an ally or an opponent on each issue. The absence of an opponent on any issue suggests that a party would be likely to achieve its aspirations on that issue; the presence of no allies on an issue suggests it faces a tough struggle to achieve its preferred outcome, unless it can influence potential allies (force field analysis might help to identify prospects and to develop a strategy).

By differentiating between importance and power on each issue the negotiation landscape diagram (one for each issue) shows whether a party is a *follower,* an ally with little power; a *shaper,* a party that cares about the issue (highly important) and has high power (could exert influence), making them natural allies or serious opponents; or an *influencer,* less concerned about the issue but with high power to influence, who could be a winning ally for your proposal, if you can persuade them to support your proposal (power balance analysis could help here).

The relationship analysis diagram highlights the situation between pairs of parties (starting with the two parties most opposed to each other on an issue) and this contrasts the importance of the issue compared to its importance for another party. This is akin to what is shown in the preparation planner diagram from basic negotiation skills texts (for example, *Kennedy on Negotiation,* Gower, 1998). It identifies the cross-matching of degrees of importance on the negotiable issues and where the possibility of bargaining, lobbying and salami-type proposals might be appropriate.

The six diagrams (more than six when all the main issues and all the parties are compared, suggesting why a computer-driven simulation analysis is appropriate) can clarify the strategic issues that may be obscured by a mass of not easily separated interconnected data. If the thought of the detailed work to look inside the black box of ignorance is off-putting, bear in mind that whether the details are identified systematically or not, their interconnecting relationships exist and operate whether you look for them or remain ignorant, and your ignorance could cost you the deal.

Activities
for Chapter 11

Activity 11.1

Recall any common maxims about who has the power, or how it should be used, that you hear around your workplace. Perhaps you have a favourite maxim yourself!

COMMENTS ON THIS ACTIVITY

We need something more reliable than untested maxims which may have variable results in practice. When circumstances change, as they must, it is risky to rely on a favourite maxim, and unless what is advised is replicable by the average person, it is of little use. There are too few geniuses around to make a difference if advice is only usable by geniuses.

Activity 11.2

Have you ever negotiated for a proposition which you disagreed with personally but which was the proposition selected by your organization to make to the other party?

How far along the spectrum on personal disagreement have you been – reluctant obedience to your bosses' instructions or considering resignation?

COMMENTS ON THIS ACTIVITY

It is unlikely that you have agreed completely with every proposal you have had to negotiate – there are always differences in a team of negotiators about the appropriate next move. When asked by negotiators new to their role in an organization about what they should do in the event that they disagree with their instructions, I have advised them to accept that differences on such matters are normal and that they should temper their reaction to differences emerging, and the uncomfortable position it might put them in on occasion, with the knowledge that, if they wish to be in a position to dictate the appropriate negotiating policy for the organization, they have to learn to undertake negotiating stances with which they disagree so that they rise in the organization far enough to be in charge of determining policy stances and to issue instructions to others.

The Negotiation Agenda

Introduction

The Negotiation Agenda originated from the singular circumstances of the state of industrial relations in Britain in the 1970s, which, by common agreement, left a great deal to be desired. Strikes, go-slows and other forms of industrial disruption were rife. Indeed, a Government policy document of the time was called 'In Place of Strife' (though the document caused so much strife within the Government that its leading Ministers eventually withdrew their proposals). A new Conservative Government, led by Mrs Thatcher and elected on a policy to reform the trade unions, implemented the fairly modest proposals of In Place of Strife and added more radical proposals of its own. Trade unions had long played a prominent role in initiating and designing legislation for previous governments, but they had practically no role under Mrs Thatcher (she simply ignored them).

In these circumstances, managements found various ways to live in peace with their employees, mostly choosing a stoic acceptance that in matters of remuneration and working conditions the unions would take the lead with their traditional lists of annual demands. This usually resulted in the relegation of management's role to the mitigation, where it could stand the strikes, of the unions' demands to something nearer the amounts that the company could afford. This was never a sensible policy, as it perpetuated the problems of wage drift, inflation and loss of managerial control of their enterprises, and incidentally exposed the basic flaw in Keynesian economics, namely that a government guarantee of full employment undermined the social policy of the same government.

Under Mrs Thatcher's three governments, the pendulum swung away from union influence, for a time. High unemployment, the contraction of UK manufacturing industry and severe decline in several traditional heavy industries (coal, steel and the docks), reduced the influence of trade unions, particularly in the private sector. Parliament also legislated to reduce the power of the unions to disrupt commerce and public services. But this did not reform the essence of industrial relations. Many employers adopted revenge-driven policies, suited to the ascendancy of the employers' relative power and the taming of employee militancy by high unemployment. Meanwhile, the unions consolidated their power base in the public sector, whilst they lost members by the thousands in the faltering private sector.

The approach

The alternative and better strategy was the development in a few major companies of a Negotiation Agenda approach applied to negotiations, which is an approach driven by the necessary changes required to operate an enterprise profitably. It was no longer sufficient merely to react to employees' annual demands; managements were urged to develop demands of their own linked to their business plans and to consolidate these demands into a Negotiation Agenda. In short, the Negotiation Agenda was not a list of demands to be imposed upon employees. Demands were negotiable and traded for the remuneration and conditions packages, which the enterprise could afford if they delivered its business plans.

To derive a Negotiation Agenda, management takes a detailed view of the future of the enterprise over a 3- to 5-year horizon. Important as wage costs are, they are not decisive because other costs, including the level of productivity, also determine the future of a business. The point about having a business plan is not merely to compose a list of activities for the immediate future; it is about envisaging where management thinks the business ought to be and what it should be doing within the next five years to achieve its objectives.

Restraining, for instance, excessive inflationary wage demands has benefits, of course, but failing to tackle a need also to restructure the composition of a business should it be necessary because of the changing markets, changing technologies and changing sources of finance, could have as devastating an effect on a business as conceding to excessive wage demands. From being mainly centred on industrial relations negotiations, as in the early years, the Negotiation Agenda method spread right across all subjects for negotiation in all functions in companies adopting the approach.

Preparatory data for determining the appropriate policies are derived from analysis and diagnosis and compiled into proposals for the Negotiation Agenda. Finally, they are prepared for implementation.

Negotiation Agendas are proactive, not reactive. They are well thought-out strategies for conducting relationships with employees, irrespective of the (passing) strength or weakness of unions, and with awkward personnel across functional divisions in the management structure, irrespective of the (perhaps passing) importance of a particular function in the business as currently operated. It may also be envisaged as part of an approach to manage changes in external relationships among suppliers or customers.

Management sets out its intentions in its business plan and then derives its negotiation objectives to implement its plan. Without a Negotiation Agenda, management makes plans in isolation and then negotiates outcomes that interrupt or disrupt the achievement of its business plan. In short, without a Negotiation Agenda the business plan is hostage to the mood, militancy and awkwardness of its employees, suppliers, customers and commercial partners. With a Negotiation Agenda the initiative passes from external third parties (for example, unions), which may be pursuing policies unrelated to the needs of a business, back to where it belongs – the management, solely responsible and accountable for the future of the business – and also away from other forces within and outside the organization, with which you do business.

Hence, vague exhortations (and related promises) to save expenditures (switch off lights, and so on), to improve productivity (be more flexible, reduce absenteeism), to accept changes in work practices, to become competitive and so on suffer the fate of all exhortations not backed by specific proposals that are time bound and scheduled; invariably, they fail to materialize, as do hopes for changes to improve quality, increase market share, redesign inputs or product or the nature of relationships and cost structures.

Exchanging specific pay awards on a promise to consider changes in work practices or, in an example of supreme naiveté, to join in a working party to examine such changes usually produces what they deserve – nothing tangible. The Negotiation Agenda is based on specific proposals for specific changes. Items on the Negotiation Agenda are traded for wage claims in the format of the conditional proposition: If you agree to our specific proposals, then we will agree to specific changes in your terms and conditions of employment.

When suppliers propose changes in their selling prices or terms, and customers propose changes in their purchase prices or terms, a Negotiation Agenda approach moves negotiation outcomes from zero- to non-zero-sum outcomes. Just as management should review its current remuneration policies in anticipation of receiving proposals for changes, so it should also review its policies for supplier and customer pricing strategies and not wait for proposals to materialize from either of these sources.

The problem in each case – and in many others that are common experience in business – is that the parties are in reactive not proactive modes in their negotiating relationships. The Negotiation Agenda approach changes reactive habits into proactive habits. It does not sit comfortably with the fire engine approach of handling problems when prompted to do so. It requires managements to examine their costs in all areas of the business carefully and to propose adjustments to these upwards or downwards with their negotiating parties, internal and external, to meet their objectives. Where necessary, to meet their goals, it will propose changes from which, superficially, it loses, if this keeps valued employees and customers and the organization functioning profitably. Adding to profitability by exploiting employees, customers or suppliers is neither necessary nor advisable.

The closer the unions, suppliers and customers come to agreeing to specific management proposals from a Negotiation Agenda, the more readily management considers seriously the demands it receives as a matter of course from these sources while running its organization. Changes that become necessary or possible in some aspect of an organization's activity do not have to await proposals from other parties whose interests may not be aligned with the organization's interests. A management happy to let your salary drift short of your value to them, or a supplier willing to exploit your ignorance, loses your respect and your custom.

A Negotiation Agenda approach anticipates changes and prepares for them, allowing proposals that serve the best interests of the organization to be introduced at the instigation of the management if it assures that its business objectives are realized.

To achieve specificity in its proposals drawn from its Negotiation Agenda it is required that management:

- have clear and detailed ideas of what it wants within the next 3 to 5 years;

- is committed to negotiating its agenda alongside the other parties' claims;

- is determined to introduce and fund what is agreed into the organization to a strict timetable;

CASE STUDY

Reactive Or Proactive?

Many (probably most) changes in existing arrangements originate from the party that expects to *benefit* from them. It is rarer to find proposals for change to originate from a party that (even nominally) *loses* from them.

Consider the following examples.

Resignation prompts an offer of a salary increase

Zhao, a talented software engineer, was offered a new job by a competing company at a salary 20 per cent higher plus a more impressive job title. He felt he was languishing in his current job at a salary which was mediocre compared to those received by his social friends and to his true value to his current employer. He accepted the new job offer and submitted his resignation.

Next day, his boss told him that, because he was a valued employee, the company did not want to lose him. He had been authorized to increase his pay by 20 per cent. Zhao declined the pay rise and left the company at the end of the month.

Threat of tendering prompting a cut in an audit fee

An accountancy firm completed its latest audit of the Little Blue Co. annual accounts and submitted its usual audit fee. It was surprised, some months later, to receive a letter from Little Blue's Financial Director, informing it that the Board had decided to put auditing out to tender.

Subsequently, Little Blue received an amended audit fee from its auditor substantially below its usual fee. Little Blue the following year awarded the audit contract to another firm.

Demand for a price cut prompting reductions

An engineering company wrote to all of its component suppliers, where it had more than one supplier for each item, requiring a ten per cent reduction in their prices from the next quarter. In most cases, its suppliers complied with the reduction. Those that did not were de-listed. Those that did were told that further reductions would be required annually when contracts were renewed and that those suppliers remaining with the highest prices for each component, after the voluntary reductions had taken affect, would be de-listed and that the others would be required to show they provided value for money to remain listed in future quarters. It advised component suppliers to pay close attention to their unit costs and not to their profits – constantly searching for ways to reduce unit costs was the best way to maintain profit rates.

Comparing notes with non-competitive associates

A mainframe computer corporation sold its products to a large number of local authorities but from its disparate negotiations over several years it arrived at many different prices and terms from its separate negotiations.

The discrepancies were tolerable as long as the deals remained confidential. But officials of public bodies hold annual conventions at which the financial directors of the local authorities mix and mingle socially. As is inevitable, FDs tend to compare notes, and not the least likely topic is to compare what others have achieved in major purchases like IT, especially when they share the same supplier.

Allowing for the usual bravado and exaggerated claims, some of the FDs realized that they had negotiated packages for their computer systems considerably more onerous to their budgets than others. One such local authority near Birmingham discovered to its horror that it had paid nearly twice as much for its mainframe system as a similar-sized local authority near Southampton purchasing from the same company (and from the same sales representative!). The computer company was contacted and the FD demanded a large rebate and credit note, and threatened to write to all the local authority FDs in the country to warn them about the company's practices.

- introduce items from its agenda as required in current or future negotiations;

- maintain a seamless connection between the Negotiation Agenda and the business plan to ensure board level support for its policies and for the implementation of its negotiated agreements.

At any one moment in a negotiation, the Negotiation Agenda is longer than the number of issues that may be placed on the table for a specific negotiation. Should it be necessary or helpful, unused items from a future Negotiation Agenda may be entered into current negotiations in pursuit of an agreement, though they may not have been envisaged to be part of the current deal when they were being prepared.

The Negotiation Agenda is a longer-term commitment than merely a list of items that are to be negotiated at the next meeting. It is not a short-term fix, but a carefully constructed agenda for, or close to, the planning period in the business plan. It supports a principle that whatever is negotiated currently should not make it more difficult to achieve objectives in the business plan that may be negotiated later within its 5 year horizon.

It is an assertion of the Strategic Negotiation Process Model approach that the derivation of the Negotiation Agenda from the commercial and operational imperatives and the business plan, and the implementation of the negotiated agenda in an organization, adds greatly to the smoother implementation of the necessary changes and to the flexibility with which adjustments can be made, should events show them to be necessary.

The Negotiation Agenda is not an excuse for reacting to the demands of people who set terms for their cooperation from a unilaterally determined price-list on their menu. Policy choices are made in the pre-negotiation phase, costed carefully and integrated into the Negotiation Agenda. If the agenda items are agreed then, allowing for adjustments that may be necessary in the

CASE STUDY

A Rose By Any Other Name ...

In long-drawn-out negotiations with the unions in an oil refinery, the management wanted to achieve certain specific flexibilities between two trade unions (the two unions at the time were engaged in merger talks with each other, which came to a successful conclusion two years later). After much negotiation, most of the management proposals (with some irritating but minor workable restrictive conditions attached) were accepted for dual roles in certain work common to both electrician and plumber tradesmen from the two unions.

However, the union representatives adamantly refused to accept that with the restrictions removed on the formerly reserved work, the employees concerned should be redesignated as 'refinery maintenance staff', and thereby subject to supervision by whichever supervisor was available, and they insisted that they remain known as either 'maintenance electricians' or 'maintenance plumbers', which continued the rule and the practice that only supervisors who belonged to the same trade as those they supervised could supervise staff. This caused problems now and again when all the supervisors from one of the trades were fully occupied elsewhere, thus delaying necessary maintenance or repair work until an apprentice trade-trained supervisor became available (under the site safety rules, all work teams had to be directly supervised) even though perfectly competent and experienced supervisors from other trades were available. The resultant downtime added to costs and not to revenues.

A Negotiation Agenda would have anticipated this problem and included it in its specific conditional proposals for exchange for what the unions wanted. Linking the issue of all-trades supervision to the pay rise could have created a tradable for negotiation.

light of negotiated changes in the original proposals, their implementation should follow the plan discussed during preparation for the negotiations.

If the implementation phases have not been properly thought through and events show that the proposals are impractical in their agreed form, the loss of the change items from the agreed agenda represents an interruption to the achievement of the business plan. It also represents a blow to the anticipated cost benefits of the negotiated agenda because the organization will get back less than what it has paid for in the negotiated exchange.

Negotiating changes in working practices are bedevilled by poor preparation by those (usually management) making proposals for changes. Where the practical applications are not thought through, often because the preparation has been rushed, the implementation phase is postponed while a working party is set up to specify how the change will work in practice. If the details prove overwhelming to management, timelines slip and the exceptions so corrupt the proposed changes that people lose interest in continuing with the meetings. Fatigue (even boredom) kills the working party and the changes never materialize.

Derivation of the Negotiation Agenda

For every change identified in the commercial imperative of the business plan there will be up to five operational imperatives identified. Tables 12.1 to 12.5 show the pro forma set that should be completed to identify the items for the Negotiation Agenda.

In practice, five to eight are sufficient to capture the main commercial imperatives of an organization over a 3- to 5-year horizon (Table 12.1).

Table 12.1   Commercial imperatives

Objectives	Commercial imperatives
1	
2	
...	

These may be identified by the management team from relatively informal acquaintance with the business and their knowledge, however vague, of the changes that are coming over the horizon. I find that even junior management grades have a fairly accurate idea of what is happening in their organization and in their business sector and, working together in pairs or small groups, they produce comprehensive lists of commercial imperatives using their experience and what they know about their business. From the more senior grades, whose jobs involve regular scanning of the business sector for trends and changes, more accurate assessments are to be expected.

Finance is a major operational resource affecting all aspects of an organization's performance. It will feature among the operational imperatives identified for delivery of the business plan. There are the direct costs of funding a commercial imperative and the indirect costs of those other commercial imperatives that are curbed, curtailed, delayed or denied as a result. Where these are negotiated within the organization's budgeting procedures, their

---

CASE STUDY

Modest Proposal

A hospital management team agreed with a staff union that instead of nurses leaving written notes on events involving patients that a 15-minute face-to-face 'handover briefing session' would be introduced for discussing patients with the incoming nurses on the next shift. The union agreed this would be good for patients because information about patients sometimes was inadequately covered in hasty notes left by the outgoing shift and the paucity of detail that this produced was detrimental to continuing with appropriate medical treatments.

However, implementation of the agreed proposal was blighted by an unanswered question asked by the nurses union: from whose shift would the 15 minutes be taken or added; the outgoing shift staying on for 15 minutes, or the incoming shift arriving 15 minutes early?

While this was not beyond the wit of those involved to solve (in practice it would not be a loss or gain to either shift, as an incoming shift became an outgoing shift eight hours later!) the whole proposal bogged down in an argument over exceptions (there are always exceptions!).

For example, a nurse had to leave on time to catch the last evening ferry to cross the bay; others could not get in before their set times due to bus timetables, school hours, dependent relatives and so on; plus those who could not stay behind, or arrive early, for good reasons.

The exceptions amounted to about eight per cent of a shift's nursing staff. Unable to resolve the exceptions, management eventually abandoned the implementation of what they had agreed to (and already) paid for.

Yet experience suggested that during any handover there was always a slight delay in attending to patients while staff prepared for the workload of the shift and in that 20–30 minute period some degree of temporary absence of some staff (certainly up to 10 per cent) could be accommodated. A Negotiation Agenda approach would have prevented the beneficial change being dropped because it would have been discussed in preparation and the trial answers developed to address it, without stalling the forward momentum for the changes.

---

advocates should prepare for their negotiation in much the same way as for other resources.

Linking financial requirements to the organization's business plan is always a good place to start and deriving negotiable objectives for the Negotiation Agenda is a fruitful way to assure close approximation between goals and outcomes. Financial evaluation of funding requirements always plays a role in negotiating for board approval. The method assures users of well-informed command of the detail sufficient to implement clear strategic outcomes.

CASE STUDY

Changes In Universities

The advent of distance education pedagogies in universities opened possibilities for new sources of revenue from students dispersed in a wider catchment area than is normal for a traditional campus university. Distance students do not need to visit a particular campus site to receive instruction. The commercial imperative might be to introduce new sources of revenue off campus to add to the university's net income stream.

This change would affect the organization and remuneration of academic and administrative staff. Faculty, instead of delivering lectures to selected groups of students on campus, would be required to prepare distance learning materials for distribution to off-campus students who would study the materials at their own time, pace and convenience. Administration staff would administer distant students using IT systems; these would require new skills and technologies. The examination systems would be affected to cope with distant exam centres, local invigilation services (proctoring), secure mass transfers of thousands of exam scripts around the world and new forms of communication to register, be accepted and processed from first contact to graduation. All the inputs required for these changes would constitute the operational imperatives to deliver the commercial imperatives and the business plan for the university.

CASE STUDY

Hospital Changes

In a hospital environment, changes in medical technology continually change the arrangements for treating patients. Large central hospital buildings, treating patients who visit the hospital for periods of treatment, staying in wards overnight or longer, and being treated by procedures initiated by resident medical staff (the norm up to the early 1990s) were subject to changes in medical practice and technology which changed treatment, procedures and location.

'Day surgery' (no overnight stays, except if emergencies developed) became possible, as did 'outreach' surgeries and clinics with medical staff visiting distant locations to perform simple procedures and major theatre surgeries using 24/7 shift working for routine operations.

All these changes (and more), if introduced, required new skill patterns (example, breaching the nurse-surgeon divide), new long-term training programmes, new overlapping of the boundaries between standard para-medical professions (radiography, pharmacy, physiotherapy, social work and such like), new organizational forms and changes within the traditional hospital hierarchies.

The resources required to effect these changes constituted the operational imperatives needed to deliver the commercial imperatives and the business plans of hospitals.

For operational imperatives, such as in

employee groups, a skill change arising from a commercial change could affect more than one group of people. Training senior nurses to take on relatively minor surgery tasks associated with warts, toe and finger nails, and varicose veins, and so on, affects the work roles of registrars, consultant surgeons and anaesthetists.

To add to the skills of one work group might have effects on other work groups that currently supply that skill (and, of course, the deskilling of a group to accommodate the change elsewhere also has implications for the group).

Similarly, different parts of the organization are affected by, say, changes in the technologies of communication channels. Database management of tens of thousands of confidential records creates compliance and user access problems. Unsupervised access to databases via dispersed desktop computer terminals changes traditional controls of access from when it was only available selectively at a special place in a building under the supervision of gatekeeper guardians with notoriously suspicious temperaments.

Training, retraining and redundancy for the untrainable (or at least sideways moves to other work roles, not necessarily of comparable skills, responsibility or earnings) create operational imperatives requiring attention and planning. The selection of policies for personnel and the reward and benefits packages of workgroups in a changing environment are HR problems best considered early on in a change programme. Table 12.3 shows the pro forma applied to the impact of identified imperatives to achieve the business plan on HR Strategies.

Table 12.2 Operational imperatives

Commercial imperatives	Operational imperatives for each user	
List each commercial imperative and derive operational imperatives for each one	User group	
1 2 ...		

Table 12.3 Impact of imperatives on HR strategies

Imperatives		HR strategies				
Commercial	Operational	Employee relations	Recruitment	Training	Organization development	Manpower planning
1 2 ...						

In Table 12.4, each commercial imperative is listed along with the operational imperatives identified as related to it. Under each (suggested) heading, from budget to financial planning, the impact of the operational imperatives is noted. The question the analysts are attempting to answer in this table is what might have to be done in respect of the current policies of the organization under each heading to accommodate the delivery of the imperatives?

Table 12.4   Impact of imperatives on financial strategies

Imperatives		Financial strategies				
Commercial	Operational	Budget	Sources	Financial evaluations	Stakeholders	Financial planning
1						
2						
...						

What is the finance department required to do to the existing budget plan? Where is the finance coming from (an agreed budget heading, new borrowing, future surpluses and so on)? What do the standard financial evaluations show (gearing, yields, payback period, discounted cash flow, net present value and so on)? How might the various stakeholders react to the proposals? How does the expenditure fit into the organization's financial planning? And in all answers the need for drafted proposals is evident.

Proposals involving a downsizing of the organization, or a substantial amount of change in its composition, would affect employee relations, recruitment (and decruitment), training, possible organizational development issues and, of course, manpower planning.

In all cases, not every column shown would be or need be affected by specific imperatives, and for many exercises, other column headings could be added or substituted to suit the circumstances within the organization. This would certainly be the case in the all-encompassing technology imperatives, which cover all the various means by which an organization transforms inputs through adding value into outputs and, therefore, for each technology subject, different lists of likely impacts would need to be identified. Because the compilers of these pro formas work within the organization, a sufficient level of command of the necessary detail to identify likely impacts must be assumed (or the necessary knowledge to do so must be acquired).

Transforming the information into a means suitable for a Negotiation Agenda requires the next step in the derivation process. Table 12.5 shows a pro forma for this exercise for HR strategy. Imperative changes in working practices, organization or technology may impact across several employee groups and a pro forma should be completed for each group and for each imperative too. This creates considerable amounts of data, at first sight almost too much to be manageable.

With five or more commercial imperatives, each with five or more operational imperatives, there are 25 or more possible headings. Complexity increases when under each of the three main resource headings in the tables (people, finance and technology), five are identified per resource; this raises the quantity to 75 possible data sets; and if a change programme involves all three resources, it rises to 375 possible sub-headings, no mean quantity of data to assemble and sort through!

Table 12.5 Derivation of the Negotiation Agenda topics

Employee group				
Imperatives		**HR strategy**		
Commercial	People	Remuneration and benefits		
		Now		Future
		Helps	Hinders	
1				
2				
...				

However, in practice, many of the headings are repetitive and this reduces the actual data requiring consideration to bounds well within the capacity of most managers. For example, training appears frequently for changes or improvements in the people resource and a whole host of headings under finance require attention to stakeholders (board, departments, shareholders, bankers and so on). When this is realized by anxious and sceptical managers, faced with the plethora of data headings, their relief is tangible, all the more so because it is so obvious from the evidence they compile themselves.

In Table 12.5, in this example for the impact of HR strategies, we are asking different questions to earlier ones. For each imperative we want to know to what extent the current remuneration package *helps* or *hinders* the achievement of the imperatives. These answers may be represented by a tick (√) or a cross

(×). Clearly, if current arrangements meet the requirements, there is no need to change them. If they do not meet the requirements – especially if they work against them – then discussion should follow on what might be done to replace them with policies that do meet them.

In short, the approach is to decide what we want the business to do and then assess how well we do things at present. This work identifies small and large deficiencies and, having agreed that they exist, we search for ways in which we can realign the way we do things currently. This leads to the discussion, given the business objectives we wish to achieve over the planning horizon of 3 to 5 years, of what we must do instead.

This way, we fill the final column, 'Future,' with potential headings showing what must be done to achieve the imperatives to deliver the business plan. The future column, when discussed and agreed, becomes the content of the Negotiation Agenda.

Content of the Negotiation Agenda

One way to illustrate the content of a Negotiation Agenda is to provide an example (disguised on grounds of confidentiality) from an actual case. Necessarily this must be grossly simplified, but it contains sufficient material to enable you to follow the format and replicate it in applications more familiar to your sphere of work.

My example comes from the interface between public and private enterprise in the UK following changes in the government's approach to the funding of public finance projects. Briefly, government expenditures are funded from taxation and borrowing from capital markets. In common with all other countries, the demand for public expenditure to supply public services eventually exceeds the tolerable taxation base and the borrowing limits that are prudent for a government subjected to regular accountability in democratic elections.

Even if a government wishes to press ahead with potential public projects for social reasons (needs exceed facilities to meet them), prudent governments feel compelled to curb their ambitions because should they continue to act in a prodigal manner beyond some acceptable level (which varies for different countries, but in none of them is it possible to sustain infinite expansion), opposition parties will gain power by attacks on the tax and spending burdens that relentless expansion imposes on the electorate. Profligate dictatorships, without the inconvenience of democratic accountability, also face international pressure from creditors who restrain expansionary behaviour by refusing to fund their programmes up to the point where they must default on their existing debts.

One attempted solution to these problems is what was called in the UK the Private Finance Initiatives programme (or PFI), now Public–Private Partnerships (or PPP). Governments traditionally raise capital for projects by raising public finance (taxation and borrowing) and invite the private sector companies to tender for capital projects. The government funds the project, selects the supplier and hands it to the department responsible for administering the project once it is built. The private firm's role ends with the handover of the finished project to the government department that supplies to the public the services provided by the project. Hence, the education department seeks tenders for a new school building, manages the selection of the builder, supervises the work and when it is satisfied that the building is ready for occupation by the school's administrators and pupils, it pays the builder who withdraws and looks for other construction opportunities.

Starting slowly in the 1990s, PFI projects grew into multi-billion pound expenditure programmes. Under these schemes, the public sector departments or agencies invited private firms to supply the capital to complete a project, organize themselves to construct it and to manage the completed project over a period of twenty to thirty years in return for an annual fee sufficient to cover their administrative costs, to earn a return on the investment and to meet the service goals (with penalties for non performance) negotiated with the government department/agency.

At the end of the 'concession period', the private firm hands the building over to the department, with some allowance possible for losing a written-down asset from its balance sheet, and has nothing further to do with it, while the building becomes a wholly-owned public asset. The government acquires modernized public sector assets without having them appear in its annual accounts paid for by taxation and borrowing. All that appears in the government's annual accounts and budget is the much smaller sum paid to the PFI concessionaire for providing the services from the assets that the public requires. From the point of view of the politics of public finance, this is a popular alternative to increases in public debt and the tax burden.

In the next few sub-sections I shall illustrate the process of completing the data for the Negotiation Agenda by making a generic example from a negotiation of an imaginary, but representative, PFI negotiation between a government agency and a commercial contractor. Each pro forma from the template will be completed for selected aspects of the concessionaire contract for each party. This is not meant to show how each party would prepare in practice – the Negotiation Agenda approach, unfortunately, is not general enough at present – but each completed pro-forma set is illustrative of what either party should be doing when preparing for this type of negotiation. By extension, the method may be generalized to any other business sector.

In what follows, then, I shall interpolate how I think each party would collect, analyse and diagnose the data in their preparation of a Negotiation Agenda.

COMMERCIAL IMPERATIVES

Table 12.6 identifies the commercial imperatives from the business plans of the two organizations (set out together for ease of presentation and to assist your understanding of the process, though you can read them as separate data sets if that assists your understanding).

Table 12.6   Commercial imperatives

Government Department	PFI concessionaire
Reduce the growth of public expenditure on capital projects	Secure with financial partners sufficient funds for large 30-year public projects
Increase availability of public projects	Programme a steady stream of profitable work for the enterprise
Maintain/improve quality of services	
	Earn sufficient annual fees for managing the finished project
Transfer capital expenditures to private sector, off Department's balance sheet	
	Ensure asset transfer is profitable over its lifetime
Secure 'Value for Money' (as defined by the Treasury)	Ensure corporate risk is acceptable

The suggested plausible commercial imperatives for the Government and the PFI concessionaire are extrapolations from an original strategic negotiation case. They did not necessarily apply in an actual case, but I would expect something like the above if each or either party had operated a Negotiation Agenda approach.

The government department's commercial imperatives are driven by government policies for public expenditures. They can usually be reviewed from documents in the public domain and in the tender documents made available to serious commercial contenders (and, sometimes, in-house suppliers in the larger government departments).

Reducing the growth of public expenditure on capital projects does not obviate the electorate's demand for increasing the availability of public projects. Aged infrastructure (roads, water, sewage, drainage, bridges, canals, harbours, airports, rail lines, buildings, hospitals, public places and so on) beyond a point becomes embarrassing for an elected government. The two commercial imperatives can come into conflict, alongside the imperative of maintaining/ improving the quality of public services and securing 'value for money' (as defined by the Treasury). Some commercial imperatives drive the needed changes; others act as constraints.

For many commercial firms considering bids for PFI contracts the concept is quite new, financially. Their funding has to be over the duration of the PFI contract (from 20 to 30 years). This may mean opening up entirely new financial arrangements with bankers or with other construction firms (mini-consortia have become a feature of this business) and with a prejudice favouring cross-EU-border alliances new organizational structures have emerged for all aspects of EU-State funds.

Another interesting development has been the appearance of a secondary market in the sale and purchase of completed PFI projects which are seen as vehicles for financial investments. Selling on a completed PFI project creates a new strategic opportunity for a construction firm because it releases tied-up capital for investment in new PFI construction projects over a 30-year horizon. A strategy of disposal by selling on its completed projects works well with the imperative of securing a steady stream of profitable work for the construction enterprise. The strategy addresses its core competences (in 'design and build') and could be more financially attractive and less risky than 'design, build and operate' projects over 20- to 30-year periods.

The commercial imperatives of earning sufficient annual fees for managing the finished project and ensuring that the eventual asset transfer to the government department is profitable over its lifetime have high relevance for a company intending to sell on its PFI projects. For a PFI project to be acceptable for purchase by a financial investor, these two commercial imperatives must be bankable. Hence, in the negotiations with the Government care is needed to ensure that a potential sale price is viable enough to be obtainable, if only because, in the absence of a sale on completion option, the construction company would have to live with a sub-optimum income level.

Corporate risks in PFI are a major issue. For the Government the transfer of risk to the concessionaire is a major incentive. The obvious need to avoid white-elephant outcomes predominates in a Government's thinking. Avoiding handing to the Opposition sticks with which they can beat Ministers in the future is an instinctive and prime motive for the Department's most careful scrutiny of a project's viability. Thus, passing much of this risk on to a commercial contractor under PFI makes a great deal of sense from the Government's point of view.

Commercial contractors earn future income from their projects' viability. If insufficient vehicular traffic uses the bridge, canal or highway, there will be less fee income from the Department under the revenue rules of PFI. If a new school building is outside the catchment area for school children (such as if it is located in a residential area predominantly occupied by retired people, commercial premises and open spaces), school enrolments will generate insufficient demand for the size of school built. When a Department assesses the future demand for a project, they apply decision rules plus public money; commercial enterprises apply similar rules but it is their money at risk if they get it wrong.

It is a similar situation for other risks like construction risk, something a commercial company should have had a lot of experience in assessing and in ensuring that it is minimized from their building practices. Under PFI, these risks are passed entirely to the concessionaire, much like a turnkey project in major construction projects. Until the project is handed over to the Department, it has no construction risks.

Moreover, because the concessionaire is contracted to supply the services from the project for 20 to 30 years, handover is delayed long past the usual time of the completion of the project. This passes the operating risk of the project for that period to the concessionaire and removes it completely from the Department, which is another benefit in the management of corporate risk of these types of project.

OPERATIONAL IMPERATIVES

Table 12.7 takes data collection another step towards the Negotiation Agenda. It derives the operational imperatives from the commercial imperatives. These are usually associated with finance, HR and technology but could encompass any functions important to the activity. For our purposes, I shall cover finance for the Department and HR for the concessionaire by selecting a single commercial imperative for each and suggesting associated operational imperatives for finance and HR.

For the Department, I have taken the commercial imperative of 'Reduce the growth of public expenditure on capital' and suggest that one of the (up to 5–8) financial operational imperatives that may be required to deliver this is: 'Identify £800 million worth of viable PFI projects and bring them on stream at the rate of £40 million a month in Year 1 and £80 million a month by year 2.' The feasibility of this outcome (my illustrations are imaginary) is driven by the commercial imperative and not at this point fitted to the capability of the Department. Naturally, an examination of the necessary outcome would lead to an intense evaluation of its feasibility, out of which would come an assessment of the suitability of the current mix of resources for meeting it.

Table 12.7   Operational imperatives

Commercial imperatives	Operational imperatives for each user
	User group
	Government: Finance
	PFI concessionaire: HR
Government Department Reduce the growth of public expenditure on capital projects	Identify £800 million worth of viable PFI projects and bring them on stream by year 2
PFI concessionaire Programme a steady stream of profitable work for the enterprise contracts	Recruit additional experienced staff for expanded tendering teams, in-house legal expertise and accountancy and in-house finance specialists to prospect, prepare and negotiate PFI

This is precisely a function of the Negotiation Agenda approach; it tests feasibility of the top-level intentions of the organization, as expressed in the business plan, and identifies what must be done to achieve them. If objectives are not feasible, given the current mix of resources, the organization faces the choice of adjusting the mix or not meeting its business plan, and the Negotiation Agenda shows exactly what has to be negotiated (and with whom) for the necessary mix to materialize.

If I may (with abject apologies to Scotland's Bard for my outrageous adaptation) paraphrase a few lines from Robert Burns ('To a Louse', 1786):

> *Oh, would some Power the gift to give us*
>
> *Better plans, not strategically hopeless!*
>
> *It would from many a corporate blunder free us,*
>
> *And foolish notion.*

There are no hiding places for infeasible objectives remaining intact in the Negotiation Agenda. Inconsistencies and outright fictions are exposed. If the plan cannot be achieved in the time horizon without significant and implausible changes in the organization's resource mix (finance, HR and technology), the sooner this is realized by those charged with implementing it, the better. The best time to start making the necessary adjustments is as close as is possible to year 1 and not in year 4.

Turning briefly to the HR resource for the same Departmental operational imperative and noting that the finance imperative is to 'Identify £800 million worth of viable PFI projects and bring them on stream by year 2', we may take a look at the HR implications for meeting such a target.

Spending £800 million may seem like a spendthrift's wildest dream, but in practice spending this amount over two or three years is not quite so easy. For a start there are restrictions on what it may be spent upon. Accountable Governments invest much time and resources checking the probity of its officials and the wisdom of the politicians as expressed in the way they recommend spending taxpayers' money (check on the Internet for reports of the UK's Public Accounts Committee for many examples at www.parliament. uk/commons/selcom67/pachome.htm).

There are also resource constraints internal to the Department and within the organizations of potential PFI concessionaires. The obvious question for this imperative is whether, with existing resources, the Department could deliver £800 million worth of PFI contracts within the time period, and if not, by when. If it is to deliver anything like the sought for amount, what does the Department need to do to gear up to speed and, given that it could acquire the necessary employee resources, by when would it be able to complete the spending programme implied as an objective of the business plan?

Assuming that the Department already does much of this type of work under the traditional public expenditure approach of annual budgets passing through Parliament (which would continue alongside PFI projects) it should have capable staff resources present to some extent for handling all phases of contracts with external suppliers. If PFI projects are going to be supplementary to traditional contracting, then it will need to recruit additional employee resources of engineers, architects, estimators, planners, inspectors and so on. If the Department envisages a run-down of resources devoted to traditional publicly funded projects, recruitment would be less of a major source for the PFI programme. It would involve induction and training of existing resources.

For the PFI concessionaire, I selected the commercial imperative of 'Programme a steady stream of profitable work for the enterprise' (Table 12.7). This imperative has clear operational resource implications, much like that faced by the Department. The HR staff would prepare an audit of existing resource capacity in the areas of expertise (and their necessary support staff) and decide upon a strategy to ensure that sufficient personnel resources were available. Unlike the Department, it would not be gearing up for such a large target expenditure (£800 million plus). Its ambitions would be confined to ensuring that it can keep its existing capacity fully employed net of any additional capacity it recruits to generate sufficient profitable work to deliver its commercial imperatives.

In HR terms, one of its 5 to 8 operational imperatives would read something like: 'Recruit additional experienced staff for expanded tendering teams, in-house legal expertise and in-house finance and accountancy specialists to prospect, prepare and negotiate PFI contracts' (Table 12.7). The pace at which the organization reacts to the introduction of PFI would depend on the sense of urgency that managers feel under to cope with what were nothing less than major changes in their traditional business of delivering construction projects to the public sector under well-established rules and conventions.

ANALYSIS TO DERIVE THE NEGOTIATION AGENDA

There is one clear area of work for which the traditional public sector private bidder is not a supplier, namely, in post-construction facilities management. The PFI commits the builder to 20 to 30 years of facilities management of the completed project. In all but title, the builder of a hospital or school will manage the physical entity on behalf of the Department much like a private landlord manages the facilities and the building it rents to other organizations.

Few traditional construction firms are geared up for long-term facilities management and, necessarily, they will require hired expertise to meet the Department's requirements and will have to offer details of their plans in their response to the RFP. This presents them with dual negotiating tasks: to arrange for the employment of resources for facilities management and to persuade the Department that the resources they acquire (recruitment or acquisition of a facilities management partner) are suitable for a 20 to 30 year contract.

Fortunately, in the cases of hospital and school PFI, the facilities management function is confined to the buildings (janitorial, maintenance, cleaning and repairs) and does not extend to the medical or teaching services that use them. The Health Service in the UK and the Education Department employ their own specialized staff in PFI-built buildings and do not require the concessionaire to extend its services beyond a traditional serviced buildings role.

Nevertheless, the concessionaire would enter in Table 12.8 under operational imperatives a requirement for facilities management resources. The basic decision here is whether to recruit an in-house force or to outsource (by partnership or acquisition). Whichever it chooses, it will need the agreement of the Department that what it proposes meets the operational needs of the users of the facility. The concessionaire can expect detailed quality control and performance negotiations in this aspect of the proposal and this implies considerable work to detail their scope and define their operability. It may be that working up a negotiation stance will influence the choice between in-house generation of a new division and acquisition of, or partnership with, an existing facilities management resource.

Table 12.8   Impact of imperatives on HR

Imperatives		HR strategies				
Commercial	Operational	Employee relations	Recruitment	Training	Organization development	Manpower planning
PFI contracts	Facilities management skills	integration	substantial	significant	new division	few internal transfers, except managers
...						
...						

Table 12.8 lists some pointers to the sub-headings upon which a new facilities management resource would have some impact. Problems of integration of a large number of recruits on employee relations need to be looked into, if only to respond to expected Departmental enquiries under this heading. The new

building may be off-site, perhaps some distance away, and the Department can reasonably ask for observations on how this is to be managed.

Even a small project normally would require noticeable recruitment of personnel, especially one intended for public access and use. A small sub-station for a sewage works requires fewer people but a large general hospital complex would soon rack up significant numbers of security, janitorial, cleaning and maintenance staff. The greater is the number of recruits, the more induction and training people will be required. Given the fairly strict quality and performance standards, backed by warranties, that the Department will wish to impose on the concessionaire, the more important is the need for substantial selection and training resources.

A major change, such as the addition of a wholly new facilities management function, is bound to impact on the concessionaire's organizational development plans. However it is recruited or outsourced, a new division within the concessionaire's organization is the most likely outcome. If the concessionaire envisages undertaking more than one PFI project (as is most likely) a new division can be expected to grow in importance within the concessionaire. That means aligning management across the old and the new entities. Because these changes involve career decisions of existing managers and some transfers of employees at all levels (manpower planning), some thought may need to be given to how best to integrate the new division within the existing organization, including addressing the question of how much the taking on of this new function will alter the balance of the company's culture from a mainly engineering towards a mainly operational service business?

This suggests another aspect of the Negotiation Agenda approach that is worth considering. By its nature, and partly illustrated in the hypothetical examples chosen here, the Negotiation Agenda approach drives managers to consider strategic questions about the kind of business they are in and how things might or should change as the business is exposed to relentless analysis on where it is going. This is of direct benefit to the management of any organization. That they can link their daily activities to the strategy of their company is both a source of comfort (it isn't the cynic's case of the blind leading the blind) and a constant check that what they are doing is driving the organization forward and not undermining its future.

In similar vein, managers can work through the entire list of operational imperatives for each commercial imperative to identify and analyse the strategic policies associated with each of them. From these analyses, the negotiation tasks become clear at main heading level. What is needed next are data for each of the headings from which you can compile specific negotiable proposals for each of the parties whose consent you require to implement your agreed strategies. Some of these would be negotiated with internal parties (across the functions, up and down the organization's HR structure) and others with external parties (the commercial PFI client, possible partners or acquisition targets, your suppliers or customers).

Table 12.9 shows a remuneration and benefits entry in a pre-negotiation pro forma for facilities managers. Because facilities management for the lifetime of the PFI contract is bound to be closely supervised by the Department (and its Departmental clients) for compliance by the concessionaire with detailed quality and performance criteria, with warranties subject to penalties (and probably expensive indemnity clauses for expected litigation in pursuit of public claims), the preferred remuneration regime is likely to be best served by some form of performance-related pay (PRP) for all levels of employees that reflects their contribution to corporate risks of under-performing or neglect of duties. This suggests that the concessionaire adopt an HR strategy that introduces PRP in its recruitment phase. How simple or sophisticated the PRP scheme needs to be would depend on the circumstances and also on experience of it in operation. In the Negotiation Agenda these details would need to be worked out and checked carefully for their robustness.

Table 12.9 Derivation of the Negotiation Agenda topics

Employee group					
Imperatives		*HR strategy*			
Commercial	*People*	*Remuneration and benefits*			
		Now		Future	
		Helps	*Hinders*		
PFI contracts	Facilities managers	X	√	Adopt performance-related pay with regular appraisal	
				Retrain + discipline code + earned bonus element	
	...				
	...				

In Table 12.10 the impact of the Department's imperatives against financial criteria is shown. Work still remains to be done among stakeholders, particularly with employees in recognized trade unions, who pursue union policies against what they see as 'creeping privatization'. PFI is compatible with continuing public ownership, and the Opposition may oppose PFI on ideological grounds, or from a desire to court popularity depending on which way the general public mood swings.

Table 12.10 Impact of imperatives on financial strategies

Imperatives		Financial strategies				
Commercial	Operational	Budget	Sources	Financial evaluations	Stakeholders	Financial planning
Reduce the growth of public expenditure on capital ...	Identify £800m worth of viable PFI projects and bring on stream by year2	√ to be	Government adjusted	√ Continuing	√ Treasury Department Regulator Ministry User groups X Unions Opposition	√

Financial evaluations are likely to remain under continuous review as increasingly refined data become available and parameters change as negotiated outcomes are reached between the parties. The final numbers, as long as they are within the anticipated ranges, may require small adjustments to the budgeted figures. Fortunately, the budgets of most organizations contain some slack to accommodate small changes. With a flagship policy like PFI, changes upwards in budgeted figures are noticed by those responsible for them because they are sensitive to media comment on the political image of rising budgets.

Assembling the Negotiation Agenda

The derivation of the impact of the imperatives on the organization produces the raw materials for the Negotiation Agenda. You can think of the Negotiation

Agenda as a list of all the changes required for the organization to achieve its business plan. That is at its simplest. Of course, even small changes involve several steps to their achievement, and translating them into practical policies takes time and planning. Then there is their negotiation.

Not all changes are minor. Some like PFI involve complete changes in a supplier's role from a turnkey builder (design, build and handover the keys) to turnkey builder plus long-term operator of the built facility. This changes the company's financial imperatives, its HR policies and practice, and introduces new technology (adding unfamiliar facilities management to familiar construction).

Growing companies also experience change in more than one area. Adding a national to a local market, or an international to a national market, is not just a matter of scale. Servicing such changes involves organizational, manpower and managerial changes. Coordination changes are added to functional changes, as well as the possibilities of integrating formerly separate entities into a new, larger firm.

The analysis and diagnosis phase of the process model will have produced a mass of detailed data. These now have to be sorted through, duplications noted and the items for negotiation assembled and allocated to the parties with whom the negotiations will be conducted. In Table 12.11, a generic Negotiation Agenda for a PFI contract is shown.

A live contract would incorporate several volumes and much greater detail than shown, but the headings should give you a flavour of what is involved. A great deal of staff work is involved in looking at issues and determining what the organization wants to happen. From this negotiation, policies are assembled and the data and arguments for them, such as in an extended force field format. Those items selected for the impending negotiations may not exhaust items on the list, it being a judgement of the negotiators that the best way to approach a final settlement on various issues is in more than one step.

The Negotiation Agenda identifies potential proposals that management intends to introduce within the horizon of the business plan when circumstances suggest that they are appropriate. It is not just a list of good ideas or fads picked up from the professional press or news releases from the Government (or worse, the boss meeting somebody on a business trip). They are carefully tied to the well-thought-out imperatives necessary for the business plan. They should be fully costed before they are introduced and the details of the data converted into a negotiation plan.

Table 12.11   Negotiation Agenda for a PFI contract

Agenda item	Staff work comments
Risk allocation	
Demand risk	Market survey for products/services, pricing
	Demography, incomes, households
	Substitutes, legislation pending in product and process, competition and so on
	Negotiation aims: avoid dependence on high demand for profitability
Construction risk	Design and build, geology, flooding, environment, access, materials, unusual features, fit for use, inhibitions, costing, contract type, planning, site management
	Negotiation aims: minimize exposure in fixed-cost projects, procedures for variation orders, interruptions to construction by unforeseen events, limited delay penalties, *force majeure*, turnkey handover by architects' certification
Facilities management risk	Performance, quality, continuous operation, staffing fit for purpose, management liaison
	Negotiation aims: performance measures, quality criteria, success criteria, tenant's contract, rewards and penalties, operating risks, programming of maintenance works, repairing works, payment for malicious damages, safety standards, redundancy for critical services and emergencies, third party use and assignment including indemnities, insurance
Payment arrangements	Negotiation aims: regular quarterly fixed payments, standing charges, performance payments monthly in arrears, amounts for payments categories, no withholding payments to exert leverage, payments regime subject to review, use of surplus land, inflation escalator
Termination handover	Negotiation aims: terms or mechanism to be outlined for end of concession, terms to extend concession period, compensation penalties for early termination from change in Departmental/ Government policy

The Negotiation Agenda is a confidential document by its nature, and premature leaking (or announcements) of its contents could cause unwelcome setbacks (the first casualty of change proposals is a willingness to consider them). Ideas have to be transformed into fully costed negotiation plans.

CASE STUDY

Annualizing Hours

An organization may see an opportunity to control and then eliminate overtime working by a policy of annualizing hours. It may place this item on its Negotiation Agenda and require HR to devise a feasible plan to negotiate such an agreement with its employees. Overtime working in certain business sectors arises because of variability in work loads between peaks and troughs. Using overtime to handle the peaks, employees are asked to work beyond their normal finishing times and perhaps at weekends and over scheduled holidays. To ameliorate the inconvenience of such requests, employees are paid premium rates for the time they work outside normal hours.

Where such overtime working becomes a regular feature, some employees are more than happy to earn extra pay for their availability for overtime; others are less keen to do so. In many jobs the decision that overtime working is needed is open to manipulation by those seeking to gain from it; indeed, line supervision may cooperate in creating spurious overtime opportunities in exchange for employee cooperation in other minor functional goals. The end result is a culture of overtime working that is expensive (paid hours exceed worked hours) and mildly corrupting when it becomes endemic.

Campaigns among management to restrict and reduce overtime working to the absolute minimum seldom succeed. Some jobs by their nature require some minimum overtime working and it would be grossly expensive to over-staff with surplus employees just to cover irregular and temporary shortages, and often grossly inconvenient to customers to operate in a five-and-finish culture. An alternative scheme uses a minimum annual hours (standard working hours per week times standard weeks per year = total annual hours) and employees agree to be available for extra hours in any week which are deducted from their available annual hours. They are not paid extra for the overtime they work but have hours off in lieu in future working weeks to the amount of hours that they worked overtime when required by the company. If the standard annual hours are calculated to be say 1880 (40 hours times 47 working weeks), then if they worked 40 hours overtime they would have one week off work with pay. Multiple variations of the simplified assumptions I made here are possible and have been negotiated in organizations operating such schemes.

Suppose an organization decides to place on its Negotiation Agenda the annualizing of hours worked as a potential scheme to be implemented in its plants and offices in pursuit of an operational imperative to achieve its commercial imperative of reducing the labour cost base. From the staff work involved in preparing the details of the scheme, it may be clear that to introduce the scheme across the organization would cost a great deal of management time, but in only 30 per cent of the organization's divisions would real and immediate benefits in cost terms be realized, and in some divisions and employment functions it is not yet clear which annualized hours scheme was most appropriate.

In these circumstances, the negotiating team may decide to introduce the new hours scheme into some divisions first, see how the arrangements work in practice and then decide whether to extend the scheme across the organization. Meanwhile, staff work would continue on investigating the operation of such schemes elsewhere to see if amendments to it might be worth introducing. The proposal for annualizing hours would appear on the Negotiation Agenda, selections from it would be introduced into upcoming negotiations and staff work would continue in compiling negotiation plans for them.

Planning template for the Negotiation Agenda

Strategic negotiators are advised to develop their own planning template to be used by the team and its support staff in their organizations for their negotiations. John Benson, for example, over several years, developed a planning template for pay bargaining negotiations, covering bargaining units of varying sizes in large companies and organizations. The template required negotiation teams to prepare and submit details on them from their organization's Negotiation Agendas. When checked for content and consistency, these were used to secure the approval of senior management for the intended outcomes and the budgets necessary to meet the commercial or operational imperatives of the organization's business plan.

From the planning template you should understand:

- the need for a highly structured framework for planning your negotiations;

- the particular information needs of pay bargaining;

- the probable sources of that information;

- the link between the strategic negotiation process and the key management objectives;

- a framework for costing the practical options behind your proposals and bargained results;

- the merits of the Strategic Negotiation planning process for your organization.

The example below is based on John Benson's Negotiation Agenda for pay bargaining and illustrates particular facets of that process, but the method used is adaptable for negotiations on other operational imperatives, including finance and technologies.

This provides guidance in turning the strategic requirements of the Negotiation Agenda into operational reality. It uses the planning template as a framework within which all aspects of a Negotiation Agenda to be used in the upcoming negotiations can be considered. It also sets out the kind of information the management team is required to know.

Specifically, the template's purposes are:

- to provide a common format for submissions to obtain authorization for the objectives of the negotiations;

- to provide a structured framework for analysis of key data;

- to clarify roles and accountability levels for negotiations in a decentralized negotiations environment;

- to facilitate input of strategies for negotiations;

- to provide an accurate record of the results and costs of negotiations;

- to provide an audit trail to monitor the implementation of the results of negotiations and the actual costs increase in the paybill (or other expenditures).

The planning template is not prescriptive. It is a framework for you to adapt and adopt in whatever way works best for your organization. Some of the descriptive language may need adaptation to suit the nomenclature of individual organizations.

At first glance, the planning template appears formidable in its detail and the amount of information required, but you should bear the following points in mind:

- The first compilation of the template will take the longest time it will ever take. Thereafter, the base data only need to be maintained and updated for future negotiations.

- The information required is that on which confident management decisions can be made. You should be wary, however, of seeking absolute perfection in your data if it is not available, or only available at inordinate cost. It is better to be approximately right than absolutely wrong.

THE BARGAINING UNIT

In pay bargaining, one planning template should be produced for each bargaining unit, defined as a group of employees (perhaps in a common grade) whose terms and conditions are negotiated collectively by the organization. They may be located at a single site or at several different sites in the organization.

The basic documents that you require for reference and familiarity include the current terms and conditions (T & Cs) of the bargaining unit. Most details of current T & Cs can be extracted from the organization's payroll, existing negotiation procedural agreements, individual contracts of employment, manpower plans and budgets. Similarly, for finance and technology negotiations you need ready access to current contracts with the other parties, correspondence and brochures, details of your current spending with them and any internal correspondence within the organization about the use of their products and services, details of faults, downtimes, backups and related costs; all should be filed.

The accurate collation of the information about current T & Cs, and similar information, is likely to be a fairly onerous exercise when undertaken for the first time, but a clear understanding of where you are in your relationships with other parties is necessary before planning how you are going to get to where you want to be in your business plan.

PAYBILL INFORMATION

The previous 12-months' total paybill costs are basic data. The total should be the actual cost of the previous 12-month's paybill. Payroll data (with clear cut-off dates) provide the most likely source for this information.

The paybill total should include all cash and related paybill items which may be subject to negotiation because knowledge of the actual annual costs ensures that all possible negotiable items have been identified. In the UK, the employer's National Insurance Contributions (an additional tax by another name) should be included in the total. This total and its constituent parts must be borne in mind when thinking about creative solutions to conditional packaging of offers.

Negotiating with unions which usually present detailed pay claims as an amount or a percentage on top of current hourly pay, requires that the negotiators cost all claims in full, including the consequential additional costs attributed to an increase in basic pay (premium rates for unsocial hours and so on). These data provide hard evidence for addressing such issues as reducing absenteeism/overtime levels, the introduction of an annual hours scheme to eliminate paid overtime or to prevent motivating its creation, and a reduction in the number and complexity of allowances, many of which are historic, their original purposes forgotten.

The template should include the actual budgeted manpower levels for the forthcoming agreement year in whole-time equivalents. Probable sources of information include (as a check to current numbers): the business plan, operating budgets, manpower plans and budgets, and the organization's payroll costs.

You should consider manpower levels to understand fully the effects on paybill costs. For example, if the business plan projects that the budgeted numbers of employees are to rise, the paybill will increase without any negotiated increase in pay or other costs. Equally, if numbers of employees are planned to fall, the paybill will decrease accordingly. This calculation establishes the correct baseline cost upon which you may negotiate increases.

With premium pay rates for unsocial hours, the basic hours worked will be less than the hours paid, and negotiators ought to have these data available to them. Probable sources of information for these data include the organization's payroll, data from attendance or time recording systems and overtime authorization forms.

Where premium paid hours (mainly overtime and other unsocial working hours) exceed the actual hours worked at normal time rates, the difference could indicate the costs of management resorting to overtime working to cover emergencies, and also the existence of collusive quid pro quo arrangements between some supervisors and employees, in which supervisors, under pressure from senior management, offer unofficially additional payments in the form of 'phantom overtime' to employees to persuade them to complete work targets.

For example, if hours paid are equivalent to 65 and the actual hours worked were 48 it might be worth investigating alternative work arrangements and considering the negotiation of changes (annualized hours?) by adding this item to the Negotiation Agenda. The elimination of paid overtime by an annualized hours agreement was a major target of a Negotiation Agenda of an oil refinery which I studied in the 1970s. I was recently (2002) engaged in a similar exercise in another oil and gas company. With a rising trend in overtime payments, what earlier intervention stopped often restarts after a while like a nuisance weed, if senior managements (and gardeners) lack the necessary vigilance.

If they show unwelcome trends the data may highlight potential efficiency problems perhaps worth negotiating about. The questions that should be asked of the data include the following:

- Which categories of employees may earn proportionately more overtime?

- Is this leading to inequities in earnings patterns of some groups of employees when they receive the same base pay increase as other categories who do not have the same potential to earn overtime payments?

- How are paid hours geared to hours worked?

- Are there any areas for possible Negotiation Agenda objectives on overtime and premium-earnings drift?

- Is there any scope for the introduction of different working patterns; for example, new shifts, annualized hours, changing the mix of full-time to part-time employees?

Answers to these kinds of questions may suggest the possibility of undertaking staff work to examine the problem and to explore possible changes for inclusion in the Negotiation Agenda for future negotiation.

Managers develop their command of the detail of the resources for which they are responsible and because the development of the Negotiation Agenda is ongoing throughout the year, and not something done in a rush a few weeks (days?) before a negotiation, it produces well-thought-out change programmes for the organization in conformity with the business plan.

A key piece of data to be calculated is the budgeted manpower levels for the forthcoming year, assuming no changes to those T & Cs which currently prevail, that is, assuming no increase in salaries/wages. This provides the best available baseline costs upon which any increases will be based – an accurate starting point for calculating and modelling future earnings. Put another way, if there are no changes in T & Cs for this bargaining group, what will be the labour costs for the next year/agreement duration?

These data also familiarize the negotiating team with the key paybill ratios by all parties and form a ready reckoner for the cost implications of any demand/offer on the negotiating table. It also generates an understanding of significant ratios which assist in identifying areas where costs rise disproportionately to any base increase, for example, where guaranteed overtime exists. This could be a message for employees if they are not aware of their average earnings; that is, in a remuneration package it is not just base pay that is important – it is the total package, including its cash and non-cash items.

A definition of 'average earnings' is 'what individual employees earn, on average, when they are at their place of work'. Note that this does not take account of sickness and holiday payments where they are not themselves calculated as a continuation of average earnings.

COMPARISONS WITH OTHER BARGAINING UNITS

Comparability claims from unions and employees are commonplace. Often the claimed comparisons are unfounded, but data are essential (anecdotes are not data!). If the claims are true, negotiators are in a better position for knowing the truth because once a claim is rejected, and is subsequently proved to be true, it is an uphill struggle to restore credibility. Of course, the fact that a comparison claim is well founded is not in itself a reason for agreeing to uplift pay! There may be compensating benefits from working for one organization that is lower paid than another (for example, better job security, flexibilities in hours of work, less onerous working conditions, non-shift work, better amenities, and such like).

The easiest information to obtain is for bargaining units in the same organization. This is true in principle for both management and employees. Management can check the pay data for different bargaining units and employees can form their impressions from what other employees claim they earn. They can also compare other terms and conditions for each bargaining group in unionized environments – the union has copies of all the employment conditions in its agreements. However, the union's information (and, therefore, the employees' information on other bargaining units) is open to interpretative errors.

For example, unfavourable premium pay rates may apply on paper, but be different in practice. Perhaps an employee group secured a premium entitlement to double time for voluntary overtime only if the notice period is less than one day, whereas another employment group negotiated double time for compulsory overtime whatever the notice period. Perhaps the compulsory overtime group rarely works overtime and then only when the exigencies of the job override all else; perhaps the other group works regular overtime and is well managed by its department, and notice of overtime is never less than one day. Which groups are better or worse off?

The data should include information on other bargaining units' settlement levels which are likely to impact directly on the expectations of other bargaining groups. The comparisons should:

- summarize the internal market comparisons;

- highlight anomalies between employee groups;

- identify equal value issues;

- identify possible areas for management planning of strategic shifts in relativities;

- forewarn and forearm against unfavourable comparisons.

The probable sources of information include commercial and government labour market reports, salary and benefit surveys, both published and from private researchers, local employers and published data in specialist or professional journals.

Negotiators (both management and union) should undertake close analysis of external market data. In several negotiations with unions that claimed 'substantial increases over base rates', their negotiators based a large part of their claim on their members falling behind the pay rates for other employee groups; the management countered with the data that showed vacancies in the group were exceeded by rising job applications at existing rates of pay.

Analysis of external market data, and close comparisons with similar organizations, should help the management negotiators to:

- understand the organization's true competitive market position in relation to the employees covered by the bargaining unit (know your markets!);

- understand the prevalence of significant differences in pay policy and practices of other organizations which may form the basis of a union claim or supportive argument.

The key objective is to consider information which will work for you and your organization and adds value to your negotiating planning and decision-making.

Considerations in assessing external data and salary survey information include:

- the necessity to compare apples with apples and ensure that job sizes are comparable with those in your organization. Accurate job matching is at the heart of the use and interpretation of survey data. Additionally, the size of organization should be comparable, and the possible influences of business sector and geographical location taken into account in making comparisons;

- the fact that published salary surveys are always out of date. Allowances should be made for the lead-time between data collection (not publication) and the time you are using the information. Adjustments need to be made on a pro rata basis in times of high inflation or high levels of wage and salary settlements and increases;

- ensuring there is a suitable comparative sample size, both within individual surveys and by the use of several publications. For example, there are surveys which mainly comprise small- to medium-sized organizations and which tend to result in aggregate salary levels lower than those of large organizations.

- understanding that no survey is totally scientific and accurate no matter how much detail is provided. Managerial judgement should not be suspended. It is good practice to take information from two or three different sources. What is needed is a broad feel of the parameters of pay and benefits for specific groups in comparable markets;

- using only the survey data relevant to your organization and the specific bargaining unit – otherwise analysis/paralysis will set in!

KEY ECONOMIC INDICATORS

You should use the year-on-year percentage increase (decrease) for the most recent 12 months available for prices and earnings index figures. For unemployment figures, the most recent seasonally adjusted figures should be used. You should be able to get these data from employment data and the business press. Because both parties may be aware of these indicators and may use them to influence the negotiations, you should be well prepared for their appearance. You should indicate any relevant and local demographic data.

FACTORS INFLUENCING THE SETTLEMENT LEVEL

You should list all the factors you see as influencing the expectations of members of the bargaining unit, either upwards or downwards. For example, significant downsizing, entry of competing employers into the area, local scarcity of certain skills and so on could influence the expectations of the negotiators regarding the likely range of settlement, either upwards or downwards. You should discuss with colleagues in which direction the trend is likely to go. This could influence the tactical decisions your team may decide to implement. Sources of information considered in these discussions include: post-conference reports of the pre-negotiation conferences; feedback from team briefings; analyses of attitude surveys; collective managerial judgements and instincts; and MBWA (management by walking about).

THE CLAIM

You should itemize the formal union claim for the bargaining unit if any, including any non-substantive elements. You should calculate the associated costs of each item of the actual and projected paybills and their percentage effect on the paybill totals.

Written appraisals of the actual level of expectations of the union and the members of the bargaining unit, for each of the items specified on the claim should be made and recorded as they change.

This analysis requires the manipulation and modelling of information. In the long term, there is a need to develop a computerized HR database and pay modelling system – either in-house, or by the adaptation of a proprietary pay modelling system.

In the meantime, data can be captured via existing payroll, HR and financial reporting systems and with the assistance of IT expertise. A suitable spreadsheet package can be set up, using the template as a basis of the specification. Alternatively, the data can be manipulated and modelled by manual calculations.

This analysis helps to:

- give a full, considered response to the claim;

- identify the high-value but low-cost items, that is, where movement may be valued highly by the staff side and where the calculations show it is not significant in cost terms;

- appraise expectations and structure the management side's thinking about the possible options.

KEY OBJECTIVES

The negotiating team should state how long- and short-term management objectives will need to be considered in relation to the negotiations; for example, costs, productivity goodwill, quid pro quos and so on. You should be specific about the aims in relation to your realistic settlement options.

Every pay and conditions bargaining exchange is an opportunity to change any aspects of the employment relationship that do not help you to meet the organization's objectives. The template should address these objectives and the quid pro quos the management side requires for any staff-desired change in their T & Cs.

Some objectives require long-term horizons for realization; others are realizable more quickly. It is always important to ensure that short-term changes do not undermine longer-term objectives. Where negotiation tactics (for example, salami) are a first step towards a longer-term objective, these should be stated explicitly and circulated for discussion.

An example of a broad need in meeting a business plan objective may be to look at the containment and control of labour costs. It is possible to review a multitude of areas that impact on this objective, including:

- multi-skilling
- work practices
- shift patterns
- annual hours arrangements
- mix of full-time and part-time employees
- overtime
- competitive local pay rates.

As an example, one of these areas might be the control of overtime costs. Within this subject area, issues that might be addressed could include:

- premium rates for overtime
- when overtime rates apply
- possible new time-recording systems
- discipline processes

- mix of labour force between part-timers and full-timers

- shift patterns

- monthly, annualized, or other contractual hours arrangements.

Each of these requires a negotiating objective attached to it and each of the objectives given a high, medium or low priority rating.

In preparation for each negotiating event, HR and reward strategies should be reviewed. The principal subject areas for negotiation should be established. These principal areas should then be segmented, as in the example above, to establish the detailed, tactical negotiation objectives. These objectives then become the specific shopping list on the Negotiation Agenda for use in a series of negotiations.

SETTLEMENT OPTIONS

The length of agreement, level of cost and the mix of paybill items combine in various different settlement options (including non-wage items). Of the three options you identify, you should indicate your most favoured option.

You should demonstrate the different options available to you, bearing in mind the key objectives and their related costs. You should include all items on which you are prepared to negotiate and should demonstrate the overall parameters within which you are prepared to reach agreement, indicating your most favoured option.

Having received and appraised the claims and drawn from the Negotiation Agenda items for the negotiations, possible settlement options need to be calculated and modelled. Your options may differ not only in cost, but also in the total make-up and mix; for example, one may emphasize cash elements, and other benefits. Options may also differ in terms of their duration – one year, two years and so on

STRUCTURE OF NEGOTIATIONS

Knowing exactly with whom a negotiating team will be negotiating can help in appraising their expectations. Hence, you should assemble information relating to the negotiating teams (bearing in mind the Data Protection and Freedom of Information Acts, and their equivalent laws in other countries) and discuss how team composition might influence the conduct of the negotiations and the practice of communication within the bargaining unit. Getting the right mix on the management side to match the staff side is important:

- List the names and titles of the other party's negotiating team.

- List the names and titles of the organization's negotiating team.

- How will the negotiated settlement be communicated to management and employees?

- How will the other party make its decision to accept the settlement offer?

Remind the negotiating team to think about a communication strategy and how to influence the process.

IMPLICATIONS FOR INTER-PARTY RELATIONS?

What is the environment within which these negotiations will be conducted and what factors which will influence bargaining unit behaviour and/or expectations? Where there are implications that could have such an influence, outline your intended approach towards the negotiations.

You should describe briefly (and be ready to discuss) the day-to-day employee relations environment in which the organization is operating and its implications for these negotiations. In financial and technology negotiations you would look at the competitive environment and at factors that influence future delivery of products or services.

Employee relations' issues that could influence the negotiations include:

- a group resistant to change

- a group which always has a significant number of grievances under discussion.

- a group that tends to follow the leadership of another (more militant) group

- hostile *v* cooperative groups

- status-conscious *v* egalitarian groups

- constructive *v* negative groups

- good negotiators *v* poor negotiators.

You should then outline the tactical approach towards the negotiations given the environment you have defined as above.

Because both of these sections are sensitive remember that if you have all of your eggs in one basket, the sensible approach is to watch the basket. Hence, restrict the circulation list, shred draft copies and, where convenient, report to non-team members orally.

NEGOTIATION AUTHORIZATION

To avoid detaching the negotiations from the line of authority in the organization it is essential that the CEO or his designate sign off the negotiation budget and approve the linkage of the Negotiation Agenda to the organization's business plan. Strategic negotiation is about uncovering those linkages and securing the commitment and attention of top-level management to the objectives of the Negotiation Agenda.

It is very easy for negotiations for any of the pillars of the organization – people, finance or technology – to become detached from the organization's strategy (many negotiations do not even start with a conscious connection to the organization's strategy), and thereby they are vulnerable to damaging higher-level interventions during difficulties when policies are suspended or reversed.

Securing budget authorization means demonstrating to the satisfaction of the top-level managers that the overall objectives of the Negotiation Agenda are aligned with their organization's overall objectives. If top-level management is not convinced before the negotiations commence, it is better to find this out and revise the planned negotiation strategy beforehand, rather than during the negotiations when correcting a strategy does most damage to the credibility of the organization and its negotiators and, importantly too, to that of top-level management.

SETTLEMENT REPORT

After acceptance of an agreed level of settlement, a 'settlement report' should be completed and copied to the organization's CEO, or designate. The report should also detail any significant variations from the options and budgets signed off by top-level management. It should cover every item of the agreement that is a cost element.

The narrative section should assist in the proper monitoring of negotiating performance and in reviewing effectiveness of the planning process of the Negotiation Agenda. This provides a follow through in the negotiation cycle and permits a review of the HR and reward strategies.

It also informs future preparation of negotiation strategies and tactics, for example, if the Negotiation Agenda objective to reduce overtime premiums is not achieved over a couple of negotiations, it might indicate that changes of strategy on working patterns, which should lead to the required changes in overtime practices, would be appropriate.

Activities
for Chapter 12

Activity 12.1

Survey your own organization and consider if there is anything you would like to change as a manager for the benefit of the organization, but because you anticipate resistance from individuals or the departments affected, or for some other reason, you feel helpless to try. This applies whether there are trade unions or not operating in your organization

COMMENTS ON THIS ACTIVITY

Management seldom has unilateral discretion to change current working arrangements without at least consultation with the employees affected and, where the changes are fundamental, without some version of a negotiation of what is intended (that is, the consent of those affected by the changes). In unionized environments, negotiation is mandatory but it is not uncommon for managements to feel constrained from attempting to open negotiations on certain issues, no matter how beneficial to the future of the business they may be, because the anticipated resistance could be more trouble than the outcome is worth.

You have been asked, in effect, to identify any such changes that you believe would improve operational efficiency. Do not select changes by first assessing your chances of obtaining them. Of course there are issues of resistance, but until you have compiled the Negotiation Agenda, it is not possible to judge what you will trade for their cooperation.

Also, do not confine your attention to possible resistance from employees or unions (should you have any operating in the company). Resistance to changes is as likely from other management grades and functions, as well as possible problems of mobilizing sufficient resources to carry them out where investment is necessary.

Activity 12.2

Have you ever been in any of the situations described on page 265 or similar?

If you have been in the situation that approximates to Zhao's (feeling resentful about your situation and someone offers you a better deal, to which the party to the current deal responds by improving your terms), did you feel grateful for their belated response or angry at them for not offering it without your asking?

If information becomes available that the commercial deal you have with a supplier is non-competitive with the potential options you could obtain from rivals, how might you feel about this?

COMMENTS ON THIS ACTIVITY

Most people react negatively to the realization that the deal they accepted is worse than what they are offered belatedly on resignation or what others have been offered.

Epilogue

The Strategic Negotiation Process Model that maps the stages of activity (Figure E.1) is the backbone of the strategic negotiation process discussed throughout this volume.

The seamless link from the organization's business plan to the negotiation agenda is the distinguishing feature that ties the work of the organization's negotiators to each other and to the organization's strategic objectives as set out in its business plan. This is the essence of strategic planning through mobilizing the resources of the organization to what it wants to achieve over a 3- to 5-year rolling horizon.

Thinking strategically is about thinking ahead. If that is all it is, it is not surprising that in (too?) many organizations a gap opens up between the intentions of strategic policy makers and their day-to-day managers. At root this is a cause of organizational cynicism; the leaders berate their staff and line managers for ignoring the bigger picture and the followers blame everybody above them in the rankings for their inability to organize a proverbial drinks party in a brewery.

But the disconnection between the bigger picture and what happens on the ground begins with the uncoupling of medium-term strategy from daily operational flexibility, also known as reacting to unforeseen, though foreseeable, events, leaving long-term strategy to wishful thinking. In fact, many strategic thinkers imagine that because they know where they want the organization to go, and sometimes share their vision with a few privileged associates close to them in the hierarchy, that necessarily it should be obvious to everybody else what to do in the meantime in whatever sphere of activity they are engaged on behalf of the organization.

Working from a Strategic Negotiation Process Model, the objectives of the organization necessarily permeate at all levels and across all functions, because

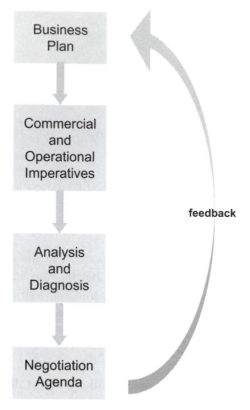

Figure E.1   Strategic Negotiation Process Model

it requires managers (strategic or tactical) to link what they are doing to the objectives of the business plan, even if this only involves considering where their activities fit into it.

If strategy requires consideration of the commercial and operation imperatives necessary to achieve the business plan (however articulated, from fully detailed plan through to broad, loosely stated wishes), then those charged with delivering any of the commercial and operational imperatives identified in the process model are more likely to be working for the objectives of the business plan than working even unintentionally against them.

The Emerald case study illustrated the disconnection between a strategic goal and its interpretation by functional managers, who saw their role merely to continue what they had been doing in land acquisition on a small scale until then and not to review it as part of the bigger picture in a changing market. To be fair, because they were compartmentalized and not privy to the board's strategic intentions, they had no channels through which to articulate alternative possibilities. Therefore they implemented their standard land acquisition policy one piece at a time from numerous individual owners, when the strategic goal ('acquire 100 sites in 1 year') would have been better served perhaps by acquiring a single business that already owned numerous sites in places where the organization wished to expand.

Strategic process models tend to raise strategic awareness across the organization and to create fora from which their functional management skills, though present and sufficient but often not used, can be drawn into thinking about better ways to achieve strategic goals and which help process ideas upwards to the strategic decision makers. It also helps them to deliver their sub-targets in alignment with those strategic goals, and enables their progress to be evaluated at higher levels from their requests for negotiation authorization and from their reports on outcomes achieved (or not achieved, and why).

Analysis and diagnosis encompasses a great deal of detailed preparation, at least the first time it is undertaken. Once completed, regular updating is much easier, or at least less cumbersome, in some cases merely requiring the adding of the latest data, or new information about what other parties appear to want or are being influenced by, for the relevant quarter or year. The negotiating team certainly is better briefed on the data and on the participants with whom they negotiate, and its members are able to speak more authoritatively across the table, always a helpful behaviour in negotiation.

Command of detail is always a powerful argument for listeners to pay close attention to what a negotiator is saying; it is much more powerful than a negotiator becoming fluent in sales speak (or its cousin, management speak) or similar such verbiage. When proposing a negotiation plan, senior managers often ask detailed questions and they appreciate clear evidence that the negotiators have thought through what they propose to accomplish, and, particularly when their proposals are closely linked to elements of the business plan, why they suggest achieving the organization's goals in the manner they propose. Waffle and bluster are easily spotted and once you lose the confidence of senior managers you also lose their close attention. What you propose will not pass their test of your competence and, if you cannot convince colleagues responsible for the organization's business strategy, you will not convince other parties whose support you need for your objectives.

To avoid detaching the negotiations from the line of authority in the organization it is essential that the CEO or a functional director of say finance or HR (if it were a negotiation about staff remuneration, for example) approve the specific linkages between what is proposed in the Negotiation Agenda and the organization's business plan, and that they sign off the negotiation budget, estimated on the basis of hard data, to achieve the relevant imperative within the stated time period. Strategic negotiation is about uncovering those linkages and securing the commitment and attention of top-level management to the objectives of the Negotiation Agenda.

It is very easy for negotiations for any of the pillars of the organization – people, finance or technology – to become detached from the organization's strategy (many negotiations of strategic importance unfortunately do not even start with a conscious connection to the organization's business plan) and thereby they are vulnerable to damaging higher-level interventions during possible local difficulties when policies are suspended or reversed: heads roll and others are demoralized.

Securing high-level budget authorization before strategic negotiations commence means the negotiators must demonstrate to the satisfaction of the top-level managers that the overall objectives of the Negotiation Agenda are aligned with their organization's overall objectives. If top-level management is not convinced before the negotiations commence, it is better to find this out at that time, and to revise the planned negotiation strategy beforehand, rather than to find this out during the negotiations when correcting a strategy does most damage to the credibility of the organization and its negotiators and, importantly too, to that of top-level management. Mishandling opportunities for change can delay, perhaps indefinitely, their introduction; where these changes are imperative for survival, the consequences may be terminal.

After acceptance of an agreed level of settlement by the other negotiating party, a settlement report should be completed and copied to the organization's CEO. This report should also detail any significant variations from the options and budgets that were signed off by top-level management. It should cover every item of the agreement that is a cost element, or has cost implications.

In addition to data, a narrative section in support and explanation would assist in the proper monitoring of negotiating performance and for reviewing effectiveness of the planning process of the strategic negotiation and the Negotiation Agenda process. This provides a follow through in the negotiation cycle and permits a review of the whole process.

Settlement reports and discussion of their main features inform future preparation of negotiation strategies and tactics. If, for example, it was concluded that a Negotiation Agenda objective to reduce overtime premiums was unlikely to be achieved realistically over a couple of negotiations, this might indicate that changes of strategy on working patterns would be appropriate, which could for example lead to the required changes in say overtime practices or shift working. The necessary staff work to identify the best way forward would be organized on the basis of shared experience and reliable data.

Strategic negotiation essentially is a practical process. It involves a great deal of preparatory staff work. It tests the realism of strategic objectives and the timescales for their achievement. It also tests the robustness of senior management's commitment and support for their professed objectives, and whether their organization can realistically deliver what they are committing it to achieve. Because it is well thought out, necessary changes can be made and phased in over a manageable period of time to bring the organization's resources, including the people who work in it, to the starting line to seize the opportunities for change.

Index

(References to diagrams are in **bold**)